For Burton
from
Jacob
VI-9-74

PUBLICATIONS OF THE AMERICAN JEWISH ARCHIVES • NO. VIII

JACOB R. MARCUS, *Editor*

HISTORICAL ESSAY ON THE COLONY OF SURINAM 1788

ESSAI HISTORIQUE
SUR LA
COLONIE
DE
SURINAM,

Sa fondation, fes révolutions, fes progrès, depuis fon origine jufqu'à nos jours, ainfi que les caufes qui dépuis quelques années ont arreté le cours de fa prosperité; avec la defcription & l'état actuel de la Colonie, de même que fes révenus annuels, les charges & impots qu'on y paye, comme aufli plufieurs autres objets civils & politiques; ainfi qu'un tableau des mœurs de fes habitans en général.

AVEC

L'Histoire de la Nation Juive Portugaife & Allemande y Etablie, leurs Privilèges immunités & franchifes: leur Etat politique & moral, tant ancien que moderne: La part qu'ils ont eu dans la défenfe & dans les progrès de la Colonie.

Le tout redigé fur des pieces authentiques y ointes, & mis en ordre par les Régens & Répréfentans de ladite Nation Juive Portugaife.

PREMIERE PARTIE.

A PARAMARIBO
1788.

PUBLICATIONS OF THE AMERICAN JEWISH ARCHIVES • NO. VIII

JACOB R. MARCUS, Editor

HISTORICAL ESSAY ON THE COLONY OF SURINAM 1788

Translated by
SIMON COHEN

Edited by
JACOB R. MARCUS
and
STANLEY F. CHYET

AMERICAN JEWISH ARCHIVES
CINCINNATI 45220
KTAV PUBLISHING HOUSE, INC.
NEW YORK 10002
1974

© 1974 by the American Jewish Archives

Library of Congress Cataloging in Publication Data
Main entry under title.
Historical essay on the colony of Surinam, 1788.
(Publication of the American Jewish Archives, no. 8)
Translation of Essai historique sur la colonie de Surinam.
Includes bibliographical references.
1. Surinam—History—1814. 2. Jews in Surinam. I. Series: Hebrew Union College—Jewish Institute of Religion. American Jewish Archives. Publications, no. 8.
F2423.E7713   988'.3'01   73-1345
ISBN 0-87068-212-1

MANUFACTURED IN THE UNITED STATES OF AMERICA

Published on the
ERNA KROUCH FUND

CONTENTS

Foreword — ix

Historical Essay on the Colony of Surinam—1788 — 1

Preface — 5

Introduction — 15

Historical Essay on the Colony of Surinam—Part I — 19

Historical Essay on the Colony of Surinam—Part II — 123

Documents — 183

Notes to the Introduction — 226

Notes to Part I — 231

Notes to Part II — 241

Index — 245

FOREWORD

In 1788, the *Regenten* or communal leaders of the Sephardim—"the Portuguese Jewish Nation"—in Surinam (Dutch Guiana) published in French a work bearing the title: *Essai Historique sur la Colonie de Surinam, etc.* This two-volume work appeared in Paramaribo, the capital city of Surinam, and has itself an interesting history. The *Regenten* had read *On the Civil Improvement of the Jews* (Berlin, 1781-1783), a book by the eminent German publicist, Christian Wilhelm von Dohm. It was a plea for Jewish emancipation, and when the Surinamese Jews wrote to congratulate von Dohm, he encouraged them to undertake a detailed study of Jewish life in their country. The *Historical Essay* was the answer to von Dohm's suggestion. The Dutch Guianese Jewish leaders were happy to publish this essay recounting their history, for they deeply resented the disabilities to which they still found themselves subjected in an age of expanding liberties in Western Europe and North America.

The history of Surinamese Jewry is the story of one of the greatest Jewish communities in the New World of the 1700's. Paramaribo, by the middle of the eighteenth century, sheltered about 1,000 Jewish souls. North America would support no community as large and as well developed until the second quarter of the nineteenth century. Jewish life in Surinam had its beginnings under the English in the 1650's and under the Dutch in 1667, when the territory was ceded to the Hollanders in exchange for English occupation of New Amsterdam on the Hudson. The Jews who had remained in Surinam or immigrated there enjoyed the *privilegia* which had been accorded them in the 1660's by the English and the Dutch. These chartered rights granted them exemptions and immunities both as an ethnic minority and as Dutch burghers, and also offered them the opportunity to live their lives as an autonomous religio-cultural enclave. The grants of the 1660's were the most liberal that had yet been promulgated for Jews in the Christian world. Not since the third century, when Rome had made it possible for her Jewish subjects to become citizens of the Empire, had Jews known as ample a political status. The English and the Dutch regimes vied with each other in emancipating their Jewish colonists, because in that mercantilistic age they needed enterprising, Spanish-speaking citizens who could produce raw materials and exploit the trade of the Spanish Main. If these charters are notable for their liberality, it is because seventeenth-century Europe had survived the tragedy of the Thirty Years' War and was ushering in an economically-motivated new world of increasing tolerance and enlightenment.

The *Essay* deals not only with the wide-ranging political privileges enjoyed by Surinamese Jewry, but also with the social and economic history of the Jews as plantation owners and urban businessmen. Many of these seventeenth-century pioneers were sugar planters; their descendants and successors left the Surinamese backcountry and its all-Jewish town, the Joden Savane. They moved to Paramaribo, where they became a lower-middle-class and middle-class white-collar group of city peddlers, shopkeepers, professional men, and merchant-shippers trafficking with Dutch Curaçao and English North America. The Jews of Paramaribo constituted anywhere from one-third to one-half of the city's white population, and the other whites, Protestants mostly, resented them as infidels and economic rivals. All told, there were about 4,000 whites in the land in a sea of about 50,000 blacks, most of whom were slaves. Slavery is always accompanied by brutality, and Surinam was no exception, as the *Historical Essay* makes plain. Servile revolts, runaway slaves, raids by the blacks increased tensions and kept the country in turmoil, especially in the hinterland. Jewish frontier rangers at the head of their own militia invaded the forests in pursuit of the marauding Maroons or Bush Negroes. One Jewish captain led more than thirty punitive expeditions into the bush against the Maroons—who were never finally subdued. The *Historical Essay* sponsored by the Regents of the Surinamese Sephardim is thus a valuable source for black history in South America during the seventeenth and eighteenth centuries.

Although Surinamese Jewry worshipped according to the Sephardic (Spanish-Portuguese) rite, there were actually two quite separate Jewish communities in the country, the "Portuguese" (Sephardim) and the "High German" (Ashkenazim). Both groups were remarkably metropolitan for a colonial outpost inasmuch as they supported rabbis as well as other religious functionaries and encouraged the establishment of social-welfare societies. They built beautiful synagogues, two of which are still standing, and maintained close religious relations with the Jews of Amsterdam. In a way, it may be said, Surinam had three Jewish communities, for the Jewishly-reared mulattos enjoyed a religious and confraternal social life of their own.

One of the virtues of this interesting study is its rather detailed analysis of the culture of all the Surinamese, and not only of the Jews in their midst. Thus the *Essay* throws light on the history of Surinam as a whole. Among the Jews was a small group of men who had fine libraries, spoke Dutch, French, Portuguese, and Spanish, and were completely immersed in the main stream of eighteenth-century humanism and liberal political aspiration. In 1785, this group founded at Paramaribo a Jewish literary association which established a lyceum or folk university offering a far-ranging series of courses and lectures. One of the architects of this educational institution was David de Isaac Cohen Nassy, probably the chief author of the *Essay*.

Nassy, the leader of the *Regenten* in the 1780's, may well have been the most distinguished Jew in the colony. He had been a plantation owner, notary, physician, scientist, publicist, merchant, and devoted Jewish communal worker, even though in his personal religious beliefs he apparently paid homage to the teachings of the Deists. Unhappy with the slow advance of liberalism in his native Surinam, he set sail for the new United States in 1792 and there speedily opted for American citizenship. The Philadelphians among whom he made his home recognized his worth and elected him to the American Philosophical Society. In 1793, he distinguished himself in the city by his tireless efforts to cope with the yellow fever epidemic; he subsequently reported his observations of the disease in a brochure which he published in English and French describing his experiences during the plague. In 1795, he returned to Surinam hoping that with the advance of the French Revolution a new day would dawn for the Dutch and their Jewish subjects in Holland and in the colonies. Nassy was profoundly influenced by the egalitarian teachings to which he was exposed at Philadelphia in the mid-1790's, and this reflected itself in the last years of that decade in his *Lettre Politico-Théologico-Morale sur les Juifs,* an apologetic work in which he vigorously defended the grant of equal rights and liberties to the Jews of the Netherlands. "All men," he insisted, "must have equal rights, equal privileges."

It is high time that the *Essay*—an exceedingly rare work—be made available in English translation. Dr. Simon Cohen, of Cincinnati, graciously agreed to assume this difficult task—difficult because Nassy and the men who worked with him were not Frenchmen, may never even have set foot in France, and expressed themselves in a French which was awkward and on occasion even invincibly unclear. Dr. Cohen has labored to produce an idiomatic, readable text, and others, too, have generously read his translation and offered many helpful suggestions. The staff of the American Jewish Archives has spared no effort in the preparation of this work. Dr. Stanley F. Chyet, the Associate Director of the Archives, has taken a deep—and time-consuming—personal interest in this book, and Dr. Abraham I. Shinedling, with his usual generosity, has carefully read the typescript and prepared the Index. To all of them, the Director of the American Jewish Archives wishes to express his most heartfelt thanks.

Jacob R. Marcus

American Jewish Archives
Cincinnati, Ohio
February, 1974

HISTORICAL ESSAY
ON THE
COLONY OF SURINAM.

FIRST PART

PARAMARIBO

1788

HISTORICAL ESSAY ON THE COLONY OF SURINAM

Its founding, its revolutions, its progress, from its origin up to our days, as well as the reasons which, for several years, have arrested the course of its prosperity; with the description and the present state of the colony, as well as its annual revenues, the taxes and imposts which are paid there, as also several other civil and political matters; as well as a picture of the manners of its inhabitants in general.

WITH

The history of the Jewish Portuguese [Sephardic] and German [Ashkenazic] community established there, their privileges, immunities and exemptions; their political and moral status, both ancient and modern; the part which they have had in the defense and in the progress of the colony.

The whole edited on the basis of authentic documents joined thereto, and placed in order by the regents and representatives of the said Portuguese Jewish Community.

[Paramaribo, 1788]

> Poor blind creatures that we are,
> Heaven will unmask the impostors,
> And compel their barbarous hearts
> To open to the gaze of mankind.

J[ean]. J[acques]. Roussseau, *Oeuvr[es]. Post[humes].*, Vol. XII, p. 460.

Dedicatory Epistle to the Noble and Very Venerable Lords, the Directors and Regents of the Colony of Surinam, etc., etc., etc., residing in Amsterdam.

Noble and Very Venerable Lords!

The Portuguese Jewish Community established in Surinam from her foundation to the present day ventures to present to you a work which in part contains an epitome of the history of your dominions in America, as well as of a people which, although unfortunate in many respects, yet counts itself fortunate to live under the laws of the Republic of the United Provinces [Holland], and under your noble protection. Your benefactions, your benevolence in regard to it, keeps this community bound to your colony, and to your interests.

Its duties towards you, the homage which it owes you in so many respects, have inspired in its representatives the courage to offer you this feeble production as a mark of respect and attachment which they and their ancestors have always had for your government. It is a duty, it is a homage, most Noble and Venerable Lords! which they hope you will deign to accept favorably.

And it is with these sentiments that we have the honor to be, with the most profound respect,

Noble and very Venerable Lords!

Your very humble and very obedient servants,

The regents and the representatives of the Portuguese Jewish Community of Surinam.

Surinam and Paramaribo
This 20 of February, 1788.

Mos. Pa. de Leon.
Saml. H. de la Parra.
Ishak de la Parra.
David de Is. C. Nassy.
David N. Monsanto.
Samuel H. Brandon.

PREFACE

It is not at all ambition, vanity, or conceit that has placed the pen in our hand to compose the work which we offer to the public. Nor would the daily example of so many bad works that issue continually from the presses, and which exist most often only as much as one has need to survey them, be able to blind us to the point of wishing to add to their number. On the contrary, the title of author is too imposing for us to wish to abuse it, and we would never have ventured to bring a literary production to light, if circumstances had not placed us in the position of having to do it. Besides, being born in a country where education furnishes nothing of all that is needed to cultivate and develop a certain spirit; deprived of the necessary knowledge, forced to write as best we can in a language [French] which, not being ours (This [i.e., ours] is Portuguese and Spanish), was taught to us less through informed principles than through a mere routine, and perhaps even a vicious one; furthermore, we are not acquainted with any other place in the universe than Surinam, the country of our birth. All these things certainly create disadvantages which should discourage us from an enterprise of this nature. But, we repeat, particular reasons have obliged us to do so. In addition, our natural resentment of the unfortunate condition of the Jews in general; truth; justice; our rights as human beings (which we were before we became Jews) and as citizens, have inspired us with the courage to profit by the happy circumstance which has been offered to us by the virtuous opinions of a celebrated political writer [Christian Wilhelm von Dohm]. And without fearing criticism, we have ventured to compose this work, the result of which and the consequences which may derive from it will perhaps contribute to some extent to the welfare of a suffering part of the human race. And in order to shed more light on the reason which gave birth to this enterprise, and which does honor to the virtue of him who conceived it and has, so to speak, inspired us, we shall put before the eyes of our readers the accidental cause which gave it birth.

The work which Monsieur C[hristian]. W[ilhelm]. von Dohm, councillor of war, archivist and private secretary of the Department of Foreign Affairs of His [late] Majesty [Frederick II ("the Great")] the King of Prussia, and at present his [i.e., King Frederick William II's] Minister Plenipotentiary to the district of the Lower Rhine, had published in German and printed at Berlin in 1781, under the title *Über die bürgerliche Verbesserung der Juden* ["On the Civic Improvement of the Jews"], then later translated into French by Monsieur J[ohann]. Bernoulli, of the Royal Academy of Sciences and Belles Lettres, etc., of Prussia, under the title *La Réforme Politique des Juifs* (published at Dessau in the Librairie des Auteurs & des Artistes, 1782, in octavo), is known to all the world.

Knowledge of this work reached us through an epitome inserted in the *Gazette Littéraire* of the month of May, 1784. Everyone hastened to order it from Holland. An unhappy person inhales; catches his breath, hopes, when he hears a voice that commiserates him, takes up his defense, or shows an interest in his lot.

The name of Monsieur Dohm, private secretary of a great king [Frederick the Great] who is both hero and philosopher, and that of the celebrated academician Bernoulli who was the translator, [being] known favorably in the republic of letters, only increased the desire of our community to read a work whose content, according to the epitome, was a rare phenomenon, even in the enlightened and philosophic century in which we live. Yet, despite our efforts, we were unable to obtain this work until February, 1786. We put it then in our College of Literature (which we call "Docendo Docemur," and of which we shall speak in this work); a reading followed; and having found it full of solid reasonings and of a luminous impartiality, which characterizes the soul of the author, the regents of the Portuguese Jewish Community in Surinam (although the reform which Monsieur Dohm proposes applies only to the Jews of Germany and Poland, and because of the immunities and rights which the Jews enjoy in Surinam, they have nothing in common with the condition of German-Polish Jewry) desired to pay the celebrated author the homage due to him as a philosopher and statesman because of the good which his work could effect in favor of their brethren in Europe. They took the liberty of addressing a letter of thanks to him dated March 10, 1786, paying homage at the same time to the memory of the translator, Monsieur Bernoulli, who had died some time previously. See the letter at the end of this Preface.

This letter was then sent by way of Holland to his address in Berlin. The regents did not think any further about the effect which it would produce, in particular on Monsieur Dohm; they were satisfied with having at least fulfilled a duty which the recognition and the love of their German and Polish brethren had inspired in them. But the virtuous heart of Monsieur Dohm, his worthy sentiments, forgetting in favor of humanity his important occupations in the service of his king, deigned to honor the regents with a response dated January 29, 1787, which reached them through Captain Dalmeyer on June 29, 1787. This will also be found at the end of this Preface. Herein he informed the regents of the interest that he still wished to take in the welfare of Jewry in general, asking at the same time for notes on the colony of Surinam and on the Jews settled there, in order to be able, through striking examples, to sustain the thesis of his work and to cooperate, as much as he was able, with any change that would be favorable to them.

The regents, persuaded by a letter that was both agreeable and advantageous to their community, complied with the duty of satisfying Monsieur Dohm on the subject of the Jews. They were in some manner compelled, despite their incapacity, to produce the present work with all possible speed and care, at the same time giving information about this enterprise to Monsieur Dohm, by another letter dated July 5, 1787, so that, after this statement, no one could rightly accuse us of vanity or of conceit, and still less of the desire of posing as authors with the publication of this work.

Our first intention was to limit ourselves simply to the history of the Jews in Surinam and to their early and modern condition, without including anything that did not directly concern us, and to send Monsieur Dohm a reply to his letter rather than an essay. But, having examined our archives and assembled some isolated facts, and having consulted fragments that were scarce and almost forgotten, we found the history of the Jews settled in Surinam so linked and, as it were, identified with that of the colony in general, and the events which distinguished the first Jews who arrived there ever since the origin of the colony so interwoven with those of the other inhabitants of the colony, that it was morally impossible for us to separate them and to produce only a special history of our community. Besides, how could a chain of petty events which happened to a handful of Jews in the space of 130 years in a part of Dutch Guiana attract the attention of the reader? Would not prejudice against the Jews and indifference towards them be sufficiently cogent to induce the reader to reject our work out of hand? Besides, since Monsieur Dohm, in his last letter, had asked us for *some historical notes on the fortunes of the colony from its beginning, together with data about its present political and moral condition*, had he not placed us under the necessity of expatiating a little with reference to the colony in general?

Having decided, therefore, to interweave anew the events that befell the Jews with those of the colony so as to make a historical epitome of all that concerned it, we have not been able to prepare this work of ours for anyone at all without at the same time giving preliminary notice to our venerable benefactors, the territorial lords of the colony in Holland, and making to them conjointly the offer of a historical epitome which will comprise the events of their colony and that of the Jews established there, as a feeble homage for their paternal protection and for the benevolence for which the Jews of Surinam have been indebted to them from the beginning of their administration as proprietors up to the present day. In consequence, we venture to flatter ourselves that Monsieur Dohm, instead of condemning us for not having sent this work to him directly, according to the contents of our last letter, will thank us for having obeyed the duty which gratitude and the acknowledgment of the benefits received have imposed upon us.

In order to fulfill this task, we were obliged to consult several works on America and principally those published about Surinam, both by Dutch nationals and by foreigners, and then to compare them with the fragments which we found in our archives. Having found, as the result of our researches, that these works are defective in several respects, we took care to compose an abridged history of the colony which, by a comparison of several events, has nothing in common with what has been written about it. And, noting, besides, that despite the incorporation of the Jews with the other inhabitants of Surinam, despite their zeal, their exploits, even their riches, they are mentioned in these works only with an indifference which clearly reveals the prejudice of these

HISTORY OF SURINAM

writers, we found ourselves under the indispensable necessity of enlarging on all that which concerns them and of recounting the most interesting facts in order to make them more particularly known, without losing sight of what concerns the colony in general.

In regard to the history of the Jewish community which we have the honor of representing at the present time as regents, we have been obliged to confirm some facts described in this work by means of authentic documents and by means of any evidence attached thereto. Though they might be superfluous or useless in any other work, they are indispensable in this one which deals with the Jews. For to report facts without proofs would be to compromise ourselves with the Pyrrhonism [ultra-skepticism] which prevails with reference to the Jews; but to confirm these facts, to develop what some authors have carefully concealed, is only to close the mouths of our antagonists; at least, they will not dare to deny everything with effrontery.

And as our community and we ourselves in general regard the colony only as a sort of political patrimony (if we are permitted to use such an expression) where we enjoy liberty and freedom, its welfare, its prosperity, and the well-being of our agreeable, though in many respects ungrateful, fellow inhabitants interest us sufficiently so that we would willingly sacrifice all that we hold most dear for their preservation. We have likewise, in many places of this work, expounded on the causes of their degeneration in general, and we have demonstrated, with all the force of which we are capable, the rights of our colonists in general, and the protection which they rightfully claim and await in accordance with the justice and equity of their mother country and the merchants of Holland, in regard to the debts on their plantations. We have therefore given details of the revenues of the colony from 1750 to 1707, the expenses, the taxes laid on their products, the profits that the [Dutch] Republic derives from the colony, and the little that the unfortunate planters derive from all their pains and from so many troubles which they continually endure there. In this picture we have not at all flattered the manners and the character of the inhabitants of the colony, either Christians or Jews, in general. On the contrary, we have disclosed their faults freely and in accordance with our judgment, without fearing criticism; for it has no hold on hearts which do not at all seek to immolate candor or truth on the altar of flattery.

In accordance with this principle, we complain at the same time about the prejudices which still prevail there against the Jewish people in general, and we have called the accusations and the apology of the Jewish people of Surinam to the attention of the enlightened and fair-minded public, in order that it may judge us according to our faults and according to our needs. At the same time, we have gloried in acknowledging, with the most complete satisfaction, the obligations which we have to the paternal protection of our venerable benefactors in Holland, and equally the kindness and benevolence of several distinguished persons of the colony, without hesitating for a moment to name them openly and to accord them the praises which are due to them. If we have wounded their discretion thereby, we beg their pardon. Besides, is it not sufficient to hide the names of our Zoiluses [snarling critics] without concealing those of our Maecenases [patrons]?

Concerning the form which we have given to this work, it has appeared to us most conformable to that of a historical essay which comprises ideas and views which are perhaps little analogous to the abridgement of the history of a colony, whose political affairs are not at all the business of the authors. And since its principal subject is the history of the Jews, we have gathered together all that we needed to take them from their expulsion from Portugal and Spain to Brazil, then to Holland, to Cayenne, until they are placed in Surinam, without forgetting the history of their first settlement in Holland, and their rights under that commonwealth. The works from which we have drawn, the knowledge of the greatest part of all that which is found in this essay, are scrupulously cited here. But without maintaining an attitude of servile respect, we have followed them, judged them, even criticized them, according to our feeble lights and our local knowledge.

In regard to the style, we have already admitted our incapacity; in consequence, we do not doubt at all that one will find here phrases that are hardly French, barbarisms as one may wish to call them; but we have endeavored, as much as was possible for us, to make it clear and intelligible; and we flatter ourselves that an indulgent public will be willing to pardon the defects that are found there in favor of the right of humanity which we claim and of motives, free of pretension, which have made us write this work.

And yet, if there are found in the course of this essay articles that are of little interest to the general reader, and many dissertations in favor of the Jews, we flatter ourselves that our venerable benefactors in Holland as well as Monsieur Dohm and true philanthropists will not take it amiss that we have called their attention to the details which concern the Jewish community in Surinam, in order that everyone, in the sphere in which he is situated and the power that he possesses, may be able to derive therefrom that which accords with his good intentions and reject the rest as useless. Besides, if it is permitted to an individual who is accused of irregularities in his manners to speak about himself and to mention the good that he has done in order to give the lie to his accusers, this defense is with greater reason permitted and even necessary for an entire people which finds itself in the same circumstances. And if, despite our few pretensions, despite the candor and truth which we have prescribed for ourselves in composing this work, the voice of criticism which is backed up by religious or national prejudices nonetheless desires to accuse us of being presumptuous and vain and, to crown its perversity, wishes to assail the community with new invectives, instead of observing its faults with the intention of correcting such as it may have, and of putting us in condition to improve our work, we shall place the critics in the number of so many black calumnies which have been spread against the Jews in general, and we shall apply to them in advance what Menippus said to Jupiter: "If, instead of replying to me, you take up your thunderbolts, you are wrong."

Letter of the authors to Monsieur C. W. von Dohm, on the subject of his work on the improvement of the Jews.

Sir!

Illustrious and worthy friend of humanity!

Imbued with sentiments which give acknowledgment to virtuous hearts, we venture to overstep the bounds of prudence in order to have this letter sent to you. The homage which humankind owes to you in such just respects, the eternal obligation which the Jewish community in general has toward you, your ideas, your philosophy, your impartiality, and your zeal in behalf of an unfortunate people, will immortalize your name. Those who are the objects thereof owe you unceasing homage. Permit us then, worthy friend of humanity, in our capacity as regents and representatives of the Portuguese Jewish Community, established more than a century ago in Surinam, in [South] America, to send you this letter and to thank you for your zeal for the work which you desired to publish concerning its political improvement, a work which, though in print since 1782, did not come to our knowledge until last month. And although, by virtue of this philosophical tolerance which is the emblem of the august commonwealth of Holland, our mother country, we have only to felicitate ourselves upon our lot, nonetheless we cannot refrain from admiring, sir, your disinterestedness, from blessing God who has inspired you with this sublime virtue which prevails in your heart, and from regarding your work as the antidote to all those prejudices which reign in the hearts of men against those who worship the same God, although in different ways, and, finally, as the scourge which will crush, in the eyes of the wise, those who persecute us, and the shield which will defend us in the eyes of the universe.

Receive then, sir, our feeble homage. May the soul of the virtuous Monsieur Bernoulli, your worthy translator, receive from our common Father the reward of his virtues, of his humanity, and of his zeal! Pardon, sir, the transport of acknowledgment which has inspired us to write to you. Accept the ardent wishes which we and the entire Jewish community express for all that concerns you. May the God of the universe give you the power and grant you the strength to be constantly the support of the unfortunate and the defender of the oppressed.

We are, with the most profound respect,
Sir!
Your very humble, very grateful, and very obedient servants, (signed) The regents of the Portuguese Jewish Community of Surinam. D[avid]. D[e]. J[saac]. C. Nassy, David N. Monsanto, J. H. de Barrios, Jr., S. H. Brandon, Mos. P. de Leon, S. H. de la Parra, Is. de la Parra.
Surinam
March 10, 1786.

Monsieur C. W. von Dohm, councillor of war, archivist and private secretary of the Department of Foreign Affairs of His Majesty the King of Prussia.

HISTORY OF SURINAM 13

Reply of Monsieur C. W. von Dohm to the Preceding Letter
Gentlemen:

Only a short time ago your kind letter with which you desired to honor me under date of March 10 of last year reached me by way of Berlin, which I left some months ago, since the King, my master, entrusted to me here the position of Minister Plenipotentiary to the district of the Lower Rhine.

I could only be agreeably surprised to learn from your letter that my writing, which regards your community as unjustly unfortunate in almost every place, has reached you. The sentiments which guided me in composing it ought to be those of all good men, of all true Christians and of all true statesmen; their simplicity, I hope, will lead to their being practiced in the future, too, by governments, and I shall always congratulate myself if I shall have been fortunate enough to cooperate herewith in some manner. But up to now I have not yet received this reward. I have just learned, on the contrary, that almost at the same moment when I received your letter my book was burned at Paris; I hope that this was done only through a misunderstanding which will quickly be made up for.

The approbation which you attest to me, gentlemen, from the other end of the world is all the more consoling to me. May you enjoy the good fortune of not knowing, other than through the traditions of your ancestors, the manner in which your community is being vitiated in Europe! Your situation furnishes a convincing proof of my thesis, that the Jews are capable, like us, of being good citizens as soon as they are permitted to be. I could, perhaps, make good use hereof if you would be willing to communicate to me some details on the advantages which your wise and enlightened government accords you. I would be curious, above all, to know if any distinctions are made, where you are, between your community and the other inhabitants. Are all occupations, crafts, and kinds of commerce permitted to you? Do you enjoy the right to own plantations in complete possession? Do you not have any special taxes? Is the number of your families restricted? Have you the right to defend the common fatherland as soldiers, and to serve it as civil or military officers?

These are questions which interest me very much, and you will oblige me by giving me an authentic and detailed answer, adding also some historical notes on the lot that your colony has undergone since its beginning, the date of which I do not know; on the changes that have been able to be made in your privileges and civil rights; on the moral and political state of the colony; and on the feelings which the justice of the government must have inspired in the Christians towards you.

If you wish to honor me with a reply, I request you to have it sent in care of Monsieur Helleman van Eickelnberg, consul of the [Prussian] King of Vlissingen [in Holland].

With most sincere wishes for the uninterrupted duration of your good fortune, I bear witness to you of the very high esteem that your letter has inspired in me.

It is with these sentiments that I have the honor to be,
Gentlemen!
Your most humble and obedient servant,
(signed) Dohm.

Cologne on the Rhine,
this 29 of January, 1787.
To the regents and representatives of the Portuguese Jewish Community in Surinam.

INTRODUCTION

The contempt with which the Jewish community is treated in all parts of the world, the hatred that is borne against them, is a fact which is as well established as it is difficult to understand, above all in this enlightened century, in which monarchs seem to vie with one another for the title of benefactors and fathers of their subjects.

The writings of Monsieur de Voltaire can perhaps give the solution to this problem of morality. This great man, made to enlighten the world, in the midst of his digressions against religions, preaching tolerance, trampling all cults under foot, conjointly took unfortunate pleasure in crushing the Jewish community and making it hideous in the eyes of the universe.[1] His worshippers, or better, the proselytes whom this celebrated man has been able to make,[2] have constantly followed the banner and the motto of their apostle. It is perhaps again he and his adherents who are the reason why the morality of Jesus Christ and the simplicity of the Gospels appear to be confounded, to the disadvantage even of the Jews,[3] and, so to speak, amalgamated with the baneful attacks of the priests. It was useless for Monsieur de Voltaire to have said [in 1771], in his "Epistle [to the Author of the Book] *The Three Impostors*" (which [epistle] begins by defending the existence of God, and ends in sarcasms against the Jews and [the Catholic apologist] Monsieur [Élie] Fréron), "Correct the valet, but respect the master" [*Corrige le valet, mais respecte le maître*]. His disciples misused his insights, and in their strayings from the truth in imitation of their apostle, they took the Jewish Community as the object of their sorry jesting. The world is, unfortunately, full of vain and haughty spirits, and it has very few real scholars. In this inequality, what hope could the Jews ever conceive in the milieu of the philosophy which is at present prevalent in Europe? It is only in the private life of each individual of which a nation is composed, a body of any society whatsoever, free of the shackles of that specious urbanity which characterizes a polished man, that one can know the distinctive character of a people. It is in their private lives, in their relations with their respective families and their friends, that one knows their morality and their manner of thinking and of living. Without this, all judgments lead to falsehoods, and all conclusions are erroneous. Such a person may be sweet, amiable, beneficent, when he is outside of his home; glory, pride, vanity, self-esteem often force him to show in appearance what he is not at all in actuality. And it is only when he is at home that from his small actions, where Nature is the only one that speaks, one can penetrate what is really his soul. Were there ever, therefore, any very disinterested persons, men passionate for the truth, unprejudiced philosophers, who took the trouble to study the Jews, to frequent their homes without fear of being blamed? Were their faults ever compared with their necessities, the large families they have had to rear with their few resources, their little satisfaction in their existence in view of so much contempt with the necessary negligence in the observance of the rules of beneficence? No, the Jews have never had that fortune. Whatever concerns them, whatever comes from them, whatever has relation to them, if it is not rigorously despised, is at least disdained. It is possible that if the two Buxtorfs [the German Hebraists, Johann (1564-1629) and his son Johann (Jr.) (1599-1664)] and [the Italian Hebraist, Giulio] Bartolocci [1613-1687), with a view to blackening the community and its religion,[4] had not studied the rabbis, the very names of the Jewish writers would be buried, just as are their actions, which could have made them be known advantageously in the history of mankind. It is for this very reason that the Jews, who have been able to distinguish themselves by moral actions and by services rendered to various powers of Europe, did not find their place in the dictionaries of illustrious men. The ingenious compilers would certainly not have disfigured their works if they had included the number of the Jews who distinguished themselves advantageously and who had the good fortune to be decorated with titles that are the glory of the community. In the midst of so many disasters: Bienvenida Abarbanel, who in the sixteenth century merited the honor of being chosen to educate Donna Leonora of Toledo, the daughter of the Viceroy of Naples and later the wife of Cosimo de Medici, Grand Duke of Tuscany, who preserved for that

Jewess the title of Mother until her death; Gracia Nassy, known in Italy as a woman of much distinction, to whom the famous Ferrara Bible of 1553 was dedicated, and who had as son-in-law her nephew, the famous Duke of Naxos; the heroism, the chastity of her daughter Esther merited being recorded; Samuel Abravanel, his heroic acts in behalf of the King of Fez, described in the Chronicle of Xarises, dedicated to Philip II, King of Spain; and many others who lived in the sixteenth century.[5] And in the past century, Alexandre and Alvaro Nunez da Costa,[6] the Machados,[7] the Count of Belmonte, whom Morery mentions in the article Amsterdam[8]; the Texeiras[9]; the Soassos[10]; the Molos[11]; the Mesquitas[12]; and again in our century Baron d'Aguilar[13]; the Gradis family[14]; and especially the Moses Mendelssohn family[15] are not unworthy of being mentioned here. The titles of barons, counts, treasurers, agents, etc., with which these men were decorated during their lifetimes by the first powers of Europe would merit being preserved, if it were only for the uniqueness of these titles, combined with the unfortunate name of Jews, which nevertheless imply even greater merits and more eminent personal virtues than if they had been given to Christians.

In contrast to all this, we have no need of presenting the history of the calamities which the Jewish community underwent, both the ancient one and the modern one, or to recall the horrors of the persecutions which it endured, of which the celebrated Monsieur Dohm has given the appalling history. Besides, it is not astonishing that in the centuries of barbarity, ignorance, and vulgarity, when the Jews were almost the sole scholars in Europe,[16] hate, envy, and, above all, avarice caused them to be persecuted with a cruelty which one could scarcely find among tigers, as the Reverend Father [Richard] Simon remarks in his *Bibliothèque Critique,* volume 1, pages 115, 116, and 118, and volume 3, pages 12-13, and several others. Pope Paul IV said, with reference to an accusation against the Jews, "Without my good Jesuit, I was damned, for I would have wrongfully killed the Jews. I pray God that He will convert them, but as long as I live" (he died in 1559) "I shall not hate them at all, nor shall I molest them."

But in the past century, the century of the fine arts, the brilliant century of France which saw Descartes, Corneille, Boileau, and Racine born, a horrible lawsuit was brought against the Jews of Metz and

Raphael Levy was burned alive on January 17, 1670[17]; Louis XIV, who confirmed the letters patent of Henry II and those of Henry III, and even extended the provisions thereof in favor of the Jews under date of 1656, brought forth his Code Noir[18]; the merchants of Paris forged atrocious calumnies against the Jews in their Request of 1765 or 1766,[19] and the libel was published, known under the name of *Observations of an Alsatian on the Affairs of the Jews of Alsace,* the author of which passes as one of the principal actors in the fabrication of false receipts; and, as the climax of the calamities, the magistrates of Essequibo and Demerary [in Guiana], subjects of the Republic of Holland, have again fabricated invectives against the Jews[20]—all this is something to astonish every man of good sense and make them shed tears for this unfortunate community. In view of so many ignominies which banish hope from their hearts which are rent by pains and cares it is only from the Republic of Holland, from the august [Hapsburg Emperor] Joseph II, from the beneficent [French King] Louis XVI, from the beloved Frederick William [II of Prussia], and from Leopold [Grand Duke] of Tuscany, etc., etc., that they await their salvation. May the works of the celebrated Monsieur Dohm, may his impartiality penetrate to the foot of thrones and, in imitation of him, may the philosophers deign to unite their voices to his in order to effect the happy revolution of banning every discrimination against a community that has been hated and persecuted for eighteen centuries.

And in order to cooperate as much as we can, despite our small knowledge, in this happy revolution, we shall place before the eyes of the public and particularly before those of our benefactor, the celebrated Monsieur Dohm, the history of the Jews settled in Surinam, for the purpose of confirming, as much as we shall be able, what he maintained in his work on political reform, "that the Jews can become generally as good citizens as the Christians as soon as they are permitted to do so." This thesis, confirmed by the facts that we have reported, and which we shall further report in the course of this work, will prove incontestably that the Republic of Holland, in increasing its credit and its commerce, has been able to make its provinces and its establishments in America the abode of liberty and the refuge of the unfortunate, who became, by reason of its benefits, useful citizens and faithful subjects of the Republic.

HISTORICAL ESSAY
ON THE
COLONY OF SURINAM

PART I

After the expulsion of the Jews from Spain in 1492,[1] to the number of 800,000 persons, according to [the Spanish historian] Father [Juan de] Mariana, and subsequently from Portugal in 1497, after having suffered great misfortunes there, as can be seen in the *Historia General d'Espagna*,[2] the Jews spread to the four corners of the world. The greater part of them emigrated to Italy, where they were received and protected by Popes Alexander VI, Paul IV,[3] Sixtus V, and others; to the states of the great Seigneur [the Ottoman Sultan], etc. They carried with them immense wealth in gold, jewels, and other articles, in addition to more than an estimated 30,000,000 ducats in coined silver.[4] The decree of expulsion of the Jews from Spain, says Father Mariana,[5] was always regarded as a completely reprehensible act; for people who were as rich as they were useful could not at all be obliged to leave their native country without causing very perceptible damages to all the provinces of a kingdom.

Those who [remained in Iberia and] had their wealth invested at interest or in real estate kept the name of New Christians. When they began to be suspected of being unfaithful to the [Roman Catholic] religion which they pretended to profess, and when their wealth aroused the avidity of their persecutors, to avoid the fatal blow which awaited them and to place their possessions where they would be safe from the pursuits of the detestable tribunal of the Inquisition, they sent the greatest part of their wealth to London and to Holland; they made use of bills of exchange which they had invented several centuries before. Later, they were admitted by all the European powers. As Montesquieu says,[6] "Philip II, who shortly afterwards extended his laws over Portugal, decreed that those of his subjects who were descended from a Jew or from a Moor could be admitted neither into ecclesiastical orders nor into public offices. This seal of reprobation which, so to speak, was imprinted on the forehead of the New Christians, made even the wealthiest loath to reside where their fortune did not protect them from humiliation, and they carried away their capital to Bordeaux, Antwerp, Hamburg, and other places where they had continuous connections,[7] even despite this decree of Philip II. It is in vain that the grandees of Spain take the precaution of changing their name and coat of arms; it is nevertheless known that they come from Jewish fathers. The monasteries are full of them; the greatest part of the monks, Inquisitors, and bishops come from this community. This emigration, as Abbé [Guillaume] Raynal remarks,[8] became the origin of a great revolution; it extended to several countries the industry which up to that time had been concentrated in Spain and Portugal, and deprived the two states of the advantages which the one [Portugal] derived from the East Indies and the other [Spain] from the West Indies." [8a]

Previously, during these last epochs the Jews whom the Inquisition incessantly persecuted were exiled in great numbers to Brazil. "Although despoiled of their fortune by these insatiable leeches, they succeeded in establishing some culture—this beginning of well-being—and caused the court of Lisbon to perceive that a colony could become useful to its mother country in other ways than by means of metals." [9]

However, although these were well-established in Brazil and living there comfortably, the contempt attached in Spain and in Portugal to the name of New Christians made them all the more stubbornly devoted to Judaism. Consequently, they sought only for favorable occasions to draw near to their brethren, and while waiting they made deliveries of bars of gold and of silver to their correspondents and brethren who had already settled in Holland and in England. The conquest of Brazil by the Dutch under the command of Prince [John] Maurice of Nassau-[Siegen] opened up for them the means of fulfilling their designs.[10]

In order to let this work proceed in a more regular manner, we must, before giving an account of the colony of Surinam and its relations with the Jews established therein, consider the primitive state of those who settled in Holland.

According to [the French historian, Jacques] Basnage [de Beauval],[11] 648 Spanish and Portuguese Jews, all circumcised, had settled there from 1588 or 1589; according to Uri Halevy of Emden and, after him, his son Aaron Levy, from 1554 on. According to the report of Lavra and d'Aboab,[12] 931 persons [had settled]. Hence it can be calculated that the number of Portuguese and Spanish Jews who settled in Holland in the course of the years from 1554 to 1588 amounted to 1,579, not including women and girls.

From this time up to the year 1595, the Jews there concealed their Judaism. The Protestants, with the rigorous investigations made by Calvinism against Papist images, suspected the Jews of being tainted with Catholicism; and therefore, on the day of their Kippur [Atonement Fast] in the year 1595, they attacked a house in which Jews were assembled to say their prayers. A crowd of armed people fell upon them, and under the threat of killing them, they demanded of them their relics, hosts, crucifixes, etc. This demand astonished them, and they declared that they were only Jews who had fled from Spain and from Portugal because of the Inquisition. The Dutch, not very satisfied with this answer, entered their homes, and having found only Hebrew books there, they let them go, but under the condition that they should pray to God every Saturday for the welfare of the government of Amsterdam.

After this period [i.e., of Spanish rule], changes occurred in the government of Holland in 1578. According to the view of Monsieur Wagenaar, the Jews there had the freedom to build their synagogue and to profess their religion openly. Monsieur Wagenaar does not mention at all the unexpected attack which the Calvinists made on the Jews, and which we have just related, but Miguel de Barrios, an author who wrote in the last century, reports the fact in full detail.[13]

Despite this admission of the Jews to Holland, and the tolerance which characterizes the Republic, and despite all that [Jacques] Savary [de Bruslons] says in his dictionary with reference to the word Jew[14] and several other political writers with reference to the profit which the commerce of Holland derived at all times from the industry and the activity of the Portuguese and Spanish Jews, their privileges as citizens there are very limited. Monsieur Wagenaar, in his work,[15] mentions merely the benefits that they have and can still have, as far as commerce is concerned; all professions, except those having connection with medicine, are forbidden to them, and they are not permitted to join the guilds.

We do not know if these obstacles did not contribute greatly to the decadence of the Jews in Holland, and to the fewness of luminaries whom the community there was able to acquire afterwards, in the midst of so much religious liberty. They are still accused of ignorance without consideration of how little profit the community would have been able to derive from its efforts in devoting itself assiduously to the arts and sciences. If, in the beginning, instead of brokerage and commerce in stocks, the Jews there had been able to have their own workshops and factories; if they had been able to join the guilds without discrimination, and thus to profit from the wealth and the luxury of their brethren, the community in Holland would not have declined to its present state, its well-being would contribute also to the advantage of the Republic itself, and the Dutch Jews who emigrated to America would have furnished the colonies with many artisans and professional men who would settle there permanently. The first ardor of religion; that attachment to many prejudices and habits which is, unfortunately, made permanent by idleness and contempt, would be weakened, would even vanish imperceptibly, to the advantage of the colonies where they would be settled. How many vigorous arms could still be employed in Holland itself to raise the deplorable state to which the national manufactories are reduced!

The sixty thousand Jews who are in the city of Amsterdam alone are a real object of concern. The States General indeed felt the necessity of reforming this branch of wealth when they adopted their resolution of July 6, 1753, emanating from the representation of the Princess [Anne] of Orange and Nassau, Regent of Holland.[16] Monsieur van den Heuvel, in his memoir which took the prize on the subject proposed by the Haarlem Society of Sciences, likewise maintained, with truly patriotic zeal, that this reform was as useful as it was necessary. He maintains, in this writing, that "the number of wigmakers, merchants of fashions, perfumers, etc., should be reduced and that the Jews in particular should be compelled to establish factories for the manufacture of tapestries, porcelain, mirrors, and other manufactures which up to the present have not been undertaken in Holland, and in which they should employ those of their religion who today (for lack of other resources) walk the streets and carry on a traffic, more harmful than necessary, in various articles of merchandise, particularly in lottery tickets, etc." [17]

Meanwhile, we are awaiting, from the wisdom of the government of the Republic, measures which can, at the same time, include both the welfare of Holland and that of a large part of its loyal subjects. It will again be this Republic which will first afford the Jews the means of their subsistence, just as it was the first to receive them in its bosom with so much love and benevolence. May the European powers remember "that this very liberty (as restricted as it is) brought to Holland a number of Spanish and Portuguese Jews who settled previously in Amsterdam, where they occupy a large part of the city, that these Jews brought there not only their fortune and their wealth, but also correspondence with foreign Jews, especially with those in the Levant, the effects of which greatly increased commerce and navigation." [18] Thus may the Jews who are scattered in the four corners of the world implore the God of Israel for the welfare of a republic which is as beneficial as it is wise!

After these Jews settled in Holland and, by reason of the wealth which they brought there, displayed a luxury equal to that of the Christians, and were able to gain for themselves a general esteem, even to the extent that in the following years they occupied distinguished positions in the service of several crowned heads, as we have already stated in the introduction to this work, several other Jews came here [to Holland] from all parts, and those who lived in Brazil sought only favorable opportunities to go there, as we have mentioned above. There were at that time in Brazil a number of those whose families were settled in Holland, and who longed for their absent brethren exposed to the terrors which the Inquisition inspires. The bravest of those of Holland resolved to go to Brazil with the Dutch fleet that was intended for its conquest, and they served as volunteers in the army. This fact is corroborated by pieces of poetry in Spanish which were composed at that very time, fragments of which are found at the end of the work of Miguel de Barrios which we have cited, and four lines of which we shall quote in order to shed more light on what we have asserted.

> *Con el Hollandio en el Brasil ardiente*
> *Se opone al Portugues la Nation sancta.*
> *Y este ane en buda al imperial quebrante,*
> *Que la amenaça con furor ambiente.*

Which means: With the Dutch in burning Brazil, the holy nation opposed the Portuguese; and in that year it routed the imperial force which wished to subjugate the Republic.

These Jews, then, meeting their brethren in Brazil, persuaded them to lift the veil which concealed their Judaism. Those of Brazil were for the most part people of substance, and well versed in commerce and agriculture, and during the eight years which followed the conquest of Brazil, Prince [John] Maurice of Nassau[-Siegen] remaining there as the governor, gathered together their wealth to await the issue of this conquest. Unfortunately, when the United Provinces recalled the prince in 1644, the Dutch forces in Brazil became so diminished that the Republic lost all that it had conquered from the Portuguese,[19] and the Jews of Brazil then made the decision to withdraw with their wealth on the vessels which conveyed the 2,000 soldiers who were under the command of the prince. The most distinguished of those who went to Holland with their families were the celebrated Rabbi Isaac Aboab, the Nassys, the Mezas, the Pereiras, and several others."[20]

It was at this time that David Nassy, his family, and his companions, already accustomed to the climate of Brazil and to the labors of agriculture, adopted the resolution to settle anew in America. The mania or the rage to form colonies in the New World was then general, and in keeping with this purpose, he obtained for himself and his associates, from the West India Company in its assembly called XVII, on September 12, 1659, the privilege of founding a colony on the island of Cayenne with the title of *Patron Master*. (See Documentary evidence No. 1, of which Articles 2, 3, 4, 5, 6, 7, and 8 are especially remarkable with reference to the subject of this work.)

The mainland of Cayenne, located between four and five leagues from the island of this name, had belonged to the French from 1624 on, under the administration of the Society of Rohan. Some years later, a new society, under the name of the Company of the North Cape, drove out the former and became master thereof. And despite the hopes which this new company conceived for Cayenne, the enmities and the quarrels which arose among the directors caused such a tumult in the colony that it was entirely annihilated at the end of 1653. The Dutch, profiting from this event, took possession of this part of Guiana in 1656 or in 1657; they established themselves on the mainland under Gerrit Spranger.[21] And it is by virtue of this possession that the West India Company granted the above-mentioned Nassy the charter of September 12, 1659, and, by Article 1, fixed the boundaries with the other colony founded on the mainland.

The Dutch, then, Christians as well as Jews, remained the peaceful possessors of Cayenne until May 15, 1664,[22] when they were driven out by the French, in the name of the Company of Equinoctial France, under the command of de la Barre, Lieutenant of Marine [Navy], who brought a large number of Christians and Jews from La Rochelle.[23]

David Nassy, by virtue of his charter, was likewise established, with a very large number of Jews, on the island which had belonged to him in his own right since 1660, and he diffused everywhere the news of his acquisition. The Jews of Livorno [Leghorn in Italy], to the number of 152, left in July, 1660, to go to Cayenne. (See the thanksgivings which they rendered to God for their safe arrival, in Spanish lines printed at the end of the work of Miguel de Barrios.) And when the French made themselves masters of their island likewise, they all withdrew with what they still had to Surinam, which then belonged to the English.[24]

If the Republic had not suffered this misfortune and if the Jews, as subjects of Holland, had not at all undergone this fate, perhaps if they had continued in legitimate proprietorship of Cayenne, the prejudice which regards them as not being at all a part of any nation would have been banished and it would have produced examples that would have been imitated by the richest men of the community. Even smaller causes have produced great events to the advantage of human beings, and Abbé Raynal, who felt this truth very deeply—he is known for it—would have seen his desire accomplished more than a century ago. Let us see what he says in his *Histoire Philosophique*, Volume VII, page 275: "May the Jewish people, at first slaves, then conquerors, and then degraded for twenty centuries, some day legitimately possess Jamaica or some other rich island of the New World! May it gather all its children there, and rear them peaceably in culture and in commerce, sheltered from the fanaticism that made them odious to the world, and from the persecution that too rigorously punished it for its errors! May the Jews at last live free, serene, and happy in a corner of the universe; for they are our brothers through the bonds of humanity and our fathers through the teachings of religion!"

From what we have just said, it is incontestable that the Jews, who knew how to make Brazil fertile, as Abbé Raynal says, in Volume V, page 9, were then in a position to make Cayenne more important than it ever became, both because of their knowledge of agriculture and because of the wealth which they brought from Portugal. And if France, instead of having driven them out of their homes because of their religion, had admitted them as subjects of France, she would have derived much more advantage from the colony, which now costs the Crown so much money, without its being able to be compared even with the smallest ones which Holland has in Guiana. And in order to judge the status of this colony, one has only to read the *procès-verbal* of Malouet, Ordonnateur [governor] and General Commissary of Cayenne, of January 7, 1777, printed at Surinam, by N. Vlier.[25]

This history, which we were obliged to give summarized in order to get to our subject, is a convincing proof that the Jews who were the first to settle in Surinam were almost all people of merit, very capable and very rich, and that as a result it is not surprising that they took the greatest part in the founding and in the growth of the colony, despite dissimulation in this respect on the part of those who attempted to write its history. We flatter ourselves that no one will call in question what we have asserted, especially about the Jews, the more so since in the archives of the community there are to be found resolutions by means of which it was established "that the ecclesiastical institutions at Surinam shall be of the same content as those which they had in their colony of Cayenne." And in another, of April, 1674, 8,000 pounds of sugar are granted to the daughters of J. Brandon, of Amsterdam, for each of his daughters who should get married, and that, this resolution adds, "because he was one of the members of our congregation of Cayenne." Hence it is as clear as day, first, that the Jews deserved to have obtained, equally with the other subjects of the Republic, grants to establish a colony, and to possess it as their legitimate property, and, second, that this charter or privilege was fully implemented, which presupposes talent and merit on the part of those who went to Surinam.

Before entering into what concerns their settlement in Surinam, it seems suitable to us (in order to comply with one of Dohm's proposals) to give, as briefly as is possible, a description of the first period of the colony, in order the better to be able to speak, in the continuation of this work, of its events both ancient and modern.

Of all the authors who have written the history of Surinam, no one, it seems to us, has attempted to investigate the etymology of this word. On the contrary, there are several who have declared that they could not even make any conjectures on this matter. Nevertheless, we shall venture our opinion. Among the different nations which occupied that part of South America, there was one which lived in a district of the Amazon country, which, according to the atlas of Abbé Raynal (Map No. 29), is only about nine degrees of north latitude distant from Surinam. This province was called Surina, and the peoples who inhabited it were the *Surines* and the *Corcipines,* nations which were, according to de la Martinière, in his geographical dictionary in folio, "the most skilful in all America, especially in woodworking; they make (he says) benches and chairs in the form of animals, etc." These characteristic aspects are still found here on pieces of wood, and notably on the clubs or the tomahawks of the Indians which our ancestors captured from them, and which some had enough curiosity to preserve. Here there are to be found figures of animals, etc., better carved than any Indian figure, and this gives reason to believe that the first inhabitants of the colony were the same, or at least belonged to the province of Surina, situated in the Amazon Country. Thus it is very apparent that the first European nation which came to these seas called the river by the name of the Indian nation which inhabited it; the more so since the word *Guyane,* already employed by the French for *Cayenne,* as Martinière again observes, could not be used *equally* for all parts of Guyane [Guiana] and thus they called the river Surina or *Surinam.*

Whatever, then, may be the origin of this word Surinam in Guiana, on the coast of South America, it is situated, according to the observation made by de la Condamine in these very places on August 28, 1744, at five degrees and forty-nine minutes north latitude.[26]

The river which gives its name to the entire extent of the country flows almost from south to north, and has its mouth between the Marony and the Saramaca rivers. Before it enters there, one finds at the left a large bank of sand mixed with mud, always known under the name of *Parhams-Punt,* or *Cape of Willoughby of Parham,* afterwards called, through corruption, *Bramspunt,* a name which it still preserves today. From its mouth up to the confluence of the Commewine River (which actually makes the richness of the colony), it is about three-fourths of a league wide. These two rivers are so deep, especially that of Surinam, that they can carry the largest merchant ships as much as four or six leagues up the river. Two and one-fourth leagues from the mouth of the Surinam is the fortress called New Amsterdam, and almost a league further up is situated Fort Zeelandia, rebuilt by the Zeelanders in 1667 several hundreds of paces lower than the city of Paramaribo, the chief place of the entire colony. At the end of this work we shall give a short description of the situation of the colony in general. Let us now look at its origin.

According to the opinion of several writers, the first nation which took possession of this part of Guiana was the French, all the more easily since no other had settled there and because the Company of Rohan had been established in Cayenne since 1624. David Pieterse de Vries in his voyage reports that he found there, in 1634, some European habitations. The misfortunes which befell the said Company of Rohan and the others which followed it in its disasters (as we have noted above) necessarily could not have any favorable effect with regard to Surinam; besides, the foul air which evaporated from the marshes and from the waters stagnant because of the small amount of clearing done, compelled the French to abandon it.

The revolution in England before and under the government of Cromwell inspired the English with more zeal to establish colonies in America. In 1650, accordingly, Lord William Willoughby departed from Europe (or, according to others, from Barbados, where he was governor) with a vessel and the necessary provisions and went to Surinam. He was favorably received by the natives, and after he had sojourned there for some time, the sicknesses which occurred to his crew compelled him to return to Europe. Two years later, he sent three vessels back there with several families both Jewish and English and loaded with munitions, merchandise, and everything they needed to establish their settlement there.[27] Despite the foul air which caused much mortality among the new colonists, the colony was at least successful enough to attract the attention of Willoughby, so that, despite what de la Martinière and several others assert, the date of the founding of Surinam can be set at 1650, although it was not until 1662 that Lord Willoughby and Laurent Hyde obtained from Charles II, King of England, the grant of all the mainland in Guiana from the Copename River to beyond the Marony, through the charter of June 2, 1662, which is to be found in Hartsink.[28] Of all the authors who have written about America, none made more inexcusable errors than de la Porte, in his *Voyageur Français*. As little as one compares what is said there[29] with what was reported before, and what one will see in the course of this essay, it will be found that de la Porte took very few pains to find out about the beginning of the colony, its first inhabitants, its climate, and the customs of the colonists both ancient and modern. This work can be regarded as a general novel of America in which historical truth and the dates of the events are confused and disfigured by peculiar anecdotes and made-up stories.

The English, as peaceful owners of Surinam, sought in every possible way to extend its limits to a habitable terrain. And since almost all the terrains from the mouth of the river up to ten or twelve leagues up the river are merely lowlands full of marshes, with banks replete with mangroves, they settled farther up along the river and along the Para, which empties into the Surinam. It was in these two places that the first habitations of the colony were established, whose number increased to forty or fifty, for sugar, with the exception of those where attempts were made to grow tobacco (which never succeeded), and of still others which made use of the timber to erect mills which were then very simply constructed and were turned by means of horses or oxen.[30] The bricks which they needed for the masonry of the boiling vats used for the refining of the sugar they made themselves. Often, a number of colonists assembled in some appointed place, and they would work jointly to make whatever they needed, and it is for this reason that various old buildings of the colony were of brick, including the synagogue of the Jews in the Savane.[31]

The Dutch, and the Jews driven away from Cayenne[32] (and not the

French, as Firmin says in his *Tableau de Surinam*),[33] came to Surinam in 1664, and increased the number of its inhabitants, until a rather considerable population was formed, principally on the part of the Jews. The latter, joining with those who had come from England with Willoughby, of whom we have documents in our archives dated from September, 1662, obtained from the English such favorable privileges that they were put without any distinction on the same level as the other inhabitants, to the point of being permitted to hold office in the colony.[34] By virtue of these privileges, and the grant of ten acres of land in Torrica mentioned there, they formed, in 1672, on elevated ground situated near these ten acres which belonged to the Jews Dacosta and Solis, a little settlement with a small synagogue where they could assemble on holidays. This was abandoned several years later as the result of the grants of the Savane made by Samuel Nassy to the Jewish community in September, 1682, and in August, 1691, according to the resolutions adopted under these dates. In this first little settlement there is still to be found today the old cemetery of the community for the interment of old families who wish to be buried near their ancestors.

This influx of new colonists aided by the means which they brought from Cayenne put the colony in a position, even from its very beginning, to become one of the most opulent in America. Unfortunately, the [second] war which broke out between Holland and England upset this entire likelihood. The states of Zeeland, wishing to attack the settlements which the English had on the Guiana coast, equipped three war vessels and several small boats manned by 300 picked soldiers, and this squadron set sail in the month of December, 1666, under the command of Captain Abraham Crynssen, together with Captains P. J. Lichtenberg and Maurice de Rame, and it arrived at Surinam on February 26, 1667. Lord Willoughby was absent at the time, and Governor Biam was in command of the small garrison which was there. Despite the number of its inhabitants, the colony had as yet no fortifications; besides, the fact that the townsmen were far away and separated because their habitations were situated up the river and too far forward on the land rendered it easy for the Zeeland admiral to make himself master of the colony, and obliged the English to capitulate. He planted the flag of the Republic on a small fort which was there and to which he gave the name of Zeelandia, which it still retains today, with 150 men to guard it.

Admiral Crynssen appointed Joseph Nassy commander of the Eracubo and Canamana Rivers, as can be seen in the authentic document which is extant in the Secretariat at Amsterdam, dated December 6, 1700.[35]

Crynssen, among various solemn declarations which he made to the inhabitants of the colony in the name of the sovereignty of Zeeland, declared in particular to the Jews that they would, in the future, enjoy the privileges granted by the English. And in the third and fourth articles of his act, dated May 6, 1667, approved by the states of Zeeland on April 30 of the following year, it is added "that the Jews will be regarded as if they had been Holland-born."[36] And, after having new works constructed at the fortress, and after furnishing it, among other things, with strong palisades and putting there a garrison of 120 men with fifteen to twenty cannon, victuals, and munitions for six months, he departed with his squadron to go to other islands, and loaded on board a flute [warship] which was leaving for Zeeland the booty which, valued at more than 400,000 florins, he levied on the stubborn inhabitants who too passionately loved the English government. If one will compare this booty, exacted from a place conquered with the intention of keeping it and even of enlarging it to the advantage of the conqueror, with that which Jacques Cassart was able, in 1712, to draw from the colony, with the intention of pillaging it, it will be seen that Surinam was proportionately richer and more opulent in 1667 than almost half a century afterwards.

In the interval between these conquests and others which Admiral Crynssen had made of other colonies, the treaty of peace was signed at Breda on the last day of July, 1667, which treaty provided, among other things, that all the places conquered by the respective enemies before May 10, should remain in the possession of the conqueror, but that all those which had been conquered after this date should be returned to their former proprietors. By this treaty Surinam, conquered in February, came into the possession of the Zeelanders, and New York, in North America, which had belonged to the Dutch, came into the possession of the English, an event which caused several persons to believe that these places had changed masters only by means of a formal exchange amicably arranged.

The news of the peace, which was then unknown to the enemy squadrons which were cruising in America, caused great misfortunes at Surinam, for the colony, which had just sustained a considerable loss when it was captured by Zeeland, had to endure the horrors of a new attack eight months later. Upon receipt of the news of the capture of Surinam by the Zeelanders, Captain John Hermans left Jamaica with seven war vessels manned by 1,200 men, and after having ruined Cayenne for the French, he arrived at Surinam in October, 1667. After some resistance on the part of the colonists aided by Chevalier de Lezy, who had withdrawn from Cayenne with 200 men, he retook the colony, where the whole was given over to pillage by the soldiers. More than 500 inhabitants, most of them Englishmen and Jews, whose sugar plantations extended as far as ten miles up the river, saw their mills, to the number of thirty or thirty-two, destroyed or carried away. After a stay of about three weeks, he returned to Barbados, where he landed his prisoners, including the commandant, de Rame, and other Dutch officers.

Willoughby, who had been very severely grieved by the seizure of the colony by the Zeelanders, nonetheless could not rejoice at its recapture by the English, because he had already been informed about the Treaty of Breda at Barbados, where he was governor, although he pretended not to know about it. Nevertheless, he had the prisoners transported to Martinique by virtue of the peace which during this interval had been concluded with France, and he at once sent his son Henry Willoughby with three war vessels and three merchant ships to Surinam, to persuade the inhabitants to leave the colony and go to Antigua and to Montserrat, and to transport their sugar mills and their slaves there. This persuasion was accompanied by a declaration to the effect that those inhabitants who refused to accede thereto would be regarded as rebels. According to Harris, 1,200 men voluntarily left for Jamaica, of whom the greatest part were those Jews who had come with Willoughby from England to Surinam. And it was again through the efforts and work of these men who came from Surinam in 1670, most of them Jews, "that the cultivation of Jamaica gave courage to, and inspired the emulation of, the other inhabitants." [37]

When the news of the recapture of Surinam by the English reached Holland, the United Provinces demanded from the British government the restoration of this place to the condition in which it was at the time of its capture by the Zeelanders, together with damages, etc., by virtue of Article 3 of the Treaty of Breda of July 31, 1667. They also complained about the despotic orders of Lord Willoughby and his son.

On receipt of these complaints, England, without hesitation, sent orders to Willoughby, most of which were of no effect, because his son, before preparing to evacuate the fortress, once again forcibly carried away 168 slaves, 126 head of cattle, 120,000 pounds of sugar, and eight mills for which he arranged transportation to Barbados.

These continual disasters caused the ruin of the greatest portion of the inhabitants of the colony, and the Jewish community, which had always had the largest part in unfortunate revolutions, again felt the effects of the confusion which prevailed in its affairs because of the departure of its other brethren for Jamaica. Since their interests were closely linked together, this capped the climax of their misfortune. But since the detailed history of Surinam is not at all the object of this writing, we refer those who wish more detailed information to the works which we have already cited, although none has fulfilled the duties of a good, impartial, and accurate historian. This has compelled us, on other occasions, to have recourse most often to various other works, principally to what we have found in our archives, in order the better to organize this writing to the best of our ability.

However, we shall observe that, despite the discussions in the Republic between Zeeland and the other [Dutch] provinces, the former nonetheless remained the mistress of Surinam; and although it was declared that sovereignty over this colony belonged to the confederated provinces and that the respective inhabitants would have freedom of sailing there and of carrying on commerce without any distinction, Zeeland alone sent Captain Julius Lichtenberg, who arrived there in February, 1669, as governor of its new colony. And despite the opposition which he experienced on the part of the Christian and Jewish inhabitants, who desired to see themselves again under English rule, and despite the void which he noticed there by reason of the departure of those 1,200 persons whom we have mentioned above, he took possession of everything and arranged matters in the most suitable manner. The rest of the Jews, who were firmly resolved not to quit the Dutch government, seeing that the calamities which they had suffered during the last war were beginning to abate, addressed themselves to the new governor and asked for the confirmation of their privileges, with new articles for their security. These were granted to them fully under date of October 1, 1669. (See Document No. 5.)

Although the colony, according to all that we have just said, already belonged to the Dutch since the peace concluded at Breda in 1667, and although Lichtenberg had already been established as governor since 1669, one can nevertheless not fix the time of the formal recognition of this proprietorship until the year 1674, by virtue of the Treaty of Westminster signed after the second war which the Republic had to wage against England. According to Article 5 and Article 6 of the said treaty, the English laid down the condition "that it would be permitted to the inhabitants of Surinam to leave with their goods and their slaves to wherever it should seem good to them." This took place in 1677 with regard to ten Jewish families and their slaves, to the number of 322 persons, who left the colony after having complained to England that the Dutch had forbidden them to leave.[38]

During this interval the United Provinces again had to settle several difficulties which arose with the province of Zeeland, which made claims on, or at least asserted rights to, the useful part of the colony, although most of the vessels employed for the conquest of Surinam under the Zeeland admiral Abraham Crynssen had been sent only at the expense of the States General, and Zeeland, so as not to expose itself to unfortunate discussions, ceded the colony to the States General under a remarkable condition, which no doubt escaped the notice of the authors of the work on Essequebo and Demmerary against the [Dutch] West India Company, which the authors of this work openly attack.

It seems—because one finds confusion among the authors cited—that this Company, on some unknown ground, also laid claim to the colony, and that, according to all appearances, it was seconded by the States General. Then Zeeland, when it saw itself compelled to cede the colony to the States General in 1670, laid down the condition "that this colony could never be ceded to the said Company, both because it had no claim thereto and because it was not at all in a position to guard it, or to protect it, or to favor the views of the inhabitants."[39] And although by virtue of this arrangement the colony was placed under its domain, the States General granted its rule to Zeeland, and after the death or the departure of Governor Lichtenberg, it appointed Johan Heinsius as governor in September, 1678, with the approval of Their High Powers.

It seems that during these various revolutions the [aboriginal] natives of the country had, for some few years, been quiet spectators, without having caused the least trouble to the whites. Finally they aroused themselves from their lethargy, for what reason we do not know. But according to what we have received by way of tradition from our ancestors, they did not want their country to be governed by any nation other than the one which had first settled there, that is to say, the English, although even in their time they had caused some damage to small houses. As a result, they began to devastate the houses and to massacre the whites who had the misfortune to fall into their hands. Since it was impossible for the colonists, in the situation in which they found themselves, to repress these hostilities, they besought Governor Heinsius to appeal to Their High Powers, who thereupon engaged the Zeeland admiralty to send 150 troops to the aid of the colony, but these were of no use at all. As a result, the inhabitants who were settled towards the upper part of the river, most of them Jews, saw themselves obliged to form small detachments in order to fall upon the Indians who were already becoming very redoubtable, and this was, in a great number of cases, more favorable to them than what was done elsewhere. At the same time and after the death of Governor Heinsius, who was succeeded provisionally by L. Verboom, the most important Christian and Jewish colonists (among the latter were Nassy, Meza, and Aboab)[40] made remonstrances to the administrative council against the administration of the colony, under date of May 6, 1680, and wanted to change everything which had been established up to that time and which in no way corresponded to the interests of the colony in general. And although the principal articles of this remonstrance were granted, everything nonetheless remained in the same state, because of the meager order which prevailed then.[41]

In that period and for several years afterwards, nothing occurred which was serious or which affected the welfare of the colony, its administration, and the mutual relationships of its inhabitants, in which the Jews were not consulted and in which they did not have the same weight as the Christians in every respect. Our archives are full of letters of petition and of communications on all sorts of matters, and although these facts are of little interest for the history of Surinam specifically, they nevertheless are of great service in that of the Jews, and if one carefully examines the various events of the colony, the character of its first settlers, their capacity and even their wealth, one will see that Surinam had the good fortune of having been founded and then enlarged by worthy people whom the persecutions of the Inquisition, that of Cromwell, the revocation of the Edict of Nantes, and a thousand other circumstances threw together there as though by chance.

It was certainly not with vagabonds and with wretches drawn from the dungeons of England and elsewhere that the colony was founded, as several others in America were. The objection will perhaps be made to us that several vagabonds from Holland were sent there, according to the permission which the States General, through their resolutions of July 20, 1684, gave to the city of Amsterdam.[42] But since this permission was not given until 1684, the colony was then accordingly more than thirty years old, and thus it was founded neither with vagabonds nor with criminals drawn from dungeons. The fact that in the course of time a large number of these kinds of people, Christians as well as Jews, came there, whether from Holland or from other places, leads to absolutely no conclusions against our assertion, and nothing is more certain than that it was with skillful agriculturists and with the money which they brought there that the colony was able to make rapid progress in a few years, which was unfortunately arrested by the quarrels of the European powers. And in order to shed more light on what we assert, principally on what concerns the Jewish community, the influence which it had in the colony, and the esteem which its merits obtained for it, we shall enter into several other details of the history of Surinam, which is, in many circumstances, closely linked with that of its Jewish inhabitants.

The goal which one unquestionably has when one wishes to found a colony; the desire which the new colonists have who lend themselves voluntarily to the views of the government; and the purpose which the mother country proposes in founding it can never be successful when one has the misfortune of initiating enterprises at a time when war dissipates all its means and, so to speak, wrings hope away from the hearts of the new colonists. The English, and after them the Dutch, felt these terrible effects; but nonetheless it is the colonists alone who experience the wound whose scar is ready to open at the least blow which it receives. The continual sacrifices which the mother country has to make in order later to draw benefit from its advances are incontestably the sole means of repairing the misfortunes which befall its subjects. If one neglects these means, the body becomes cacochymic [anemic]; one lives and breathes, but always languishes in a pitiable state of distress.

Because of the war which the States General had to carry on during the past century, it did not suit them at all to take the colony under their immediate domination in order to repair its misfortunes by dint of benefits whose happy effects the United Provinces would later have felt. Zeeland, for its part, could not or did not wish to conserve what it had conquered, whatever its reasons might have been. This province, despite its declaration, made in 1670, to the disadvantage of the West India Company when it ceded the colony to the States General, informed the States General, in 1679, that it intended to cede the rulership and its useful domain of the colony to the said company in return for the payment of two hundred and sixty thousand florins, under conditions that are found in Hartsink,[43] and the States General acceding to this agreement, the Company concluded its purchase on June 6, 1682, just after being released from the heavy burden of its debts, which nevertheless could be settled only little by little and with great delays.[44] And the States General, approving this cession, accorded to the proprietors of this colony a grant dated September 23, 1682, which ought to be regarded as the constitutional law of an establishment which, in a certain fashion, repaired the breaches made in the commerce and in the navigation of the Dutch,[45] and which, in addition, gave the colonists protection from every kind of vexation.

The West India Company, foreseeing the expenses which it would be obliged to incur for the advancement and the maintenance of the colony, according to the very contents of its grant, resolved the following year to cede, at the same price at which it had made the purchase from Zeeland, one-third of its property to the city of Amsterdam, and another third to Sir Cornelis van Sommelsdyk, who together formed an association relative to the colony of Surinam known under the name of the Chartered Society of Surinam, which in 1778 was changed to that of Directors and Regents of the Colony (*Directeuren en Regeerders der Colonie*).

The States General approving this new acquisition on the part of those two co-proprietors, the Zeelanders, who so greatly feared that Surinam would fall under the administration or into the power of some Roman Catholic owner, gave their consent, in the assembly of the States General, only under the express clause "that no direction or administration in the said colony would be granted to any person of these provinces or resident in Surinam itself who professes the Roman Catholic religion; and that no person of the said religion would ever be able to participate in the said association or company or to retain the part which he might already have there. Resolution of the States General of October 5, 1686." [46]

Monsieur de Sommelsdyk, then, as co-proprietor of Surinam, according to Article 6 of the agreement made between the proprietors of the colony, left Holland on September 3, 1683, with 300 troops, to go to Surinam and to assume there the office of governor general. He arrived there on November 24 of the same year, the commandant being L. Verboom, who in 1680 had succeeded Heinsius in the rulership of the colony.

Surinam was at that time in a very unfortunate state. The government had neither form nor rule. The confusion which was caused in the government by the remonstrance which the colonists had made to the administrative council in 1680 after the death of Governor Heinsius, which we have related above, and the change which it was proposed to make, and which was applied only at the beginning, disgusted the colonists to a very perceptible degree. In addition, the continual losses which the war had caused them, the number of people who left for Jamaica, and the continual hostilities which they experienced on the part of the Indians—all this combined to make the colony seem two finger-breadths away from its ruin.

Consequently, at the beginning of the year 1684, Governor Sommelsdyk, to the satisfaction of the inhabitants, established an administrative council and a council of justice, and made laws suitable to render the colony flourishing, if its state of health could support violent remedies. The character of Monsieur de Sommelsdyk was, in addition, very austere. He wished to make the colony, suddenly or as though by means of enchantment, the most considerable and the best governed in all America. Besides, he had the very ardent zeal to make religion respectable and even redoubtable in the eyes of the colonists, most of whom were not Calvinists. He was the first who tried to counteract the privileges of the Jewish community with regard to working freely in their settlements on Sundays, and to set limits to the liberty granted by the privileges with regard to marriage contracts which took place among them in accordance with their laws, ways, and customs. These moves perceptibly troubled the Jews, because they added to the loss of their privileges the foreboding of a still more baneful future, the more since they saw in the person of the governor a co-proprietor, and consequently they inferred that he had unlimited powers. The decision which nonetheless was made by the members of the proprietory association in Holland on December 10, 1685, concerning the general privileges of the Jews, and the response which they later made, under date of August 19, 1686, concerning the prohibition, by the governor, of their working on Sundays, in regard to which he was informed that they could not consent to the revocation of this liberty, inasmuch as it would not cause any scandal to the detriment of the religion of the country (Documents Nos. 6 and 7)—all this quieted the Jews, to the extent that they congratulated themselves on the change of master and on the proprietors of the colony in Holland. Happily, this good fortune was realized in the future, and it never experienced any other shock on the part of the government from that time to our days. It was also this felicity which inspired them from that time on with the courage to add some suitable ornaments to the synagogue which they had built in the Savane in 1685 on a small mountain with twenty-five acres of neighboring land which Samuel Nassy had granted to the Jewish community. We shall speak further and at greater length about this edifice later; let us return to the general affairs of the colony.

The ill-humor which Monsieur de Sommelsdyk showed at each contradiction which he experienced on the part of the colonists and his haughty and austere character caused him to be regarded as a man little suited to lay happy foundations for a colony which, although almost thirty-six years old, should have been considered still in its cradle because of its disasters. Consequently, many complaints were made against him in Holland. But let us pass over facts not very interesting to resume our history.

The city of Paramaribo has an Indian name, about the origin of which name there are several opinions. Some maintain that it is an allusion to the name of Willoughby, who called himself *Willoughby of Parham,* as if it meant the City of Parham. Others suppose that it was only with reference to the river or creek of which the Para is nearest the city, and the first to be settled of all the colony. Others, who are still more ingenious, maintain that this name is composed of two Indian words, *Panari* and *bo,* applied particularly to the place where the Europeans contracted the alliance with the natives of the country, and that for this reason the Indians called this village (for there must have been one before the arrival of the Europeans) *Panari-bo,* which means place or village of friends, and that later on it was corrupted to that of Paramaribo. The first word, *Paramari,* has no meaning in the Indian language, but *Panari* means friends, and *bo,* village or hamlet. It was then only a small village. There was only a small fortress there, which afterwards was given the name of Zeelandia. The capital city was situated from ten to twelve leagues from the mouth of the Surinam. It was called Paramburg, or according to the old registers of the Jewish community, Surinamsburg, later changed by the Zeelanders to that of Nieuw Middelburg. The remoteness of this city and the obstacles experienced by the vessels that came there from Europe forced the inhabitants to establish the town near their little fortress four leagues from the mouth. However, at the time of the arrival of Monsieur de Sommelsdyk it was only a hamlet of 100 to 120 houses without any form or order whatsoever, and it was through his efforts that the city, called Paramaribo, had a beginning, in regular form. It afterwards became one of the most beautiful in America, and we shall speak of it later.

Monsieur de Sommelsdyk, after having given his orders for the necessary work on the fortress, and having arranged as much as possible the other branches of his government, turned his attention to the damage which the Indians were wreaking on the plantations. But, not having sufficient forces to check their hostilities, he resolved to seek means to make peace with them. The Jewish community, according to its traditions, still takes pride in having greatly facilitated this peace, since Samuel Nassy, who had known these Indians since the time of the English (when they were on friendlier terms with the whites), persuaded them to put aside their evil intentions towards the inhabitants. It was through him, too, and by means of a great number of gifts, that a sort of preliminary peace was concluded which could not be accomplished in any other manner than on condition that the head of the colony should marry the daughter of their chief; for without this tie, they said, we cannot trust the whites at all. On this report, de Sommelsdyk concluded the generally desired treaty of peace, and in consequence took the pretended Indian princess as his concubine, who did not fail to contribute to the maintenance of this peace. This woman was still alive, more than eighty years old, in the time of Monsieur Mauritius, and she was living with Madame du Voisin, widow of Monsieur de Cheusses, governor of Surinam, who was a member of the household of Sommelsdyk and whom she called by the name of daughter.

The storehouse of provisions for the military establishment was poorly stocked. Besides, the immense labors which the soldiers were obliged to perform on the work of the fortress caused a revolt which ended only with the massacre of the governor. One day (July 19, 1688), while on parade, the soldiers addressed themselves to him and made their remonstrances to him, with the request to lighten their labors, and to increase the amount of victuals which were distributed to them. In reply, the governor, in accordance with his character, which was proud and hot-headed, drew his sabre, when all of a sudden several gunshots felled him lifeless on the square. This volley also wounded Commander Verboom, who was much beloved by the soldiers, so seriously that he died therefrom on the 28th of the same month, nine days after the governor.

In spite of the austerity of character which Monsieur de Sommelsdyk possessed, he certainly did not deserve so tragic an end; and if the colony had had the good fortune to have had him as governor a few years later, instead of having him in the time of confusion and disorder, it would have experienced the happy effects of his rule. Despite his impetuosity, he had the most distinguished zeal for the welfare of his inhabitants, and his capacities would have enabled him to correct his faults and to make the colony a flourishing one.

After this action, the rebels, to the number of nearly 200 men, took possession of the fortress and of all the munitions of war. The commander, wounded as he was, but wishing to appease this tumult and to prevent still more fatal consequences, incessantly had peace proposals made, and offered the rebels a general pardon, which their mistrust rendered useless. The principal inhabitants of the colony and several members of the council were, as usual, at their settlements on the Surinam and Comowine rivers, and those who were in the city at once gave information everywhere as to this fatal event, principally to Councillor Bagman and to the captain of the Jews, Samuel Nassy, so that each of them, for his part, should come to the defense of the country. The alarm was then general, and the citizens assembled in haste from all sides and unanimously disapproved of the peace offer which the commander had had made to the rebels. The first to come to Paramaribo with his citizens was Captain Nassy, followed by Monsieur Bagman. These, having learned that the rebels had taken possession of a vessel which lay in the roadstead, put some people on two other ships, named *Sara* and *Samuel,* belonging to the said Monsieur Nassy; and as a result of the sacrifices which they made, exposing their lives to the greatest dangers, they arranged their attacks with the council, which were so well ordered that they succeeded in forcing the rebels to deliver the assassins over to justice, on condition of the pardon which the council offered then to the others. However, fifty of the most stubborn of those who had seized the vessel remained firm, but seeing themselves unexpectedly attacked by the two other ships, they surrendered, and those who were guilty, to the number of eleven, were punished with death on the 3rd of August following, six days after the death of Commander Verboom and fifteen after that of the unfortunate Monsieur de Sommelsdyk. Although Samuel Nassy had performed memorable deeds in these circumstances, according to a contemporary manuscript written in Portuguese which we have before us, nevertheless the historians of Surinam have failed to report them. But since the truth always pierces the darkness eventually, Monsieur Hartsink[47] reports, on the subject of the war with the Frenchman du Casse, which took place in 1689, "that the principal post of the fortress Zeelandia had been entrusted to Captain Nassy with eighty-four of his Jewish citizens, because of his faithfulness, and the bravery of the said captain at the time of the assassination of Governor Sommelsdyk." This report confirms all that we have said about him.

Thus, on learning of the tragic death of Governor Sommelsdyk, the directors and proprietors of the colony in Holland offered the governorship thereof to Monsieur de Chatillon, the son of the first governor [Sommelsdyk], who later became vice-admiral in Holland, and died generally regretted in 1740. Upon his refusal, there was appointed as governor Monsieur Jan van Scherpenhuysen, at the time when war was declared between France and Holland. He arrived at Surinam with a reinforcement of troops on March 8, 1689.

A few days after his arrival, he wrote to Europe "that he had found the colony in the most deplorable state, the fortress in such poor condition that it was not capable of making any resistance in case of the slightest attack; the magistracy without any order or form whatsoever; enmities and dissensions among the church people; finally, that the Jews, on their part, had revolted against their Captain Nassy, on the ground that he wished to govern them despotically, and to impair their privileges and their religious ceremonies." [48] We cannot conceive whence Monsieur Hartsink derived all this, nor how Monsieur Scherpenhuysen could have made such a report to his masters in Europe. For as far as the general affairs of the colony are concerned, we have already seen that Governor Sommelsdyk, although of a hard and inflexible character, had introduced into Surinam some very good orders, and had reformed the magistracy to the satisfaction of all the inhabitants. Besides, he had had work done on the fortress, since it was in a position, as we shall say later, to rout the squadron of Monsieur du Casse, two months after the arrival of Monsieur Scherpenhuysen in Surinam.

As regards the Jews, all that he says about them is contradicted by what we find annotated in the archives of the Jewish community. We agree, in accordance with our traditions, that Captain Nassy tried several times to remove the force of the prejudices of the Jewish community, principally with regard to the great number of their days of festival, which are commanded in the Sacred Books. But nothing important ever happened, and a letter of the rabbis of Amsterdam, written to the regents and the original of which is in our archives, in which they reproached the Jews for not being willing to recognize the benefactions of Monsieur Nassy, calmed the few murmurs which occurred at that time. As a result, just praises were later bestowed upon him for the repeated gifts which he made to the Jewish community. Thus in 1677, in the midst of the horrors of war, after having paid to the colony the arrearages which the Jewish community owed, according to the registers of May, 1677, he established an educational institution on the Savane which belonged to him then, as can be seen from the dedicatory epistle of a work on the Pentateuch by Dr. Diaz of Amsterdam, printed in 1697. And at the time of his departure for Holland (in March, 1694) he had been charged, again, with the care of the Jewish community in the presence of our masters in Holland. But what is certain is that Monsieur de Scherpenhuysen had persuaded himself that, in having great disorders marked down at the beginning of his rule, no matter how little he would be able to do later on, he would enhance his credit with his illustrious employers, and since he was proud by nature, he had great contempt for the Jewish community and a great aversion for its. Captain, as we shall say afterwards.

The Jewish population at that time, as far as could be calculated from the list of the contributors, amounted to ninety-two families, not counting ten to twelve German Jews who were then united to the Portuguese there by bonds of marriage; and about fifty bachelors who did not belong at all to these families. Thus, allowing five persons to each family, the total of the Jewish community would be about 560 or 575 persons.[49] They already possessed forty sugar plantations, almost all of them with mills turned by animals, and more than 9,000 black slaves. For in July, 1690, the Jewish community contributed, in proportion to the other inhabitants of the colony, fifty slaves for the work on the fortress, and in 1691 another eighty-six, besides giving gratis 25,905 pounds of sugar for the construction of a new hospital. They also took, while waiting, at their own expense, twelve soldiers and an adjutant to feed them and to provide for their care.

At this same time in the month of May, 1689, two months after the arrival of Governor Scherpenhuysen, Monsieur du Casse, chief of a French squadron, attacked the colony almost by surprise with nine war vessels, a bomb-ketch, and several other ships in which, besides the troops, there were a goodly number of volunteers who had come from Cayenne because of the lure of the booty which they expected to take.

Monsieur de Chatillon, the son of Monsieur de Sommelsdyk, was then in Surinam, having come there to settle the private affairs of his late father.

Monsieur du Casse had a letter sent by an Indian to Monsieur de Chatillon, whom he treated as lord of Surinam, in which he testified to being delighted to meet so gallant a man in the colony. But this Lord, who, despite his youth, had already given striking proofs of his sagacity and of his activity in the marine, instead of being surprised by this beautiful compliment, at once put the colony in a state of defense, and therefore placed the artillery in the fortress in the most suitable manner, together with almost 250 soldiers, and 231 citizens to guard it, namely, eighty-four Jewish citizens under the command of Captain Nassy; sixty-nine others under Captain Lucas Coudrie; and seventy-eight under Captain Swart.

The continual fire from the artillery as well as that of the troops and of the citizenry against the enemy squadron, which had approached very close to the land in order to demolish the bastions of the fortress more easily, was so lively that despite more than 2,000 cannonballs and 137 bombs which the enemy fired against the fortress, they were routed so thoroughly that under cover of the darkness, on Wednesday, on the 11th of the same month of May, they withdrew precipitately with the loss of a considerable number of their men, whom they threw into the river tied together two by two and with large stones around their necks so that they should sink to the bottom. This was apparently for the purpose of preventing the colonists from learning about their losses. Besides that, their vessels were greatly shattered by the artillery.

The *Histoire Générale des Voyages,* Volume 21, page 48, reports that most of the volunteers who had come from Cayenne in Monsieur du Casse's squadron were taken prisoners, but we have not found this at all in Monsieur Hartsink's work, or among the details of the combat which are to be found in the archives in a Spanish manuscript which is supposed to be a sort of journal of Captain Nassy made on the spot and at the same time, and which has furnished us with particulars that are not found at all in Hartsink. And without dwelling on what is here reported above, it is incontestable that the citizens, on this occasion, braved all perils and showed courage and fidelity for the safety of the colony. Monsieur de Chatillon distinguished himself in this combat with a heroism above his age, to the point that, confronting all perils, he himself charged and discharged the cannons, so that unfortunately a shot having been sent off too soon, he was wounded in the face and hands, to the great regret of all the inhabitants, but he happily recovered in a few days. And the besieged did not lose a single man in this attack, and there were only four wounded, three Christians, and a Jew named Mesquita.[50]

The details of this action prove, without any doubt about it, that the fortress was not at all in such a poor state of defense, and that there did not prevail in Surinam any such kind of anarchy among the colonists in general as Monsieur de Scherpenhuysen tried to persuade his masters. For, two months after his arrival in the colony, it was in a position to rout a squadron of nine war vessels, a bomb-ketch, and several other ships, as we have shown. But the desire to find faults often gives birth to imaginary faults.

After this triumph, Monsieur de Scherpenhuysen showed zeal for the welfare of the colony. Unfortunately, however, his haughty ill-humor and the lack of mildness which prevailed in his orders most often rendered his attentions less useful than reproachable. Moreover, despite the exploits of the Jews, their fidelity and their attachment to the colony, the governor had an aversion to them and principally to their chief, Samuel Nassy, whose influence and wealth gave him umbrage. The least trifle, a little disorder, even a mere nothing which occurred among the Jews was capable of arousing him against the Jewish community, as can be seen from various letters full of complaints which he addressed to the regents and which are to be found in the original in the archives of the Jewish community.

Samuel Nassy, foreseeing from all this the destiny of the Jewish community under the rule of Monsieur de Scherpenhuysen and not wishing at all to expose himself to becoming the victim of his bad humor, courageously resolved to leave the colony forever and to go and settle in Amsterdam, in order there to enjoy his possessions, which were still huge despite his losses. Accordingly, he left for Europe in March, 1694.

Scarcely had he left the colony, when Monsieur de Scherpenhuysen and his administrative council—who were not at all unaware of the previous decision of the lords of the colony with regard to the privileges of the Jewish community, and in particular with regard to Sundays, made in December, 1685, and in August, 1686—restored that same prohibition on July 10, 1694, and made another decision, to take away from the syndics of the Jewish community the title of Regents which they had had since the beginning, by virtue of their privileges. One will recognize once again how scanty were the means which the governor knew how to employ to conciliate the affection of those of the Jewish community in the fact which we are going to cite in order to protect ourselves against any sort of accusation of prejudice in respect to him.

There is, in the archives of the Jewish community, a letter of the said governor, written to the regents, dated May 16, 1695, in which he requests the Jewish community to contribute generously to the collection which was being made to build a new hospital at Paramaribo, and in the same letter the governor continues: " I have found it very strange that you despotically arrogate to yourselves the title of Regents of the Jewish community [*Régens de la Nation*], and in consequence I inform you that I have found it good to forbid you to bear this title from now on, for there belongs to you only that of Regents of the synagogue. You will therefore receive a resolution of the council, etc. to that effect, etc." Is it not peculiar that at the time contributions are requested, as an act of benevolence, reproaches are made on a matter in which there was basically no harm at all? But this governor had another aim in view; he wanted to meet with refusals on the part of the Jews in an affair which concerned the colony. But these, despising the trap which had been set from far off, and seeing nothing but their duty, contributed generously according as their means permitted them to do. (Note of June 28, 1695, which we have cited above.)

The Jews, dejected also by the departure of Monsieur Nassy, who served them as a palpable support, and seeing themselves molested in their rights and not being able to bear the damage which would be caused them by the loss of one more day of work each week, wrote at once to Samuel Nassy and to Baron de Belmonte, Count Palatine, their deputies, in Holland, and requested their good offices before the Lords of the Colony for the reparation of these grievances. Monsieur de Scherpenhuysen, on learning of this, assembled the council and tried to institute a criminal proceeding against the regents because they had had the audacity to make complaints to Samuel Nassy against the edict of July 10, 1694, and particularly against the person of the governor. According to a letter of March 10, 1696, the regents were summoned to appear in person before the council, and to bring with them a copy of the letter which they had written to Holland, together with its Dutch translation. (Registers of the Jewish community dated April 25, 1696.)

The Jews were alarmed by this accusation, which was as unreasonable as it was despotic, since it impaired the natural liberty that the subjects of any place and of any condition whatsoever have of bringing their complaints to the attention of the sovereign in order to be protected from the despotism of his subdelegates. They sought specious reasons to avoid appearing before the council, declaring nonetheless, in a letter, that they had requested Samuel Nassy to take care of the maintenance of the privileges of the Jewish community, and that if Samuel Nassy had brought complaints against the governor in particular in the matter of his rule, that was not their fault at all. Happily, before new orders of the council could cause the Jewish community any new alarms, Nassy and Belmonte obtained the reparation of all these wrongs, and in the month of June, 1696, the council, without making mention of the orders which came from Holland with the new governor Paul van der Veen, declared by means of a publication that the edict of May 10, 1694, had not been directed against the Jews, and that it was solely with the intention of avoiding scandal against religion on Sundays in the City of Paramaribo, etc. See Document No. 9 and the original letter of Samuel Nassy from Amsterdam dated December, 1695, in which he informs the regents "that at consecutive conferences which he had in Holland with Monsieur Valkenier, president of the council of the Lords of the Colony, in the presence of other members, in reference to the Jewish community and to the colony in general, the grievances of the Jews were redressed, and that Monsieur de Scherpenhuysen had lost his position, whom Monsieur Paul van der Veen was to succeed, in whom the Jewish community would find another Lichtenberg, that is to say, a man sweet, lovable, and beneficent." [51]

Monsieur de Scherpenhuysen was in fact recalled to Holland to purge himself from several accusations that the colonists had brought against his government.[52] He arrived in Holland, after having been made a prisoner of war by the French, in October, 1696, and Monsieur Paul van der Veen succeeded him as governor on May 14, 1696[53] [serving] until his resignation in 1706; he had as his successor Monsieur Willem de Gooyer.

Surinam, as far as its agriculture was concerned, had become at that time very flourishing, although only the planting of sugar was as yet known, and several parcels of beechwood. "The Dutch nation," says an author, "destined to cultivate marshes, brought to Surinam the genius of their country," and it was only by means of this that on a soil humid and muddy (avoiding the enormous expenses and the large number of workers required by the method of the English), they succeeded in establishing a colony worthy of causing envy to all the others in America. Yet despite the advancement of the colony in this respect, and despite the remonstrances which the colonists made after the attack of Du Casse, which one finds in Hartsink[54] and in the *Tableau de Surinam*,[55] the means of rendering it secure against enemy invasions were completely neglected, to the point that seven years after this attack it saw itself menaced again by a new attack by Monsieur de Gennes, admiral of a numerous French fleet which was then, in 1696, at Cayenne, whose governor, Monsieur de Féroli, was supposed to accompany him on this expedition with a part of the garrison, but when he learned that there were two large war vessels in Surinam with seventy pieces of cannon, ready to set sail, the French judged that circumstances were not suitable for the execution of their enterprise.

The war with France was rekindled. France, a power which knew, better than any other (because of its proximity to Cayenne), the importance of Surinam as to agriculture, and the small force which was there to oppose any enemy attack, allowed Jacques Cassard, chief of squadron, to go there. He arrived there, indeed, in June, 1712, but met with no success at all. However, four months later, having returned with a fleet of eight war vessels, seven barks, and thirty flat-bottomed boats carrying 3,000 men, he succeeded, after a courageous resistance made by the citizens, in subjecting the colony to a levy which amounted, in slaves, in sugar, etc., to the sum of 622,800 Dutch silver florins, which, according to the calculations made by the administrative council later, formed almost 10 percent of the capital belonging to the settlers who were in the easiest circumstances.[56] The efforts which the inhabitants made to shine on this occasion for the defense of the country, among whom the Jews, under the command of their Captain Ishak Pinto, distinguished themselves advantageously, are found in detail in Hartsink's work,[57] where, among other things, it is found "that they were obliged by the council to guard the fortress, which was then without a garrison, because the Christian citizens absolutely refused to go there."

According to the traditions and what is found in the archives, the Jewish community did not have anything at all to complain about against the French after they had made themselves the masters of the colony. For Monsieur Cassard, even before the terms mentioned in the act of ransoming had been delivered to the proprietors, had restored to the Jews all the things which the soldiers had taken from the synagogue in the Savane, among them the silver crowns (with which the Scrolls of the Law are adorned), together with an order that the synagogue and the ceremonies conducted there were to be respected.

This war, which marked an epoch in Surinam, must rightly be regarded as having stopped the course of its prosperity. For besides the enormous expenditures which the colonists had to make at a time when their successive losses had not yet been recovered, as well as the levy paid to Cassard, as well as the disorder on the plantations, and the continuous alarms during the time that the enemy remained, from October to December, they still had the misfortune to see that a bold spirit of revolt reigned among their slaves, which ceased only with the flight of a large number, who later formed colonies in the midst of the forests, leaving the impression of the revolt in the hearts of those who in appearance had remained faithful to their masters. If this blow did not completely ruin the colony, it at least placed it in a very sad state. To crown the misfortunes, the colonists at that time made the yoke on their slaves all the heavier, believing that fear alone, and the examples of horrible punishments, would be the most capable means of turning them away from their natural inclination to seek their freedom, and instead of treating them with more mildness, they only sought such means as would render slavery harder and more unendurable. These mistakes, this specious policy which made one believe that the least sign of mildness toward the Negroes implied fear or weakness on the part of the whites, had a contrary effect, to the point where the woods became filled with runaway slaves [*Marrons*], who found there a ready asylum among those who had preceded them. Let each one recall the past of the colony, and then draw the parallel with modern times, on the subject of slavery. It will be found that it was not until after the attack by Cassard that the flight of the slaves and the tyranny of the masters became more frequent; and that if we have the misfortune of still feeling the effects of the wickedness of our slaves, we have not, generally speaking, had to reproach ourselves at all for some years for tyranny against them, despite the calumnies of several political and journalistic writers in this regard.

It is, then, very unfortunate for those who are the objects of continual reproaches, that when one experiences, generally, the same disasters whose effects are the same everywhere, one has the bad faith to blame the Jews of Surinam for the flight of the slaves in the time of Cassard, asserting that *those who increased the number of the runaway slaves since the time of the English belonged for the most part to the Jews.*[58] We would pass over this reproach in silence if we did not still hear several persons of distinction maintain this opinion with an obstinacy which revolts honest hearts, adding to it, as the crown of misfortune, the title of tyrants and of hangmen of their slaves. But in order not to break the thread of our history, we will reserve the development of this matter, in order to put it in its proper place, remarking only that nothing serious occurred then (even since the time of the English) of which the regents of the Jewish community were not aware, and which was not finished by them, and of which they did not keep exact accounts. And that when it was a question of some revolt on a plantation of a Jew, or some case which was to be referred to the jurisdiction of the superior magistrate, the council always referred to the regents the task of terminating the affair, adding in its letters (these are the very words): *Do your duty so as to spare expenses to the Jewish community; otherwise it would pay to the official solicitor that which accrues to him for the emoluments of his examinations, etc.* (Original letters which are found in the archives from 1680 to the year 1720.) *O tempora! O mores!* So we must have had at least in part the knowledge which the one who furnished memoirs to Monsieur Hartsink had in order to compose his history, and who perhaps gave occasion for the nasty writing of Messieurs [the magistrates of] Essequebo and Demmerary, which was presented to the tribunal of X in Holland in 1775 or 1776, and which was printed in Amsterdam in 1785. (See the Introduction to this work, Note 20.) We do not even know how much the blindness of these gentlemen attributed to the influence of the Jews the revolt of the Negroes which took place along the Berbice river in 1763.

Despite the duty which we have imposed upon ourselves, in composing this work, not to make observations on the political condition of the colony, we cannot, under the actual circumstances, resist the desire to venture several ideas as to the moral and political causes which contributed greatly to its ancient disasters, the more so because the happy changes that later took place, despite our taxes and the clamors of several caustic spirits, produced the advantage which we always expected from the wisdom of our lords. We shall therefore take the epoch of the invasion of Cassard as the most suitable place for the development of our observations, from the beginning of the colony up to that time, that is to say, from 1650 up to 1713.

We have seen that the colony, despite the feebleness of its first ten or twelve years, grew, after the date of the charter of Charles II to Willoughby and Hyde, to the point of giving the most flattering hope to these two proprietors, who were indisputably in a position to make it the most flourishing [colony] in all South America, without excepting even the Portuguese and Spanish colonies. What happened after the English reconquest from the Zeelanders, the number of people who left Surinam, the pillaging which Willoughby and his son did, and even the booty which the Zeelanders took from the inhabitants in 1667, [these] are proofs of the rapid progress that the colony made in a period of twelve or fifteen years.

Let one recall the state in which Holland found itself at the time of the capture of Surinam: the breach that must have been made in its commerce by reason of those 350 ships which the French had taken from them in 1657; the formidable league between England and France to weaken its commerce; and the wars which the Republic was forced to wage, from 1660 even up to 1721, against almost all the powers of Europe—a circumstance certainly not very favorable for the formation of new colonies in America.

Furthermore, Zeeland, which had taken Surinam from the English, was not in a position to render it flourishing, for the interests of this province were no longer in having establishments so far away where its subjects (according to even the nature of the federation of the seven United Provinces) were not at all able to carry on an exclusive commerce. Again, despite all this, if the Republic, instead of acquiescing in the acquisition of this vast country by the West India Company, had taken it as one of the provinces belonging to the confederation; or if, instead of making more grants to the company of those three co-proprietors which was being formed at this time, the city of Amsterdam, powerful and rich by reason of its commerce, had taken over the proprietorship thereof, perhaps the colony would not have experienced any of the misfortunes which it later suffered. What garrison did it have for its defense from the conquest of the Zeelanders up to the invasion of Cassard, to oppose the Indians? Upon the remonstrance of the colonists, Zeeland, in 1679, sent 150 troops there; Monsieur de Sommelsdyk brought 300 more men (the greater part of whom, because of their revolt in the assassination of the said governor, were condemned to withdrawal from the colony), and, finally, Monsieur de Scherpenhuysen brought another small reinforcement. And if we may believe the author of *La Richesse de la Hollande,* the Lords Proprietors, already in 1688, found themselves impotent to send the necessary provisions to the garrison which was then in the colony.[59]

When one considers these misfortunes, and the combination of so many disadvantages, one is surprised to see how the colony was able to raise itself up again from its fall, to form new settlements, to increase the amount of its revenues, and to become, in fifteen or twenty years, richer and more opulent than it had ever been. And if one also considers how this same colony, after having fallen upon new misfortunes, which did not have causes as complicated as in its penultimate fall, instead of flourishing, could not raise itself up again or return to its first state (although at the present time it is beginning to reestablish itself by reason of the advantageous prices of its products), one would be still more surprised.

However, it seems to us that we have fathomed the cause thereof, and this cause is luxury, unrecognized then, and adopted later on; for (1) generally speaking, one did not know what money borrowed on interest was; (2) the superfluous was abhorred, and one lived in the abundance of objects of primary necessity. There was nothing at all of unfortunate distinctions among the inhabitants, and nothing at all of that vain and haughty ostentation which brings with it a destructive luxury upon the settlements, the effects of which became more noticeable after money had been borrowed at interest from Holland. We shall speak of all this in greater detail, and we shall demonstrate that our ideas are correct; in the meantime, let us continue our history.

A little before Cassard's attack, the inhabitants of Surinam, seeing that their remonstrances to the council had had but little effect, addressed themselves to Their High Powers, under date of September 17, 1712, and made complaints against the Lords Proprietors, and against the administrative council, both in regard to taxes contrary to the grant, as well as in regard to the bad state in which the fortifications were at that time.[60] And on October 12th of the same year, at the time of Cassard's arrival, the Captains of the Citizens protested against the damages that the colonists had suffered because of their negligence, and in consequence they refused to guard the fortress, which, at their refusal, was occupied by the Jews, as we have observed above. The administrative council, in its turn, brought complaints against the colonists who obstinately refused to contribute to the necessary work on the fortress. The States, after having heard the Lords Proprietors, ordered the inhabitants to contribute with their contingents, and to obey the orders of the council.[61] New complaints arose again the following year. The planters wished to be indemnified for all that they had contributed to Cassard for the ransoming, since it was because of the bad condition of the fortifications which, according to the grant,[62] the Lords Proprietors were charged with maintaining, that Cassard had made himself master thereof.

On these new complaints, the States, on July 28, 1713, again condemned the colonists to pay the expenses of Cassard, and ordered the council to impose new moderate taxes upon them, in order to provide for the needs of the colony.

In the meantime, and in the midst of all these quarrels, the Jews, whom the austerity of Governor Scherpenhuysen had rendered fearful that the old persecutions would return, and who, despite the truly paternal protection of the Lords of the Colony which they unceasingly experienced, believed that the monster of envy and prejudice still breathed, like the hydra of the fable, which grew new heads as they were cut off, decided, therefore, to obey the regulations of the council, and to attach themselves strongly to these Lords as their sole supports. And upon the communication which the council (original letter in the archives) had made to the regents in May, 1713, of a plan for the fortifications, after having given their opinion, they immediately contributed to everything that was demanded of them. But since the rest of the inhabitants evaded their payments, the plan had no effect at all at that time.

The spirit of concord which then reigned among the Jews and the faults of their fellow-inhabitants, who had cast themselves down into an abyss of discussions, opened the eyes of the Jewish community, which remained quietly on its habitations, and placed its individual members, despite the disasters of the colony, in a very flourishing state again. And the new assurances, which they had received some years before, of the protection of the Lords Proprietors in Holland by a letter of Monsieur Geronimo de Haas de George, former mayor or Amsterdam, written to Governor de Gooyer,[63] in particular to maintain the Jewish community in its rights and privileges, which letter had all the success which was expected of it, quieted the Jewish community on all these points.

It was then that the community renewed the affection which it had always had for the well-being of its fellow-inhabitants. For the Jews aided the Christian planters with everything that was in their power. We shall mention some of their beneficent acts.

On June 12, 1707, they gave to Governor W. de Gooyer twelve good carpenters to finish Government House, and in July, 1710, according to the registers of that date, they gave him a further present of seventy-two barrels of sugar, to aid him in his private affairs. Governor Coutier, who succeeded the latter, received four cows and two heifers, as well as fifty barrels of sugar, according to the registers of November, 1719, and the Commandant de Rainevalk, ten barrels of sugar. In addition, the said governor was given twenty-four good Negro pioneers to labor on his plantation until the work was finished. Commander de Vries also received twenty-four good Negroes for the same purpose, and the reason why he requested them from the Jews is contained in his letter of September, 1731, because his Christian friends had failed to make good the promise which they had made to him. In addition, there were materials for the buildings, etc., which we omit to mention, in order not to swell the number of these gratuitous gifts, or to make an ostentatious display of a proper and indispensable duty among true and useful colonists who ought to treat each other mutually as brothers.

We avow solemnly before the Supreme God that we have not at all reported these facts in order to reproach anyone, but we are forced to demonstrate by authentic proofs that the Jewish community does not at all abhor (as its antagonists maliciously assert) the subjects of the sovereign who tolerates them; that on the contrary, it loves them, and that whenever it was in a position to do so, it gave most outstanding proofs of its attachment towards them. If, unfortunately, it is not in a position to do so, its misfortunes are the cause thereof, but not its good intentions.

Surinam at that time, and before the year 1720 or 1721, knew only the cultivation of sugar. Many attempts were made to grow tobacco and roucou [annatto, a tree producing a dyestuff], but these, according to the authors, had no desirable results. It was not until 1720 that the first attempts to grow coffee were made in Surinam from some small plants which a certain Hansbach had brought from the *Hortus Medicus* of Amsterdam,[64] although the *Tableau de Surinam* attributes his progress to Monsieur *de Neale*.[65] This plant, later on and for many years, made the wealth of Surinam, although at first it caused the ruin of several sugar plantations, whose owners had abandoned them in order to devote themselves to its cultivation. Sugar is a commodity which, with means sufficient to maintain it, is indeed a more definite and a more assured source of wealth than coffee, despite the cost of the [sugar] mills and the difficulties which this commodity experiences as to prices in Europe, principally in time of peace.

From this period on, the colony became still ampler [economically] through the cultivation of cacao, begun in 1733, and of cotton in 1735.[66]

According to the very exact calculation derived from the *Carte Générale de la Colonie de Surinam* by Lavaux, and from other old writings, the number of plantations which were to be found in Surinam in the year 1730, large and small, amounted to 401, namely, along the Surinam, three leagues from its mouth up to twenty leagues above it (including the Para river and other creeks), 224; and along the Commowine, its rivers and creeks, 177. Of this number, the Jews at that time possessed ninety-three settlements on the Surinam river, its creeks, etc., and in Commowine, Sarua, Cassewine, etc., twenty-two. This adds up to 115 settlements, most of them in sugar, and without a penny of debt, because the advances later taken from merchants in Holland were not known then. Besides, their mode of living was very simple and regular, luxury was a stranger to them, and their settlements were never embellished with ostentatious or useless buildings. Cleanliness, the conveniences of life, and some profusion on their tables on holidays in the Savane: this was their entire luxury, their entire prodigality. When the holidays were ended, each person returned to his settlement to see to its cultivation himself, and this was approximately also the mode of living of several Christian planters of that time.

And despite the difficulties which the Jews experienced from time to time on the part of the council, they nonetheless led a very tranquil and even happy life, until the flights of the slaves and the very frequent attacks of the runaway Negro slaves on their settlements caused them to lose their peacefulness and the ease of their rural life.

From the time of the English, even before the period of 1665, there had already been Negro runaways in the woods. Let us listen to their history in an abridged form by Monsieur Hartsink himself,[67] who on page 756 attributes everything to the Jews. As we have remarked above, his account will bring his contradictions to light.

"The Negroes of Saramaca," he says, "derive their origin from several black slaves who, having escaped from the domination of the English by flight, later established themselves along the Saramaca and Copename rivers, in regions that were very thickly forested. There they formed a sort of republic, already at the time when the English were still possessors of this part of Guiana. Some of these Negroes found the means to entrench themselves in Para under a chief named Jermes, a Negro of Coromantin, and from there they would come to insult and disturb the neighboring plantations." Note that the Jews never had more than two plantations along the Para river; their settlements were only at the upper part of the Surinam river, six leagues distant from Para. It was not until several years later that they began to cultivate the lowlands, after the Dutch cultivators showed them the possibility and the usefulness thereof, and then they nonetheless had settlements only from the Gelderland Plantation, four leagues distant from the city of Paramaribo.

"The number of these [Negro] fugitives," he continues, "was estimated at five or six thousand in 1701 and in 1702. Having fallen upon Para, they massacred the proprietor of one plantation there; the carpenter of another met the same fate in 1713. Several years later, they attacked a plantation situated in Tempaty, wounded the owner there, mistreated his wife, and finished by carrying everything away. During the regency of Monsieur Temminck, in the year 1721 or 1722, they pillaged not only in Commowine the plantation of a certain Ridderbak, but also carried the slaves away into the woods. These cruel visits increased from year to year, and became more and more destructive. Before and during the time of Monsieur de Cheusses in 1730 and 1734, these fugitives ruined various plantations in Para, in Tempaty and in Peninica, and there they slaughtered not only all the whites whom they found there, but even some of the slaves, carrying away with them afterwards everything that they believed could be of service to them. They also attacked the Bergendaal Plantation, belonging to the said Monsieur de Cheusses."

Behold the revolts, the flights and the massacres which befell the settlements of the Christians through their own slaves, who certainly increased very greatly the number of runaway slaves even in the time of Cassard. Hence the report that Monsieur Hartsink makes on the subject of the Negroes of the Jews is not correct, and his assertion is all the more uncertain as he ignored even the hostilities of this nature which befell particularly the settlements of the Jews. We shall relate them (without fear of giving weight to his report) exactly as we found them in our archives, so that impartial people may be able to see whether one can attribute to the Jewish community the cause of the colony's misfortune in this regard, or accuse them, in consequence, of more tyranny towards their slaves than one attributes to the other inhabitants of the colony. With the exception of the flight of two or three slaves, which often happened on the plantations in general, there was, in the year 1690, an uprising on a plantation situated on the Cassewine creek, behind the Savane, belonging to a Jew named Immanuel Machado, where, after having killed their master, they fled, carrying away with them everything that was there. And in 1738, another one, belonging to Manuel Pereyra, experienced the same fate. The first misfortune of this nature, which befell the Jewish community in the person of Machado, is especially remarkable for a feature which proves the hatred which Governor van Scherpenhuysen bore towards the Jews: he left the task of repairing this misfortune to the Jews alone, and he informed them in a letter dated February 18, 1690, that they could avenge the death of their brother, if they wished, in the same manner as if Machado and his plantation did not form a part of the colony at all. The Jews obeyed him fully, and in an expedition which they undertook against the rebels, killed many of them and brought back several who were punished by death on the very spot. A parallel exploit was made by the Jewish community in 1738; it was then that a man named Pereyra lost his life, a man of whom no historian of Surinam has deigned to speak. We shall return to this in its place.

From that time on, and up to the period of the peace which the colony made with the two villages of runaway slaves known under the names of Saramaca and Juca, there were continual attacks on the plantations, and it is properly from this time on, and not from the time of the invasion of Cassard in 1712, that the number of fugitives increased. We shall not count at all the attacks in which a tremendous number of Negroes fled into the woods. In the year 1749, the Negroes of the plantation of Monsieur Roma revolted, and after a thousand hostilities they fled, and they joined those [former slaves] of the Jews and of a man named Salmer. The Negroes had a little village situated on the Juca creek, about twenty-five to thirty leagues distant from the bank of the Surinam river in the interior of the woods, of which we shall speak in greater detail later. They increased this settlement, which was then nothing but later became redoubtable, principally after the flight of the Negroes of six large settlements who revolted at the same time in 1757 at Tempaty (a place where there was never any settlement of Jews). [The Negroes] belonging to Martin Pater and others amounted in number, together with those of Toma [Roma?], perhaps without exaggeration despite what Monsieur Hartsink says, to [from] 500 to 600 slaves. In the following year, they attacked the Palmaribo Plantation situated beside the Savane of the Jews, whose Negroes, who were leagued together with them, fled, to the number of almost 150. The Providence Plantation in Surinam and the Onobo Plantation in Cassewine, belonging to the Jews, underwent the same fate in the same year, and after the rebels had burned the buildings, they carried away with them about 120 slaves in number.

We have seen, by what has just been said, the old state of the colony in general and in particular, as well as that of the Jews with reference to their wealth, from the beginning of the colony up to the year 1712. Let us now see their political condition of that time, their influence, their power, and the mutual benevolence of the colonists in general.

The justificatory documents which contain the privileges of the Jewish community indisputably show that the Portuguese Jews settled in Surinam on a happier and more favorable basis than in any other place in the universe. In a word, they were placed in the rank of the colonists of the Protestant religion, without distinction. All employments and even some public offices were open to them without any restriction, according to the contents of the privilege granted by the English, and later approved and augmented by the Lords Proprietors and by Their High Powers the States General. Besides, they had a tribunal of civil justice constituted in the most legal form up to the amount of 600 florins, without it being permitted to any Jew to assign another to appear before another higher or subordinate tribunal (according to the old registers of the Jewish community) for any case in which the amount of the claims was less than 600 florins. Their individuals formed a company of citizens under the direct command of a captain and his officers, and these were under the orders of the council. Thus the entire Jewish community was subordinated to a number of persons who formed the political, civil and ecclesiastical tribunal known under the Hebrew name of *Mahamad,* or regents and deputies of the Portuguese Jewish Community; and all that which did not at all contradict the laws of the country and the dispensation of which was not expressed in the privileges was judged by the regents as a court of final resort. And by virtue of the grant made by Their High Powers to the proprietors of the colony in 1682, they contributed equally, in their quality as citizens, to the nomination of the political magistrates of the colony. And if the Jews, from the beginning, had not renounced having jurisdiction in the criminal cases of the Jewish community, at least as the first resort, the right of autonomy anciently known of them in the time of the Romans would be complete there in all its circumstances. And although, in the matter of honorable and lucrative positions in the colony, the first Jews, rich and comfortably situated and, besides, ignorant of the language of the country, did not at all take the trouble to fill any of them, according to their rights, the Justificatory Document No. 3 nonetheless shows the honorable and distinguished position which Joseph Nassy had, in virtue of the commission of vice-admiral Crynssen, and in the course of time we again find in our archives that the regents created the positions which they needed for the service of the Jewish community. Samuel Nassy, besides his posts, and Jeos. Sarvaty were notaries public known under the name of *Jurator*, and Ab. Nunes in January, 1682, was made a sworn land surveyor, who served the Christians and the Jews equally and whose maps are still today acknowledged by successive land surveyors to be among the most accurate.

Their marriages were performed among them at that time with the right of complete legitimacy, and their marriage contracts, drawn up before their rabbis according to their ritual, had the right of preference over all debts, in favor of the women. Their income from personal property, arranged simply among them, had the right of ownership as soon as it was registered in the archive of the Jewish community. The same was the case with regard to their wills, and other provisions, without their ever having to fulfill the formalities exacted by jurisprudence, which had become a chaos and a plague for the inhabitants of the colonies because of the delays which they experience in their affairs and the enormous expenses which they have to pay to the secretariat. However, as we are informed, this abuse is about to be remedied, at this very moment, by measures which have been proposed for the approval of the Lords Proprietors.

All this would still not characterize the golden age in Surinam of the Jewish community if it did not enjoy conjointly the consideration of the colonists in general, loved, even revered, by them. They enjoyed the most complete happiness; for what would the privileges of a community signify, what would its rights amount to, if it was not at all able to win the affection of the people among whom it lives? Our privileges would today certainly form the happiness of the Jews of France and of Germany, and perhaps even of those of Italy, without excepting [even] those who live under the rule of the beneficent Leopold [Grand Duke] of Tuscany. At the sight of the place, the scene, where their ancestors were persecuted because of the same religion which today tolerates them, they should consider themselves happy. But for the Jews of

Surinam, [who, though] accustomed to seeing themselves esteemed, become poor after they have been rich, and, to complete their misfortune, [become] disdained and without any other resource than that which their industry affords them, they certainly do not find themselves in the same circumstances as their brethren in Europe. One needs philosophic eyes that know the character and the innermost recesses of the human heart, to feel this truth in all its force. Besides, every man and every nation must go back to the cause which has produced its immunities and the cause which has made them lose them. And if the character and the prejudices of the greater part of the peoples among whom they live are found to be in contradiction to the sane views and the distinguished protection of those who give us the law in Europe, and if this law, because of the distance from the place where the legislative power and benevolence reside, is weakened, the mass of the evil increases, and the spite which morale experiences is reflected even in the physique. The continuation of this work will show if we are mistaken or not. Let us continue.

In consequence, the privileges of the Jewish community did not suffer any essential change except only in one point. In the beginning the Jews contracted marriages among themselves in conformity with their laws, between close relatives. The States General, for reasons reserved to sovereignty, found it good to ordain, by a resolution dated May 30, 1704, that from then on no inhabitant of the colony could marry except in accordance with the contents of the political ordinances of the States of Holland and of West Friesland of the year 1580, declaring nevertheless that the marriages which had been contracted up to the date of the resolution, together with the children born therefrom, were legal and legitimate. As for those contracted thereafter, they will not be regarded at all as legitimate, unless the alliance has been made before two magistrates of the colony, according to the law of the Republic. This ordinance had its effect, and when a Jew wished to marry a relative permitted by the law of Moses and forbidden by the law of J[esus]. C[hrist]., they would petition the council to ask for a dispensation, according to the example of what is ordinarily done in Holland; and the request was always granted, by means of a gratuity which one gave to the public prosecutor of the colony. But for some years now, the prosecutor currently in office, Monsieur Karsseboom, after having given favorable opinions on this matter in the preceding years, has been finding it good, at the present time, to indicate doubts (perhaps well-founded) in the reports that he gives to the council. [What opinion he might incline to in a report] is not known to us, with the result that before a Jew can marry by virtue of the privileges, he must await the dispensation of the States General, who in their goodness and benevolence never fail to grant the request which is made to them, but this occasions much expense.

Here is the place where we ought to speak of the German Jews, who in 1690 numbered only forty to fifty persons, but increased to the point of forming, at the present time, more than half of the number of their Portuguese brethren. They were then dependent upon the latter, who helped them in everything that they needed. Since their profession was that of commerce and of trade, they settled in Paramaribo. Aided thereafter by the work of their hands, without running the risks or the disasters connected with agriculture, they began little by little to improve their lot, their number increased by those of their brethren who flocked in from Europe. Their religious ceremonies were after the style of the Portuguese [i.e. though Ashkenazim, they had adopted Sephardic usages], and they did not know at all those ridiculous manners which distinguish them [Ashkenazim] so greatly from the Portuguese Jews, such as Baron de Bielfeld notes.[68] And although they never had to meddle with the rule of the Jewish community, nor intermarried with the Portuguese, they nevertheless lived with them in good understanding, as a part of the number of the individuals of the Jewish community.

But as soon as they began to feel a little more at their ease, they started quarrels with the Portuguese, and obliged the latter, in order to avoid results that could become dangerous, to separate completely from them. They therefore appealed to the lords of the colony, who made an arrangement between them according to an authentic act inserted in the book of Privileges, under the date of September 10, 1734, to the effect that these two Jewish communities are from this time separated, each having its synagogue and its regents, independent of each other. And although the Privileges were granted to the Portuguese, they [the German Jews] enjoy all sorts of immunities, both as Jews and as citizens, except that of having property in the Savane and the right of having a civil and citizen tribunal of justice, which is peculiar to the [Sephardic] Jewish community. Although none of them are as rich as some of the Portuguese, this part of the Jewish community generally not having had occasion like the Portuguese to sacrifice a part of their possessions in order to maintain the privileges of the Jewish community, nor the need to interfere in the quarrels of Governor Mauritius (the details of which will be found in the course of this work), the German Jews are in much better condition than the Portuguese. Perhaps one cannot find anywhere German Jews in general who have the manners of those of Surinam, and the reflections of those authors who remark on the difference between these two Jewish communities could very well be out of place here, for with the exception of several ridiculous superstitions, and a little too much bigotry (generally speaking), the difference is not very perceptible, and it would not at all have been noticed if a prodigious number of Polish Jews [fellow Ashkenazim] who came here at intervals had not, so to speak, harmed them by introducing their manners.

We have shown, by the above account, the state of the colony in general, in relation to what it had to undergo from its beginning up to the unfortunate event with Cassard. Let us now see the result of these events, which produced discontentment and complaints against the Lords Proprietors with regard to the state of the fortifications and the supreme orders of Their High Powers in 1712 and 1713.

Whatever these orders were, several more years passed before anything could be agreed on, and it was not until the end of 1733 that the lords of the colony and the colonists decided on several articles which were approved by Their High Powers under date of December 19 of the same year, and by virtue of which "the colony, in the period of seven years, was to be put in a good state of defense by means of fortifications which it was proposed were to be constructed there. The directors undertook to send there from Europe the workmen and the necessary materials, and the colonists would furnish a suitable number of slaves to labor on these works, and that during these seven years the directors would contribute annually the sum of 20,000 florins, and the settlers that of 60,000, collected from a tax which was to be imposed on the agricultural products, and from the settlers who were not included in the class of the planters." Several disagreements which since arose between the two contracting parties on the subject of the execution of this agreement gave occasion for new articles signed at Paramaribo on March 6, 1748, and later ratified by Their High Powers on January 16,[69] with the result that Fort New Amsterdam, situated in such a way that it protects the mouths of the Surinam and the Commowine rivers, was not completed until nearly sixteen years after the date of the first agreement.

It was extremely good fortune that the colony was not attacked at all from the time of Cassard up to that time. This would have had a very sad result, in view of the dissensions that prevailed for thirty years between the colonists, the magistrates of the colony, and among some of the latter with the governor, all the more since the raids of the runaway slaves had become so frequent that no one dared to stay very long in the settlements situated near the upper reaches of the rivers.

The colony, having become the theatre of a perpetual war, and the inhabitants, seeing themselves thus being troubled by their own slaves, were compelled to have detachments of troops march against them, in order to subjugate them by force of arms.

Several campaigns were consequently mounted, which cost immense sums, the greater part of them without success. From time to time the colonists themselves pursued the rebels under the command of the captain of the Jewish citizenry, David C. Nassy, and of Lieutenant Is. Carrilhos, for the Surinam river, and Messieurs van Vheelen and Lemmers, for that of Cottica. The latter with his detachment set out in 1730 on a stubborn chase in which, after having crossed more than thirty-six mountains, he entered the abodes of the runaway slaves without finding anyone there. However, he destroyed their foodstuffs and everything that he found there, and burned their cabins, and after his return to the city, the council despatched Captain Nassy to hold firm there with a detachment of his company of citizens. In the same year in the month of July, a large detachment was again sent under the orders of Captain Bedloo and of the military ensign Swallenberg. This detachment cost more than all the others, and yet achieved no results, whereupon the Lords Proprietors adopted the resolution to have only soldiers march against the runaway slaves. These at that time had less success than the civilians, and this subsequently caused them [the Proprietors] to return to them [the civilians]. In an expedition which they made to Saramaca, they took twenty-six Negro runaway slaves alive, and sixteen dead, and these detachments were continued later by Beinet, Nassy, Visser, van Gieske, Metschler, Knoffel, van Daalen, Brouwer, etc.[70]

In the account which these authors give of the civilian expeditions against the runaway slaves, the Jews are mentioned only indifferently [insubstantially]. Nothing of all that they did before and between these dates [the authors thought] deserved to find a place in their writings. Thus we shall endeavor to bring to light the most successful expeditions which they undertook against the common enemies of the country, daring to maintain in the face of the entire universe that if their detachments did not make more progress and at less expense than all the others, they at least knew how to equal the Christians in courage, in discipline, and in their burning zeal to serve the colony.

Captain David C. Nassy was at all times a robust man, accustomed to the work of the plantations and of intrepid courage. He had, besides, a special inclination to converse often with the Indians who were in great numbers in the settlements, and with whose language he was familiar. It is known that these Indians, although weak by temperament, are the most adept at discovering the tracks of the runaway slaves in the woods, and since they [the Indians] were afraid of falling into their hands, they placed spies in the forests in order to reconnoiter the place of their dwellings and all the movements that they made.

Nassy knew the use which he could make of these Indians. Being then very rich and in a position to make many expenditures, he gave them firearms, taught them to use them as well as a soldier, and, seeing his little troop in a position to support his views, he put himself at their head in order to make use of the liberty which the administrative council had given by its publication of 1717, "to whoever wished to undertake raids against the runaway slaves, at fixed prices according to the progress which they would come to make."[71] At that time he was only a subaltern officer under the command of Jacob d'Avilar, the captain of the Jews. In consequence, he mounted, in the year 1718, in the Saramaca river region, an expedition against the runaway slaves of this river region, accompanied by eleven Jewish citizens, a troop of fifty good Indians, and several of his best slaves. This expedition had the desired effect; he attacked the rebels, killed many of them, and brought back several alive, without the colony's having to spend a penny for the expenses of this expedition. This resulted in his meriting being appointed first lieutenant by the council, in the same year, instead of the plain subaltern officer which he was. And then [he was appointed] captain of the company of citizens of his Jewish community.

The good fortune which he had in his first expedition encouraged him to such a degree that no other expedition at all was undertaken in which he was not the first to present himself to march against the runaway slaves. And, according to what is found in his old papers and in the book of the citizenry, he led in his lifetime more than thirty expeditions both great and small, which caused the total dissipation of his wealth.

We shall relate several of the most remarkable ones. In 1731, the council ordered the officer of the citizenry of the Christians, Monsieur Boeyé, to organize an expedition against the runaway slaves, and ordered Captain Nassy to form a detachment, composed of his citizens, to reinforce Boeyé in case of attack or of discouragement. Nassy, following his orders, left, accompanied by his Indians, and in the middle of his journey, he encountered Boeyé, who was precipitately retreating because he had had the misfortune to have a man killed on his route by several fugitives, who by chance met his detachment on the road. Nassy in vain begged him to continue the expedition with him, since he was going to attack them in two or three days' time. Boeyé flatly refused, so that Nassy took it upon himself to march alone with his detachment against the enemy. He had the good fortune to attack them in their settlements, where he took several prisoners and killed a good number of them. In the meanwhile, a criminal process was brought against the officer Boeyé, who in his turn accused Captain Nassy, and in the proceedings which the prosecutor initiated against the two of them, Monsieur Boeyé was declared guilty, and was then punished. This fact is attested by praises and ballads which were composed in honor of Captain Nassy in Spanish by a Jewish poet by the name of Bienvenida del Monte.

In the year 1738, the Negroes of a plantation in Sarua, belonging to the Jew Manuel Pereyra, composed of Negroes of Coromantin, the most formidable of all these Africans, revolted and killed their master, as we have noted above. Monsieur Js. Arrias, a former officer of the

Jewish citizenry who had two large settlements in the neighborhood of the place of the revolt, dispatched a number of volunteer citizens under the command of two subalterns, Isaac Nassy and Ab. de Britto, in which expedition Monsieur Arrias furnished at his own expense everything which the detachment needed. He furthermore sent all the good Negroes whom he had on his holdings. The expedition was so successful that after six weeks of absence, without anyone knowing the fate of these volunteers, the detachment returned with forty-seven prisoners and six hands of those who had been killed. Therefore the council, according to our archives, in order to repay them for their exploits, made a gift of seventy-five florins to each of the officers, of thirty-six florins to each civilian, of twenty florins to each armed Negro, and of five florins to each Negro porter of victuals. But the generous Monsieur Arrias, to whose holdings this expedition caused great loss, had no recompense, as far as we knew, not even thanks in writing on the part of the gentlemen of the council.

Monsieur Hartsink has a report, furthermore, about a village of the rebels, known under the name of Creoles (a name which is given to those who are born in the country). They are the most redoubtable of all the [Negro] enemies, because of the ruses and the knowledge which they have acquired through commerce with the whites since their birth. Their village was attacked in the year 1731 and utterly ruined by Captain Bley. However, it is known that this troop of Negroes always followed his train in the hostilities against the whites, and that it was not until the year 1743, in the time of Governor Mauritius, that it was annihilated to the point that from then on the village was no longer known under the name which it had before, and this again through the intrepid courage of Captain D. C. Nassy. The latter, although already very old, left in the month of August of the said year with twenty-seven civilians, twelve soldiers, fifteen Indians, 165 Negroes, and sixty canoes, following a plan which he had formed and had presented to the council on July 1, 1743. He went up the Surinam river and after he had passed several cataracts which are met with as one goes up the river, he began his march, and the enemies were attacked on the day of *Kippur, or of Atonement of the Jews,* and without any regard for this sacred day, he pursued the enemies, set fire to their cabins, utterly ruined the village, tore out of the ground the roots of their victuals, took fourteen prisoners, and killed a large number.

This exploit astonished the whole colony, and the envy which for a long time had been expressed against the actions of this captain had something on which to exercise its baseness because of several mistakes committed by the said captain, despite so brilliant a success.[72] Here are the facts: the captain had orders to enter the village of these Creoles, to attack them, to destroy everything, and to give notice thereof immediately to the council, without leaving the place before new orders. But instead of following these orders, his troop (among which were one of his brothers and a son), whom the Indians and the Negroes persuaded that the runaway slaves had poisoned the creeks and that they would not have any water at all to drink in the drought under which they were laboring, began to murmur so strongly that he was forced to return with his prisoners and himself to bring the news of his expedition. On his arrival, which was on October 14 of the same year, his friends informed him of the mistake which he had made, and that he had to prepare to exculpate himself with at least the appearance of reason, because his enemies and enviers were ready to traduce him before the council. But he, flattering himself that the success of an expedition which was regarded as almost impossible would enable him to obtain some indulgence on the part of the council, presented himself there a few days after his arrival with all the confidence possible. The council, principally Governor Mauritius, overwhelmed him with a thousand accusations, among others that of having taken away, from the hands of the Negroes belonging to Christians who were in this expedition, the booty which they took from the runaway slaves, in order to give it to those of the Jews; and that of having consumed too many victuals which he had carried to the woods. And without hearing his defense, he was condemned to make reparations for the pretended wrongs done to the Negroes and to several Indians, and a criminal process was prepared against him. This reception and the unexpected accusations, which brought the entire edifice of all his glory down at one and the same time, had so terrible an effect on the heart of this brave man that he caught a fever which ended his days at the age of sixty-seven. By reason of his death, Monsieur Js. Carrelho was elected captain in his place, according to the act dated December of the same year, 1743.

Despite all these expeditions, sometimes very successful on the part of Christian and Jewish citizens, the woods were filled from day to day with new fugitives, and the roads to the retreats, or the knowledge of the forests, had become very easy for the slaves because of the continual expeditions which they made with the whites and which, so to speak, taught them the secret paths by which they could join the runaway slaves. This fact and many others led Governor Mauritius to conceive a plan, in imitation of Jamaica, of making peace with the runaway slaves of Saramaca, who were very numerous, and then, with their aid, to destroy those of the other side of Surinam. This plan was proposed to the council, and after a thousand debates, it was approved and put into execution. However, it lasted for only a very short time, because the disagreements which arose among the governor, the councillors, and the inhabitants had immensely grievous results, and were the cause why none of the promises to the Negroes were kept. They [the Negroes] feared, besides, that the peace proposed and concluded was only a trap which the whites wished to set for them; they suddenly broke the peace, and the hostilities began on both sides with more rage and fury than ever.[73]

The council, not knowing then what to do, resolved in 1749 to send at one and the same time two large detachments of citizens to march against the Negroes of Monsieur Coma, one by the Commowine river under Captain Rynsdorp and the other by the Surinam river, behind Cassewine creek, under the Jewish Lieutenant Captain Mos. Naar (who, despite his age, offered to make this expedition, which was his seventeenth, under the late Captain Nassy), with orders that these two detachments were to join together in case of need after some time, at a certain place on the upper reaches of these two rivers. Monsieur Naar had the good fortune to come upon tracks of fugitives, and, marching along these tracks and following them, he discovered a large tribal settlement which he attacked and reduced to ashes, having taken thirty-seven Negroes prisoner, among others the chief of the rebels, named Coridon, whom the council had ordered to be taken alive, if this was possible. Furthermore, he left a strong detachment to pursue those who had escaped; this brought in twenty more Negroes alive, which made a total of fifty-seven, besides a large number whom the detachment of Monsieur Naar had killed on that occasion. Those of the rebels who nevertheless escaped from the attack had the misfortune of lighting

HISTORY OF SURINAM 71

on the side where Monsieur Rynsdorp was marching; he took a large number of them prisoner. This fact is confirmed by a present of the value of 150 florins and a silver coffee-pot with the arms of the colony engraved on it, which the council gave the said Monsieur Naar.[74]

The rage which the whites conceived against the Negroes, the cruel punishments they made the deserters suffer, only helped increase their audacity and the inclination which they had towards desertion, as we have already observed. Among a large number of villages of the rebels scattered in the immense forests of the colony, situated twenty-five to thirty leagues distant from the settlements, there was a little village on a creek called Juca, behind a prodigiously high mountain. These Negroes, as we have noted above, were, until 1749, not at all sufficiently numerous to carry on hostilities, but since, in that same year, their number was increased by that of the Negroes of Toma, they had the courage to attack the settlement of a Jew known under the name of Auca, situation above the Savane, where there were fifty slaves without any defense. There they burned the houses, pillaged everything, and carried away almost all the Negroes who were there, men and children. This was the first raid which this village of Juca, which became so redoubtable after the flight of the Negroes of Tempaty in 1757, had made, and although this attack astounded and alarmed all the inhabitants up the river, they supposed nonetheless that it was caused by the Negroes of the settlement itself who fled thence, of their own accord, without having been captured by the runaway slaves. The officer of the Jewish citizenry Monsieur Is. C. Nassy, still young and without experience, unfortunately encouraged by this last supposition, and furthermore, knowing how little strength this settlement of Auca had, assembled in haste a dozen of his friends. All young people, accompanied by their best slaves, and with few munitions of war and provisions for ten to twelve days, they left without loss of time in pursuit of the fugitives. Following their tracks, they found out that they had to do with a sizable troop of armed people. The intrepidity of the officer led him, instead of retreating, to attack them and to suffer one of the bloodiest of skirmishes. Although their strength was so unequal, the whites kept the fight going from the morning until the evening, but having had the misfortune to see fall at their side the civilian Abm. de Britton, a mulatto Jew, and three or four of their good slaves, they lost courage. Officer Nassy, who had received a musket shot in the leg in the action, made great efforts to reanimate his people, but this was in vain; they took flight in the greatest disorder, so that the poor officer, who could scarcely walk because of his wound, deserted by his friends, was taken alive by the enemies, who (according to the report which these inhuman people made after the peace concluded with them in 1760) forced him to suffer a most cruel death. They assured us several times that they had lost in this encounter more than twenty men, among others two of the principal chiefs of their village; and that if it had not been for the death of these chiefs, whose families were set upon taking vengeance on the whites, they would have tended to Nassy's wounds and kept him, in order to have the pleasure of being served by a white man.

All these exploits and many others of the Jews (which, although known to the Jewish community, we shall not describe at all, since the archives of the colony were not opened to us at all and we cannot mention the dates of the expeditions or the number of fugitives brought back by various officers of the citizenry) certainly merited being recorded in the history of Surinam, all the more so since, of all the deeds that are reported there, none are accompanied by as much progress [success] as those of the Jews which we have just mentioned. And if we have resolved to clear up the chaos of our old archives, to examine the various papers of the captains and officers of the citizenry which each respective family took pains to preserve, and to inform ourselves about our old men who are still alive, this is not at all with the intention of enhancing the merit of the Jewish community above that of our Christian compatriots, but it is with the view of making known the dissimulation or, rather, the ignorance of the authors who have written about Surinam.

The Jews have at all times contributed of their blood [and] of their money to the well-being of the colony. They have braved all perils, sacrificed their religious prejudices, a sacrifice due, without flattery, to the protection which the Lords Proprietors have always accorded them, although [this protection has been] a thousand times evaded [locally], unknown to them [the proprietors], through the hate and envy, happily very groundless, which people bore to them. We flatter ourselves that no one will be displeased with us for having tried, ourselves, to justify the Jewish community to which we belong by means of a report of the true facts. Besides, in reporting what the Jews have done, we do not at all diminish the merit of the brave Christians who have done everything in their power for the welfare of the colony.

This kind of victory won by the [Negro] enemies, and their number which became prodigious after the year 1757, as is noted above, increased the courage of the runaway slaves, and put the colony on the brink of ruin, to the point where there remained no other resource than that of making peace with them. As a result, that which dissension, or, better said, the spirit of contradiction had rendered vain in the time of Governor Mauritius was finally regarded as a supreme good, all the more so since it appeared that the enemies themselves were asking for peace by means of several notes which were often found in the places where they carried on their raids, written by one of them named Boston, who had learned from his master to scribble before his flight. In consequence, proposals of peace were made, which was agreed upon in 1759 and 1760 and reported in full by Hartsink.[75]

If this peace did not entirely bring about the welfare of the colony, it at least contributed to the tranquillity of the colonists. We shall have occasion to speak about its results more in detail; let us cast our eyes on the domestic dissensions of the colony, which were very onerous for it.

The agreement which the colonists made with the Lords Proprietors in 1733 on the subject of the fortifications, approved by Their High Powers under date of December 19 of the same year, and which some difficulties prevented from taking place, as we have said above, was always the seed of the discord. By the said agreement, the colonists were to contribute annually for seven years the sum of 60,000 florins, and the Lords that of 20,000. Some other disagreements which had arisen between the two contracting parties on the subject of the collecting of this money and the execution of this agreement gave occasion to new articles signed at Paramaribo on March 6, 1748, and ratified again by Their High Powers the States General on January 16 of the following year. Thereby Articles 27 and 30 of the grant of September 23, 1682, which declare *that the fortifications would be under the charge of the Company, and that no one at all would be authorized to levy any taxes except with the approbation of Their High Powers,* were tacitly revoked by the voluntary judgment of the colonists, all the more so since, according to Article 30, the agreements were confirmed by the approbation of Their High Powers, the States General. However, the colonists sought the thread of Ariadne in order to withdraw from the labyrinth in which they had entangled themselves. And, finding themselves caught therein without resource, they made an outcry over trifles of little consequence, often seeking quarrels against all those who seemed to them to be attached to the Lords Proprietors. And, combining these disagreements with personal particularities, they formed a chaos of complaints and of bickerings against Governor Mauritius and several councilors on the subject of the peace which they had made with the runaway slaves of Saramaca, which we have reported above, and on the subject of several taxes which they wished to place on the colony's objects of luxury in general. The policy of Monsieur Mauritius, his capacity, since he possessed more knowledge of letters than all his opponents together, and whose poetic spirit sometimes made him utter expressions which were a little mordant and satirical against those who opposed his ideas, which were too subtle to be felt at first, excited hatred against him. And, attributing all his actions solely to his inclination to dominate, they began to regard his administration and that of his masters [the proprietors] with too much prejudice. Monsieur Mauritius, at first tranquil and later agitated by passions, equally lost sight of the limits of discretion, and everything was placed in a state of complete discord. Each party sought only to increase the number of its partisans, in order to tear the other to pieces by means of writings that were fulminating and licentious in the full force of the term. The departure for Holland, in 1747, of Monsieur Du Plessis, a mortal enemy of Monsieur Mauritius, to draw up complaints against him furnished favorable occasions to add thereto new ones against the governor and against the Lords Proprietors.

"The Jew," says Monsieur [Isaac] de Pinto, *Lettres de quelques Juifs à Monsieur de Voltaire,* Volume 1, page 13, "is a chameleon who everywhere takes on the colors of the various climates in which he lives, of the various peoples with whom he associates, and of the various forms of governments under which he lives." Consequently, in the midst of so many discussions, the Jews were not able to remain neutral. The party opposed to Monsieur Mauritius was able to win over Monsieur J. Carilho, captain of the Jewish citizenry, a rich man highly esteemed among the Jews and with whom austerity of manners and intrepidity took the place of politics and sagacity. This man, then, joined the party opposed to the governor and signed various writings against him in the name of the Jewish community. Monsieur Mauritius, considering the harm which could be done to him in the opinion of his masters in Holland by the complaints of an entire community whose members were numerous enough to form more than a third of the white population [in Surinam], complained to the regents of the Jewish community. These men, who in their quality as regents are, according to the privileges, the sole representatives of the Jewish community [and] do not need the agreement of the captains of the citizenry, brought suit against Monsieur Carilho, as much because of the power which he had assumed to sign requests in the name of the Jewish community as because he had contributed to making their privileges and immunities of doubtful legality, to the disadvantage of his brethren. The two parties which vilified each other among the Christians took under their protection their adherents among the Jews and placed the whole Jewish community in the midst of the most unfortunate dissension, even causing thereby intense discussions on the internal rule of the synagogue, the nature of their constitution, their privileges, and their religious ceremonies—but not the common cause which they claimed to defend. As a result, Megaera [jealousy] and the monster of fanaticism arose among the Jews, and rendered their settlements, like the colony in general, the theatre of discord.

From this moment on the States General saw themselves overwhelmed with requests on one side and replies on the other, until finally Their High Powers, on December 20, 1747, adopted the resolution to send all the documents written by Du Plessis and Carilho to Governor Mauritius, with orders to send them his defense as soon as possible, etc.

In the same year the Jews, fearing the fatal results of what was taking place in the colony and the harm which this could do to their privileges, addressed a letter to the Lords Proprietors, to request them to intercede with Their High Powers. They received, by way of the governor, their assurances in this regard through a letter dated July 6, 1747, in which these Lords approved the conduct of the regents exercised on this occasion.[76]

After a thousand debates of this nature, matters nonetheless remained in a state of indecision until February 3, 1750, when Their High Powers found it suitable to send all the documents of the lawsuit back to the High Council in order that, after examining them, it should dispose of the suit as it judged proper. Meanwhile, by another resolution of May 22 of the same year, the States General having requested and authorized His Highness [William IV] the Prince of Orange to take measures immediately which he should judge to be most suitable for the reestablishment of tranquillity as well as of the security of the colony which was then strongly troubled by the incursions of the Negro fugitives, His Most Serene Highness was of the opinion that commissioners should be sent there with some troops. A regiment of 600 men drawn from all the garrisons of the state was formed. The command of these troops was given to Baron de Sporcke, Major General of Infantry, with the title of First Commissioner, to whom were joined in this latter quality Monsieur Boschaart, pensionary of the city of Schiedam, and Monsieur de Swart Steenis, councillor of Gorcum, who were charged with taking notice of the state of affairs in the colony and with taking such steps there as they should judge to be necessary.

These Commissioners, having arrived at Surinam in the month of December, 1750, issued a proclamation there couched in these terms on April 14 of the following year:

"The Deputies of His Most Serene Highness Monseigneur the Prince of Orange and of Nassau, etc., make it known that after having obtained the necessary information on the subject of the troubles that have arisen between the regency and several of the proprietors of the plantations of this colony, the Commissioners Boschaart and Steenis are resolved to return to Holland as soon as possible to make an exact report thereof to His Most Serene Highness, as well as of the various complaints which have been brought before them in the name and on the part of several of the inhabitants of this colony. And, in order that His said Highness may judge of them in accordance with his great wisdom, etc., and, finally, as we have judged it necessary to send to Holland Monsieur J. J. Mauritius, governor of this colony (saving his honor, and the maintenance of his appointments), we have provisionally charged with this post Baron H. E. de Sporcke, Major General in the service of the Republic and Commandant of the Troops which are at present in this colony, conferring upon him the same power and the same authority which Monsieur Mauritius has had up to the present."

These last two commissioners, having returned to Holland in the month of August following, with Monsieur Mauritius, remitted, together with other documents, a remonstrance signed by citizens and containing complaints in fifty-two very detailed articles. Therein, Articles XII, XIII and XLIII manifest all their hatred against the Jewish community in general, without consideration for Carilho, who was of their party. But, the first fire of passion having passed, they no longer had need to regard a Jew as one of their partisans. If one draws a parallel between this remonstrance and the request presented by them themselves in the name of forty-one citizens in favor of Monsieur Carilho in October, 1747, which is found in the collection of Monsieur Mauritius, one will see very clearly how much they contradict and belie themselves in speaking of the Jews: an observation which should furnish enlightening lessons to the Jewish community to teach it to be on its guard in similar cases. However, if it is not permitted—if it is even worthy of condemnation—to persecute or to calumniate an entire people without valid cause, it is with all the more reason still more condemnable to try to slander the Jews of a colony whose origin and progress are indebted to them in many circumstances and to whom the Sovereign and the Lords Proprietors have often given signs of contentment, permitting them to enjoy all their protection. Besides, what crimes had the Jews committed that one could slander them to the point of accusing them, as was done in these articles, principally in Article XII? In this article, their Savane is compared to a den of thieves, and it is supposed that their votes in the nomination of the administrative councilors were bought for the governor.

If, instead of yielding to the solicitation of individuals, the regents, not knowing at all the talents of those intended for nomination, ask the governor which person it would be most suitable to name, and when the Jewish community settles on its choice, the union of its members causes their small number to triumph over that of the other colonists who are often divided and form little cabals, is this a crime? And supposing, again (that which is by no means proved), that the governor requests their votes, would it still not be a duty of the Jewish community, when it does not at all condemn its conscience, to be more attached to the governor than to the others who at all times have sought to heap contempt upon him, while the protection of those whom this same governor represents had sheltered them from being persecuted? And, again, what does this privilege of contributing to the nomination of the magistrates of the colony mean? Does not a free Negro who has a hovel or a small piece of land in his own right enjoy the same right? Is this sort of democratic liberty, which the legislative power has granted to the inhabitants of a colony who work equally both for their own welfare and for that of the mother country, susceptible to observations which are both puerile and unjust? Monsieur Hartsink, without being willing to sense the truth of this fact and being perhaps carried away by his own prejudices, says[77] *that this liberty given to the Jews still wounds the hearts of the other inhabitants.* Why did he not add there the word *unjustly* to show his impartiality?

The three articles mentioned above which will be found in Document No. 12, combined with the facts that we have cited in this writing, will justify what we have just said, and the illogical reasoning, the passion, and even the hatred that are to be found there are the best proof that the Jewish community can have to demonstrate its innocence. Also, the decision of Their High Powers, placed side by side with these three articles, and their resolutions of April 24, 1755,[78] again seal this truth, and cause the Jews to triumph in this regard. But let us return to the affairs of Monsieur Mauritius in order to revert to that of the Jews who in this case are found identified with all that which occurred in Holland at that time on the subject of the troubles of the colony.

The judgment of the High Council in Holland on the subject of the lawsuit that was begun for and against Monsieur Mauritius resulted in the disclosure of the innocence of the said governor. However, we shall not at all conceal the fact that, according to reports which we have seen, Monsieur Mauritius, in accordance with his custom, was a little inconsistent, but not at all of so reproachable a character as is supposed by the authors of the *Letters on Essequibo and Demerary* which we have cited. And we think that if the colonists, with less passion, less impetuosity, and more moderation and wisdom, had only made their remonstrances to him, his zeal for the colony would have made his government missed for a long time. Besides, Monsieur Du

Plessis, who was the chief of the party opposing the governor, was not of a suitable character for such commissions. They—he and his adherents—offered so many puerile arguments against his adversary that the policy which Monsieur Mauritius had taken in regard to them appeared justified. Thus the public prosecutor for the Government at once began criminal proceedings against Monsieur Du Plessis (who had already been put in prison). He [Du Plessis] got out of the affair only by virtue of the general amnesty of July 20, 1753, which Their High Powers were willing to let him have at his request, but nonetheless on condition that he pay the costs of his arrest, and under the express prohibition of his ever returning to the colony.

Scarcely had the two Commissioners who had returned to Holland made their reports to the Prince Stadtholder [William IV], when the death of His Royal Highness, which occurred on October 22, 1751, delayed for some time the question as to which measures it would be well to take in consequence [of the reports]. And at the request of the principal interested persons and inhabitants, Her Royal Highness [Anne of England], the Governing Princess, had been requested, by a resolution of the States General of October 20 of the same year, to take charge of the commission until all the matters had been completely decided. And on the proposal of the late Her Most Serene Highness, it was decreed, on June 22, 1752, to continue for a year the stay of the troops of the State in the colony, as well as to see to the funds intended for their maintenance.

The regents of the Jewish community were, during this interval, in conflict with Monsieur Carilho, who was boldly supported by the party hostile to Monsieur Mauritius,[79] who, after the departure of the said governor, was still further supported by Baron de Sporcke, because of the strong recommendations which had come to him from Holland in favor of Carilho on the part of Monsieur Soaso of The Hague, an intimate friend of the said Monsieur de Sporcke. This so emboldened Monsieur Carilho that he again knew how to have Monsieur Abm. Dacosta dismissed from the post of regent, under the pretext that he was too young to be entrusted with it. Hereupon the regents adopted the resolution to send commissioners to Holland in the name of the Jewish community and commissioned for this purpose Monsieur Isak Nassy, who left Surinam in the month of July, 1751. Therefore Monsieur

Carilho, six months later, sent his son Monsieur de Barrios, provided with a power of attorney, to cope with the commissioner of the regents, who was followed by young Dacosta himself. As a result, everything that concerned the affairs of Surinam, both the general and the particular affairs of the Jews and of the Christians, was equally represented in Holland, and was defended by the committees of all the parties. And although the affairs of the Jewish community equally occupied Her Royal Highness and formed a very perceptible part of the troubles of the colony, no historian of Surinam has deigned to make the least report thereof, apparently in order not to publish the privileges which the very sovereign had granted for their happiness and their tranquillity, as can be seen by the justificatory documents[80] of which we shall soon speak.

In this mass of discussions which characterizes in a truly singular fashion the weakness of the human spirit, its errors in morals at the expense of its tranquillity and its welfare, and which also shows how greatly caprice alone and the passion to dominate have been able to change the simple manners of the inhabitants of an agricultural colony, both Christians and Jews, and to produce such unfortunate effects, we can only say about them, with [the first-century C. E. Latin poet] Statius:

Excidat illa dies aevo, nec postera credant. ["May that day be forever forgotten, and may later ages take no notice of it."]

Their High Powers put an end to this affair by means of a resolution dated July 20, 1753, which contains, in the greatest detail, the measures concerted between the Commissioners of Her Royal Highness and the deputies of the Lords Proprietors. Here is the summary of this document: the first point dealt with the satisfaction to be given to Governor Mauritius, to whom was to be paid a one-time sum of 15,000 florins; the second, third and fourth points concerned the recall of the troops of the State and their replacement by 300 men to augment the corps of those of the Lords Proprietors, that is to say, 125 at their expense, and 175 at the expense of the planters and the inhabitants; the fifth point relates to the change of the regency of Surinam; it was agreed to dismiss all the present administrative councillors and to replace them, *for this time, and without consequence for the future,* by nine new councillors who were to be chosen by Her Royal Highness, taken from the list which she had drawn up together with the Lords Directors of the colony, and several of the principal planters and inhabitants, while ordering Monsieur Crommelin, the ad interim governor (by reason of the death of Baron de Sporcke), to have them take the ordinary oath; the sixth point concerned the means of defense and of improvement of the colony; and the seventh gave the force of law to the decision of Her Royal Highness on the fifty-two points of the remonstrance of various planters and inhabitants. As for that which concerned the Jewish community, Monsieur J. Nassy, after a thousand debates which he had to carry on against Messieurs de Barrios and Soasso, who defended with zeal all that their friend Monsieur Sporcke had done in Surinam, Her Royal Highness, in the same intention and without any difference either in the terms of her decree or in anything that could have revealed that she had conceived any indifference towards the Jews, whose tranquillity should equally serve the welfare of the colony in general, wrote a letter to the regents of the Jewish Community, dated May 27, 1754. Among various other articles, Her Royal Highness declared to them that, in accordance with the arrangement which she had made with the Lords Proprietors and the committee of the Jewish community through Monsieur Is. Nassy, she had taken it upon herself to make a new election of regents *for this time, and without consequence for the future,* according to the nomination enclosed therein, etc., further ordering them that, in view of the complaints made against the privileges of the Jewish community, the regents were to be charged with sending her immediately the collection of all these privileges, so that they might be examined.[81] Then Her Royal Highness, in order to give more basis to her disposition and to shelter the Jewish community from every kind of persecution, made an investigation of the ecclesiastical-political institutions of the Jewish community and of those which have reference to her tribunal of civil procedure, contested several times by the administrative council, and by the remonstrance of the planters, Article 12 of which we have spoken above. And after having heard the two parties, she gave her approbation to this body of laws known under the Hebrew name of *Ascamoth.*[82] There remained, for the purpose of putting an end to these disagreements, only the examination of the collection of the privileges of the Jewish community (according to her letter of May 27,

1754), from the English government up to this time. And despite the unjust observations of the greatest part of the colonists, Their High Powers, on the examination of all the dispositions made by Her Royal Highness, after having thanked her for the care which she had had for the welfare of the colony, gave their approbation to the privileges of the Jews.[83]

It would perhaps be useless for us to expatiate further on the objects of these unfortunate discussions which struck fatal blows at the well-being of the colonists and led to the birth among them of a decided penchant for procedures which exhaust their finances, and make their manners less gentle and less praiseworthy. He who would wish to have the pleasure of knowing about these affairs in greater detail can consult the five folio volumes which were printed in Holland in 1752, and the *Histoire Générale des Voyages,* Volume XXI, from page 104 to 112. This knowledge, though thoroughly sterile, would nonetheless be of some utility for the present inhabitants of the colony in general; for in considering the defects of our ancestors, the evils that their caprices and their passions caused them, the shame of so many insults and ignominies on both sides which filled five folio volumes, they would be given very edifying lessons as to how to avoid the reefs which intemperateness of passions offers us in every moment of life and which would, so to speak, put morals into action in this respect.

The colony, despite these dispositions and the care which Their High Powers and the Lords Proprietors took for the welfare of the colonists, did not derive any profit from all these arrangements. Besides, the debts contracted by the colonists in their past proceedings; the constant flight of the slaves; the incursions of the runaway slaves; the little care which, for all these reasons together, they were able to give to the cultivation of their settlements; and, as the climax of misfortune, the luxury which had been introduced several years previously and had increased prodigiously after the arrival of the commissioners of Monseigneur the Prince of Orange and after the sojourn of General Baron de Sporcke, put the colony into a condition that was but little favorable. In order to relieve so many inconveniences and to replace the deficiency of Negroes on the plantations, there was no other means than that of taking advance-money from the merchants of Holland. Amsterdam at that time was in a position to put out much money at interest and, persuaded that the tranquillity which was to prevail in Surinam after all these times of storms would improve the settlements and extend the cultivation of coffee and of sugar which would yield so much benefit to the mother country as soon as the proprietors of these plantations had the means to obtain the advance-money to increase the number of their slaves and to provide for the other necessary expenses, [Amsterdam] conceived in consequence the idea of offering money at six percent per annum interest under legal mortgages; and it was the Burgomaster Deutz who was the first to form the plan of this advance-money which was imitated at once by negotiations on the part of the other provinces of the Republic.

The colonists, further intoxicated by their madness and already accustomed to everything which could give them lustre, received this offer with avidity; and all the planters, Christians and Jews alike, took part in these new negotiations and mortgaged their plantations. The ease of having everything that they needed by merely filling out a half sheet of paper which constituted letters of exchange drawn on the correspondents; the object, hard cash which would not at all strike their eyes [i.e., which they would never actually see and possess], caused them, so to speak, to despise money and to spend their credit with prodigality. The oddness of the human spirit, the stupidity of people, the childishness which is often found combined with mature age, these made themselves felt in a thousand ways, and if one takes the trouble to examine their origin, one will find that more innocent and simple causes have given birth to many revolutions and to fateful prejudices. Does not the same thing happen in our own days (generally speaking) with regard to our paper money? Does one take the same care in getting rid of a ten-escalin note as of a piastre of silver when one buys on credit? Does one who is the most thrifty, and even the one who is most stingy, look as closely at his purchase as when he makes it in ready cash?

If, then, the necessity of making up for the stupidities committed during a period of ten to twelve years had been felt for a longer time, and if reasoning had shown the colonists that it was on nothing but continual labors on their settlements that their resources depended, perhaps the colony would not be so much in debt as it is at present, and the colonists, with less of annual crops and with less income, would retain the ownership of their settlements, and the colony would still have its proprietors instead of agents who have charge of the administration of the greatest part of the plantations, whose owners are in Holland.

But instead of having felt this need, to experience later on the felicity of being wise, and instead of the money offered on credit, payable in twenty years, having been employed to increase the number of their slaves so as to enhance cultivation, they abused the credit which was open to them; and that which, in another time and in other circumstances, would have led to the welfare of the colony only contributed at that time to beautify it externally, it is true, but at the same time to run it into debt to the detriment and ruin of the planters, who displayed on their plantations an excessive luxury in useless buildings and in showy gardens which surpass the best [elsewhere] in America. This scourge, all the more greatly felt in a colony which ought not and cannot be regarded as anything except an agricultural one, accompanied by the flight of the slaves of six large settlements situated at Tempaty in 1757 and the hostilities committed by the runaway slaves of Palmeneribo, Providence, Onabo, and several others in Cottica and Commowine, as we have noted above,[84] utterly completed the ruination of the colony, despite all the beautiful appearances which the new credit offered, or at least prepared the nucleus for the deterioration and the disaster which broke out only a few years afterwards, the blows of which are still felt and which will continue to be felt for a longer time unless the merchants of Holland lend themselves to the means of remedying them.

Fortunately, again, the continual alarms into which the inhabitants found themselves plunged because of the incursions of the fugitives forced the administrative council to make peace with them. Their number, according to the calculations of authors who have been cited, mounted at that time to more than 20,000,[85] with the result that what caused so many quarrels and so many expenses against Governor Mauritius, as we have mentioned in its place, was finally admitted to be a supreme good fortune, and his plan was followed almost to the letter by those who had so foolishly rejected it. The preliminaries of peace were signed in October, 1759, by two citizens appointed by the administrative council, Messieurs Aberombi and Sobre. Herein the condition was laid down that for one year a suspension of all hostilities would be observed on both sides, during which the whites would send the Negroes the presents agreed upon. However, before sending these presents, the council dispatched commissioners in April, 1760 (and not in 1761, as Hartsink notes, page 797), to arrange several articles of the agreement which had not yet been finally concluded. And in October of the same year 1760 (and not in 1761, as Hartsink further notes),[86] Major Meyer left with a large detachment laden with the agreed upon presents. It was then that the Negroes failed to comply with the orders of the council, which were not to deliver any present to them without first taking a sufficient number of the children of principal families as hostages, to be delivered into the hands of the whites. With the consent of the said Major Meyer, they took everything intended for them, under the promise to bring, themselves, to the whites the required hostages, [a promise] which was kept after the departure of the detachment. It is then, and not before, as the said Monsieur Hartsink says,[87] that the chief of the Pomo Negroes entrusted one of his sons to the whites, to be educated by them, which would have been impossible before the peace had been concluded in all its formality. The date thereof, despite what this author says, ought to be fixed (as far as the village of the Negroes of Juca is concerned) at the end of the year 1760. This later effected the good fortune of the concluding of peace also with those of Saramaca, done in 1762.[88] And if one wishes to find out more in detail about the genius, the ruses, and the prepossessing policy of these Negroes (who are treated everywhere like beasts of burden), one can consult Monsieur Hartsink,[89] where one will find, together with the description of their dwellings, the contract they signed with the whites, as well as other very curious anecdotes, especially for those who do not know the character and the genius of the Negroes in America.

What we have just reported on the subject of the colony in general forms equally the picture of the state of the Jews in particular—foolish, gloomy like the other fellow inhabitants, identified, so to speak, with them [i.e., with Christian settlers] when they were needed by each party to crush the opposing party, and despised afterwards as soon as this unfortunate need ceased. They must have brought more misfortunes upon themselves because of the blind prejudice which is held against them. Besides, who does not know the influence of the government on the citizens and on the people of any place whatsoever? Who does not know, again, the power which the sentiments of the great have upon the opinion of the people? This truth was so well felt and observed by great authors that we do not at all dare to develop our ideas about it. It suffices for the enlightened man to recognize that, whatever the errors of the Jews may be, [whatever] their passions, their crimes, and their virtues, they are in every sense the same as those of the other peoples in general; and if one, further, takes the trouble to examine, with eyes however little philosophical, the effects produced by indigence, contempt, invectives against an individual, against a group of people, or against any nation whatsoever, and if one thereafter calculates the errors, the offenses, and the pains of those who are the objects thereof, the result of these observations would perhaps pronounce more in favor of the Jews than in favor of any other people which would find itself in the same circumstances.[90] But let us spare ourselves the trouble of these sad observations, and let us pursue the thread of our history. The present time of the colony will furnish us with materials wherewith to cast a general glance over our state.

These various treaties with the Negro runaway slaves of Juca and Saramaca, which we have mentioned above, did not entirely assure the tranquillity of the colony, or prevent the flight of the slaves. For in the year after the conclusion of the peace in July, 1761, there were entire families of plantations which revolted and many Negroes deserted at intervals, among others the plantation "Retour," belonging to Monsieur Sal. de la Parra, a Portuguese Jew, whose Negroes, old and young, to the number of about sixty, took flight without having done the least harm to their master. The sons of this settler, accompanied by their young friends and by several volunteers, to the number of nine whites and forty-eight good Negroes of their neighbors who assembled in haste, marched immediately in pursuit of the fugitives, whose tracks, despite all their searches for almost three weeks, were not discovered at all. And since their provisions were already failing, they resolved (in order not to expose themselves any longer to some misfortune) to repair to the village of Juca.[91]

The new allies were very astonished to see them, and after a long silence they showed great satisfaction, saying "that as soon as a handful of whites had the courage to penetrate as far as into the heart of their dwellings without any apprehension, this was a convincing proof that the whites had confidence in them, and that the peace was based on candor, and not on the dissimulation of the whites, as the greatest part of them still feared." In consequence, they entertained these Jews in every possible way, and each one hastened to lavish foodstuffs upon them and to offer them, as a mark of unlimited affection, their own wives and daughters. The day after the festivities, one named Fosso, the absolute chief of all the Negroes, [a man] who formerly belonged to the Jews, declared to his confrères the pleasure that he had felt at the good reception which they generally gave his old masters. However, their guarding and their preservation belonged to him as a legitimate right, all the more so as the Messieurs la Parra belonged to the family of the Nassys, whose slave he had once been. After much discussion, the care of the whites was left to the said Fosso. Nevertheless, they reserved for themselves the liberty of doing together with them all the services which depended on them.

And as this was the first and the last time that the citizens visited these new allies, it seems to us that no one will take it amiss that we are expatiating a little on this subject. As soon as the protection of the whites was confided particularly to the old man Fosso, he sent his armed Negroes to maintain there a sort of continual guard, and in the mornings and in the evenings, while they were occupied in saying their prayers in the Jewish manner and while they were chanting in a loud voice more hymns than ordinarily, this chief was at the door of the house which he had had vacated to serve them as a dwelling, expressly to impose silence until the prayer was finished. One Thursday afternoon, he had it announced everywhere that there should be brought to the whites fowl and everything that was necessary for them to be able to prepare their food on the following day for Saturday. This was so punctually observed that the Jews did not know what to do with the large quantity of fowl which everybody ordered killed in order to have the pleasure of saying that the whites profited from their presents. On Saturday morning, their house was surrounded by a number of people to hear the chanting of the prayers, and after it was finished, they came in crowds to wish them a good day. It was then that the old man Fosso began to speak, and said to them: "See, my children, what I have told you a thousand times about the Jewish people, my old masters; they are not like the other white people whom we have seen; they love God, and they will never do anything before praying to Him and serving Him with respect. Let us try, then, for the love of this God Whom they worship, to employ the means to aid them in their enterprise." This speech had penetrated the souls of all the Negroes in favor of the Jews, all the more so since the latter, having perceived, from the very first days, their [hosts'] penchant with regard to religious ceremonies, displayed many more mannerisms and bowings than ordinarily. In consequence, their [i.e., the Negroes'] assembly held a session, of which Arabi was the chief, and they had the whites sit with them, to deliberate in their presence, and they decided to give an escort to the whites, with the provisions necessary to take them to a place of safety, and that, furthermore, they would send another escort to look for the fugitives.

While the preparations were being made, the lieutenant of the citizenry, Monsieur Grenada, who had marched at once with a detachment of civilian volunteers against the fugitives (two days after the departure of the son of the said Monsieur la Parra), had the good fortune, after six days of marching, to encounter the same fugitives, in a place opposite the road which the first detachment had taken, and to take, jointly, thirty-eight prisoners and to kill several. And, knowing that the first detachment had taken the route for the village of Juca, he dispatched a notice to the children of Monsieur la Parra, to give them knowledge of his happy success. This news was received with acclamation by the new allies, and it hastened the departure of the Jews who were there at that time. After having thanked them for their good reception, they departed, followed by their escort, with all sorts of provisions, and they had the good fortune to meet on the road and to take prisoner thirteen of their fugitives, several of whom were punished with death by a sentence of the court. We have derived all this from the journals of these two detachments, and from the report of the persons themselves, most of whom are still alive.

This good fortune of which we have just spoken was not general in regard to the other flights which took place on the plantations, so that the new runaway slaves increased considerably, and since they could not at all trust those of Juca and of Saramaca, they tried to form new villages. The immense forests of the colony, the extent of the terrain, the swamps which are to be found everywhere there, the prodigiously high mountains which serve them as a rampart and whose valleys are very fertile for planting foodstuffs there—all this rendered their sojourn easy and assured, so that there was formed at the source of the river Marony a redoubtable village, known under the name of Negroes of Bony (their chief). Another on the west bank of the Saramaca river and several smaller ones scattered behind the settlements were on both sides of the rivers, hidden far forward in the woods. These made continual incursions against the slaves whom they met occupied at their work, and whom they carried off to increase their settlements.

In order to counter these raids, therefore, the colony needed to implore the help of the Republic. On the plea that was made about it to the States General, Their High Powers sent there, in 1772, a corps of 500 troops under the orders of Monsieur Forgeoud, a man of merit, who in 1763 had been employed in the Berbice colony, on the occasion of the revolt of the slaves. The sojourn of these troops was very necessary at that time, for the continual incursions which Monsieur Forgeoud made into the woods without interruption, repulsing the enemies with a patience and a courage worthy of his character, to a considerable distance from the cultivated establishments of the Colony, and everywhere ruining their villages and their foodstuffs, guaranteed the colony, for an interval of almost three years, against all hostilities on a large scale. The colonists, struck by this good fortune, paid their thanks therefor to the court, and on the rumor of their [Forgeoud's troops'] recall protested against their departure. There were, unfortunately, among the partisans of Monsieur Forgeoud several restless spirits who had had, for a long time, a secret hatred for Governor Nepveu. Monsieur Forgeoud, more soldier than politician, engaged himself imperceptibly in the snares of the antagonists of Monsieur Nepveu; and he interfered in the political affairs of the colony which were not his province at all. This caused him much harm even in Holland. As a result, if the spirit of the greatest part of the colonists had not been, so to speak, weakened by the remarkable deterioration in their private affairs, one would have seen reborn the horrors of the dissensions which had taken place in the time of Monsieur Mauritius. But they did not at all succeed in sparing themselves from tearing each other to pieces by means of writings here as well as those which were sent to Holland.

During the time when these quarrels were continuing, measures were taken in the colony to protect it from the hostilities of the Negroes, by means of a cordon of defense which it was proposed to form there. Upon the report made to the States General, Their High Powers yielded to the urgings of the magistracy of Amsterdam and gave orders to have the troops return. The city of Amsterdam then furnished its part of the expenses of the sending of the reinforcements. However, new representations on the part of the colonists to the administrative council caused these troops to remain for some time yet. Although it was claimed that the troops of the State were of no utility in the operations against the Negroes, it is nevertheless certain, as the author of the *Richesse de la Hollande* observes, that Commandant Fourgeoud, with the aid of the troops of the Lords Proprietors which were to be found in the colony, and of the bravery and the good dispositions of several officers (among others, Monsieur Frederici, at present lieutenant colonel of our troops, and who, in addition to his amiable personal qualities, possessed surprising skill in making incursions into the woods and in ferreting out the most secret stratagems of the Negroes), brought it about that the runaway slaves came to fear the arms of the Republic, and that the plantations were guaranteed against hostilities, which before him were very frequent. But nonetheless, without taking any side or giving credence to the garbled and exaggerated statements of the friends and of the antagonists of Monsieur Forgeoud, we are not at all afraid to say that thereafter Monsieur Fourgeoud should have been able to do better than he actually did, for the extirpation of the runaway slaves, our redoubtable enemies, should have been (in our opinion) the basis of all his operations.

However, we do not deny that the idea of sheltering the settlements from their insults was a fortunate thing for the colony. But to confine oneself solely to this idea during the period of four years, to range the woods, to fatigue his troops without interruption and without thinking that neither he nor they would be able to act in this manner perpetually and that forcing the runaway slaves to move further off was certainly not the same as extirpating them so that they should not be able to reassemble later on and become more agile and more crafty and therefore more dangerous—this was an idea which, if not devoid of good sense, was at least very strange. Besides, why (without one's being able to penetrate into Monsieur Fourgeoud's reasons) carefully avoid all the opportunities of striking terrible blows against the runaway slaves? Why always avoid attacking them? Why spare their hearths? Why, again, flattered to guarantee the plantations (which could not always be done), show in some ways, in the last two years of his sojourn, a sort of indolence against these rebels, and of a decided apathy towards his own antagonists? Why, then, all this? Because Monsieur Forgeoud was of a very gentle character and facile to follow the caprices of his friends who wished to vex Monsieur Nepveu. Without this, perhaps, his plan, better conceived and better organized, would have had a happy success. He would not have been thwarted at all in his operations, and the colony would later on have been less exposed to the pillage of these same fugitives, who became so redoubtable later on.

The plan of the cordon was, then, put into execution in 1774, and from the Savane of the Jews, to the source of the Commowine river, and from there down to the sea which cuts in the rear all the plantations situated on the left bank of the Surinam river, and on both sides of that of the Commowine and of the Cottica, it was made up of small, strong palisades at intervals and guarded by soldiers in proportion to the strength of the colony.

This undertaking experienced strong opposition from the very beginning because of the enormous expenses which it would cost the colony. But if, on the one hand, the taxes for its maintenance increased, the market in wood which the settlements found therefrom in the sale of these kinds of products, and of other things indispensable for the maintenance and the renewal of their buildings, and above all the tranquillity which the settlements which are below this line of defense experienced later on, caused this plan to be regarded as the best and the most useful for the preservation of the colony. And since it is not proper for us to enter into the least political observation in regard to the internal rule and the policy of the colony which approaches our time, we shall leave this subject to Monsieur Fermin, who has already treated it in his *Tableau de Surinam*. But we must caution the reader not to let himself be surprised by the reasoning of the author, so as to believe blindly all that he says there. For Monsieur Fermin has seen many things there with too much prejudice, and has composed his work only on the basis of information by persons prejudiced against the internal and external rule of the colony. Besides, several objects of his criticism depend rather on other causes than on those to which Monsieur Fermin attributes them. In order not to compromise ourselves in any way towards him, or towards anyone else, we prefer rather to be silent in place of developing our observations on this subject, and we shall content ourselves solely with recommending at the same time that Monsieur Fermin read a certain work printed in London in 1779 under the title of *Remarques Critiques sur le Tableau Historique et Politique de Surinam* ("Critical Remarks on the Historical and Political Picture of Surinam"). Though the author thereof is declared to be anonymous, it is a certain Monsieur Sansini, an Italian ex-Jesuit, who lived for some years in Surinam. This author, in taking up the many errors of Monsieur Fermin on the political material in his work, himself falls into other faults which are still more condemnable, that is to say, of ingratitude towards the inhabitants of the colony and of a blind passion against everything that was good there. And hiding, with a revolting malignity, the good side of the inhabitants, he has only developed with bitterness all that there was of bad, which is, however, only too common, perhaps, to all the colonies of America in general.

The result of all that which we have said in this work was sufficient to plunge the colony into a not very happy state. Nevertheless, there was still needed the appearance of a future good fortune to plunge it back again later into new disasters, besides the pains and the continual fatigues which were experienced because of the flight of the slaves, which as a result got the designs of the planters off the right track and perceptibly diminished their incomes. The merchants of Holland who had made advance-loans on the settlements without touching their annual interest sought only the means of prosecution in order to recoup their losses. The countinghouse of Monsieur Deutz, known afterwards under that of Marselis, opened the scene, and from 1765 and 1766 on, one saw nothing but plantations sold and placed in sequestration for debts contracted under mortgages. Those of the Christian planters, administrators and employees, who had resources elsewhere, were able to ward off the blows for some time, but those who did not have any of these resources at all saw themselves stripped of their possessions.

One can consider that the Jews were not the most spared in these misfortunes, and it was then that they lost the greatest part of their settlements, almost all of which fell into the hands of the agents of the countinghouses, nonetheless without freeing themselves from the balance which they still owed. Almost all their settlements were sold for a third or a fourth of the amount of their debts.

In addition to these truly fatal misfortunes, a new attack was made by the runaway slaves in Para. The Negroes of a certain Planteau ran away, or were taken by the runaway slaves. Who is there, then, who would not say that, in view of these disasters, credit for Surinam was finished forever? But no; still greater misfortunes were destined for it. Holland wished to invest money elsewhere, and the examples of what had happened previously with other commercial houses were nothing in the eyes of the merchants, who supposed that the colonists would have their eyes opened by their past prosecutions, and would consequently become wiser and more circumspect in their affairs. But the blow which took place in Para put the merchants in a state of indecision. A fortunate expedition which the council caused to be made against the assailants, in which the Negroes of the above-named Planteau were recaptured (news which was exaggerated in Holland beyond the truth), accompanied by two years of favorable coffee crops, rekindled the desire of the merchants to invest their money again in Surinam, and in the year 1769 and at the beginning of 1770, one heard no other news in the colony than that of the plans for advancing money to the planters.

It seemed then that the golden age had been renewed for the colony in general. The evils of the past war, the disasters, even the hostilities of the runaway slaves—all, in a word, was forgotten, and the colonists again, in their intoxication, already accounted themselves the most fortunate of those in America. To cap the climax of the calamities, the greatest part of the funds which had been destined in Holland for Surinam was nothing less than based on good principles and on stable and permanent assurances. Nevertheless, in every street of Paramaribo there were to be found only agents furnished with powers of attorney to offer money on credit to the first comer. This intoxication struck not only the eyes of the last class of planters and inhabitants of the colony, but it even had the same effect on all the inhabitants in general, and from Governor Nepveu down to the last citizen, all were pitifully blinded. The rich, or those who possessed two or three settlements, and those who did not have more than one, sought only to sell their effects at an enormous price, and to buy others more suitable to their views. Money was on hand, there was no lack of purchasers either, but to procure the means of having as much as one needed to make these purchases was the most difficult point.

This Gordian knot was at first courageously cut; appraisers in large numbers knew very well the secret of the philosopher's stone, and as a result the plantations were appraised at three to four times their actual value. The ordinances which the government of Surinam had passed in this regard, the punishment which even several appraisers suffered, prove the truth of this fact. The famous Monsieur la Croix, the craftiest of all the agents that there ever were, had orders to dispose of unlimited money for the account of an ephemeral butterfly, that is to say, a countinghouse in Holland established under the name of *Schouten and Valens*, and by means of a certain sum which was to be paid to the said agency in particular, everybody could be aided at first. Then, Christians, Jews, professional people, even shoemakers who did not even have a penny to purchase the hides necessary for their trade—all wished to be planters, and Monsieur the agent, with a stroke of the pen, made agriculturists and planters more quickly than Pyrrha made men by throwing stones, so that one heard nothing else than purchases and sales, and one saw only shoemakers, dandies, and butchers become great lords. In consequence, prodigality, profusion and an immoderate luxury inundated the colony.

The change of masters on the settlements which followed without cessation led to the fear of some misfortunes with regard to the slaves who (to use their own terms) considered themselves as *fowls which go from one hand to the other, until they come to the table to serve as food.* Thus this appearance of good fortune lasted for only a short time, for the letters of exchange which the new planters had drawn on their correspondents, to the order of their agents, principally those of la Croix, were all protested [declared unpayable], so that what had appeared good in the preceding year was then nothing but tragic confusion, foreclosures, executions on these same effects, and prosecutions against several other inhabitants, who in the assurance that these letters of exchange were valid, had not hesitated at all to endorse them in order to circulate them more easily. Several other purchasers of plantations, who had had the good fortune to have taken the money from other countinghouses, also suffered the same fate (although their letters of exchange were paid in Holland), because of the prodigious price which they had given for the plantations, and the immoderately high price of the slaves. Let one imagine a colony burdened before this time with a debt of more than fifty million florins to the merchants of Holland, and especially plunged into the abyss of prosecutions because of the event of 1770; and then one will know the state in which the colony in general found itself, without forgetting, however, what happened in the year 1773 up to 1776 because of the discussions which took place in the time of Monsieur Forgeoud, which we have cited above.

According to these observations and according to the facts which we have just set forth, which are known in the colony and in Holland, and which no one can call in question, the most prejudiced man will recognize at once that a large part of the misfortunes which befell the colony take their source from the very colonists in general. The deterioration of the plantations, the flight of the slaves, the increase of debts, the impossibility of paying the interest owed the merchants of Holland, the foreclosures which they suffered, the change of masters—all was felt equally by all the classes of planters and of the inhabitants of the colony without any distinction whatsoever. Nevertheless, all that happened to the Jews and what is still happening to them now was without fail attributed to the ignorance of everything pertaining to agriculture which everyone imputes to them, and also to the bad management which they employed towards their slaves, and even to their religion, in regard to their festivals and to their manner of envisaging things.

This supposition, which, under the appearance of pitying the Jewish community, plunges the dagger into the heart of its individual members, did much harm to the Jews at all times, for in denying them thereby the means of employment on the plantations, one takes away from a part of the cohabitants of the colony one of the easiest and the most useful resources, causing them, besides, to be regarded as useless members for all the agricultural colonies. To combat this supposition, which is as weak as it is absurd, it suffices us to cite what Abbé Raynal said about the Jews of Brazil and of Jamaica, which we have cited in its place, and what happened in Surinam with regard to them, from the time of the English until their last misfortunes. We would still pass over in silence all the bad reasonings which one employs to overwhelm them still more, if they were not accompanied by a recent writing, presented in 1776 or 1777 to the West India Company in Holland by the council of a colony belonging to the Republic and a neighbor of Surinam.

This writing, as we have said in the introduction to this work, is found in the first volume of the *Letters of Aristodemus and Sincerus*. It was a case concerning the admission of a Jew from Holland, named Isaac Azevedo, who wished to pass to Essequibo or Demerary [in Guiana], but was forbidden to make his trip because of this remonstrance, which was full of gall and bitterness, and although, after having knowledge of this writing which was introduced into Surinam in 1786, we would have taken the firm resolution not to lower ourselves by replying to such atrocious calumnies as one finds spread there, we still cannot conceal the pain which it has caused us in regard to what it says there about agriculture, *"founded, as they say, upon exact information which they had received from Surinam, realized by daily examples of what is happening there."* [92] Thus, since we are on the subject of agriculture, with regard to the suppositions that are made about the Jews, we will make known our observations about it.

With regard to the agriculture in the hands of the Jews: they have had, from the beginning of the colony, as large settlements and in as large numbers as the Christians. It is true that they did not have the knowledge, then generally unknown, of clearing the lowlands, and as a result they settled only upstream on the Surinam River. Several years later, recognizing their mistakes, they themselves established plantations from the one called "Gelderland," situated four leagues from Paramaribo, to others several leagues up the river. Their products then yielded in no respect to those of the Christians. They made crops six times more abundant on their plantations than when these same settlements [later] passed into the hands of the Christians. The desertion of their slaves and the raids which these committed were proportionately less among them than among the other inhabitants, so that their misfortunes came neither from their ignorance in the matter of agriculture, nor from their festivals, and still less from their bad management towards their slaves, as their blind adversaries suppose of them.[93] The cause of their misfortune, the decadence of their property, had reasons which were very common and very material, which every impartial man will at once recognize.

The lands along the Surinam River, having been the first to be cultivated, were necessarily the first to lose their fertility, and this is very natural since the lands in Surinam are not manured at all, and no attempt whatsoever is made to improve them, as in Europe. However, the Jews, with no other resource besides their agriculture, preserved their property without debts and without liabilities until the end of the year 1750. But the continual loss of their slaves, as much by reason of deaths as by that of flights, obliged them, in imitation of the Christians, to take part in the offer which the countinghouse of Monsieur Deutz caused to be made to the planters. This was the fatal blow for them and for their descendants, all the more so since the principal ones among them found themselves already ruined by the enormous expenses which the lawsuits of the time of Monsieur Mauritius had caused them. This advance money, taken with avidity, put them under the necessity of taking it anew, and in this manner the growing infertility of their lands, the small amount of products which they derived from their settlements, the interest which they had to pay annually to their correspondents, the decline in the price of their commodities, and the increase of expenses in Holland, of which the correspondents knew how to make their account, undermined them little by little until their debts entirely crushed them, and their effects have been sold through foreclosures from 1766 up to these days.

Have these vicissitudes not been felt equally by the other inhabitants? And is there any difference, anything more beautiful, more moral or more noble in the history of the decline of the Christian planters of the colony? One will perhaps tell us: *the Christians nevertheless maintained themselves and still maintain themselves, their plantations are still in their hands, and the Jews have almost none of them any more.* Here are arguments by means of which the common people are dazzled to the disadvantage of the Jewish community. The mistrust which the furnishers of money on credit conceived against the Jews, the unfortunate effect of the difference in religion, the prejudice of several agents of the colony who, themselves feeling their own faults, furnished bad information against the Jews, caused them to be refused the credit necessary to buy slaves and to provide for their other needs.

But the contrary happened with the Christians. Their credit was unlimited, and it is for this very reason that on each plantation of Christians that was sold through foreclosure, the merchants of Holland lost and still lose more than on ten of the Jews together. Furthermore, let us be shown (and on this we challenge the best planter in Surinam) what the progress is of the other colonists, with all their credit and their other resources? If one plants sugar cane in Surinam, coffee, cacao, etc., does one work the land in another manner at present than formerly? The plans, the new ideas, the too greatly praised discourses on agriculture which one hears extolled everywhere—are they carried out on the plantations? All the differences which one actually sees on the settlements are deeper or shallower trenches, constructed to the right or to the left, horizontally or crosswise, etc., etc. But the effects, the results, where are they? Nowhere. If the ignorance of the Jews, their stupidity in the matter of agriculture, were the cause of their ruin, why did the Christians, great agriculturists, not become rich? Why is it that the number of proprietors of plantations residing in Surinam (among the number of more than 500 plantations which there are) amounts to no more than eighty or ninety altogether? Where, again, is the progress that they have made on these very holdings which formerly belonged to the Jews? All one can do, in regard to the Jews and even in regard to the Christians, is to perceive in all this a natural course of events connected with the physical condition of the plantation.

Monsieur Gootenaar, for example, bought for a very moderate price the plantation "Nieuwe Star," and the Messieurs Arlaud and Baek rented to him the "Gelderland," "Drie Gebroeders," "Descanco," "Goosen," "Cabo Verde," "Caap de Goede Hoop," "Guilgal," and "Boa Vizinhanca," all of which, [plantations] of good and fertile land, fell under the control of the Christians. However, where is the progress which they made on these fields that once were the best of the entire Surinam River? Their science, their art in the cultivation of the lands, their management, calculated in superior fashion, ought to display themselves in one way or another, in order for someone to be able, with good reason, to stigmatize the Jews with what they are accused of in this respect. The difference which one notes in their present state of decline compared to that of the others [Christians] does not yield any result either. If there had been among the Jews individuals who had earned from ten or twenty to fifty thousands florins a year managing plantations whose proprietors are in Holland; if, again, they had earned from three to fifteen thousand florins annually through the profits which several posts in the colony pay, they would still be in the same state as the others. And if the contrary had happened, that would be the time to regard them as useless beings in an agricultural colony, if in America (just as these gentlemen of Essequebo and Demmerary claim) all the members of the colonies, without exception, must be laborers before being able to be admitted there.

On the Cottica and Commowine rivers and their branches, which now form the largest part of the wealth of the colony, the Jews have never been able to obtain lands. They had to content themselves with those which they had possessed for a long time in Surinam. Four or six persons of the Jewish community, however, who were able, with a great deal of trouble, to acquire some [land] there [along the Cottica and the Commowine], have made as much progress as the Christians. Witnesses are the plantations of Aron Polak, of Pardo, of Hartog Jacobs, heirs of Gerrit Jacobs, etc. (all governed, worked, and administered by Jewish managers), which yield in no respect, either in cultivation or in order, to those of the other inhabitants. On these two rivers, the clearing of the first of which was not done until nearly half a century after those of the Surinam, the greatest part of their settlements produce, at the present time, some of them only half, and others only a third and a fourth of what they produced in the beginning, an evident cause of the decline of the plantations of the Jews in Surinam, felt twenty-five to thirty years beforehand.

Aside from this, the ownership of the Savane and the establishment of the synagogue have also been held to blame for the ruin of the Jewish community. Attachment to this place [the Savane], it is said, brought it about that the Jews could not quit their plantations situated along the upper reaches of the Surinam, twenty years older than the Savane, in order to settle elsewhere. [Those who argue this way] assume that with great determination they [the Jews] would have been able to acquire lands on the Commowine, which is very doubtful. They fail to consider that large estates already formed and a prodigious number of slaves to be transported there, who leave their hearths only with regret, would make this enterprise morally impossible, a difficulty which has been felt by the Christians who had their plantations at the source of the Surinam, which they still maintain without having had a Savane to attach themselves thereto. To this reason has been added, furthermore, that of prodigality in their festivals, etc., which is anything but well-founded; for an extraordinary expense of 200 to 300 florins which the excesses of these festivals would annually cost each family would not be capable of ruining them, even less the loss of several days of work of several of their slaves for the needs and the conveniences of these holidays. We have shown, besides, their manner of living when they were well off; consequently they cannot be accused of luxury or of inordinate prodigality on their plantations or elsewhere. Whatever, then, the efforts of envy may be to find special reasons to which to attribute the ruin of the Jews, one will find only reasons that are common among non-Jews, too.

If the ruin of the Jewish planters, then, has been caused by physical misfortunes, if the Christians established on the Surinam river experienced the same disasters, if the disorder in their affairs has struck both groups equally, why charge the Jews in particular with a misfortune common to all the planters in general? Let them cease, in Holland, to advance more money and to prolong credit to the planters of Cottica and of Commowine; let those who still hold onto their properties, although burdened with debts, do without the profits of their management; finally, let them have, and in every sense, as few resources as the Jews, and we would see if many plantations would remain in the hands of the present proprietors.

This suffices to demonstrate that the Jews and the Christians have had misfortunes, have made mistakes, have lost plantations, have been ruined, both groups for the same reasons and for the same causes; and that the dogmas of the Jewish religion, its festivals, the customs of the Jewish community, their Savane, etc., have contributed nothing to all this. The Jews have made, as we have already proved in several passages of this work, the same progress in Surinam as the Christians; they were as rich there, and as good planters as the Christians, and, like them, they have become impoverished. It is true that at the present time there are few plantations which belong to the Jews, and that the greatest part of those that they have had are at present in the hands of the Christians. But let one consider that when these latter lost theirs [properties], they came again under the control of other Christians, in the quality of agents of the merchants in Holland; and that if the suppliers of this money given at interest had been, for example, Jews or Turks instead, and not Christians, would not the matter have changed in appearance, and would not half of the estates of the colony belong at the present time to these two circumcised peoples? Besides, how will the Jews in Surinam be able to disprove, by actual examples, the ignorance which has been attributed to them in the matter of agriculture? Were there ever (at least for a long time) any of the Jewish community employed as directors or as managers on any plantation belonging to Christians?

This effort, which would perhaps open the eyes of the most blind prejudice, would without doubt cost a great deal to make. But prejudices ought to be sacrificed in favor of reason. It is not generally known that, in order to work the forests of Charpente, the Jews, with a very small number of Negroes and of animals, make much more income per year than the large plantations of the Christians which are devoted to this kind of work? Why are they not employed somewhere? Why are they consulted, why is their capacity for the work of the forests made use of, under the false promise of favoring them with directorships, only to reject them later because they are Jews, as has happened very recently? Does anyone know that the Jew who lately suffered this rejection is capable of making in one year more income than another person in three years? If, therefore, the negligence of the Christian director established there would then be recognized, would it not always be good fortune for the proprietor in Holland to employ the former? And in one case or another, would it not, again, be very just to consider that the Jews deprived of positions in the colony and not always needing to be present in the city are more masters of their time than the other managers, and that in consequence they would be able to give more care to the work of the plantations?

If the profit which these ministrations produce were distributed better and more wisely, many advantages for the colony in general would result, for (1.) in place of one or two employees on a large number of plantations, twenty-five or thirty persons, Christians or Jews, would be able to have their subsistence in the distribution of the total sum which a sole administrator draws annually, which would contribute (2.) to the well-being of a large number of inhabitants, with reference to other profits which would necessarily follow. For any place at all is richer with a quarter of fixed income shared among its members than with ten times as much among a very small number, while the rest of the individuals are in a state of poverty. And (3.) the plantations would be managed with more care, because one who had the small resource of two or three plantations to administer would in his ambition employ more zeal in discharging his duty than [if he] had forty or sixty. But this truth, which will strike every reasonable man, will not be realized at all, because the fear of some revolution to come has given weight to the calumny of ignorance and of dishonesty on the subject of agriculture which has been spread abroad against the Jews. In consequence, then, of this deception which, unfortunately, we are forced to present in its full light, would we not then be able to add to all our observations the discourse of a peasant on agriculture which is found in *L'Esprit des Journaux* of the month of May, 1787, page 384, and to say with the honest laborer and with changes suitable to our subject: "Well, in our situation can we do it? A household to be maintained, children to be reared, wages to be paid, our buildings to be repaired, our animals to be replaced, our day laborers to be satisfied, our occupations, our tools, our clothes, our sicknesses, our taxes"— we can add the expenses of our festivals, our marriages, our burials, the maintenance of our synagogues, a number of poor to feed, etc. Here, briefly, continues the honest peasant, "are our needs, our duties, and our situation, and what are our resources, great God! Our genius, our industry, and, more than all that, our resignation! Speak, gentlemen, is it not senseless and wicked to blame us for our misfortunes?"

We have made, as far as it was possible for us, an exact and faithful statement on the principal events of the Colony of Surinam from its beginning up to this day, with the abridged history of its Jewish inhabitants, in regard to their privileges, and the fortunate and unfortunate revolutions which they experienced there. And we dare to maintain that we have presented nothing except what is true, that we

HISTORY OF SURINAM

have said nothing with prejudice, or employed sophisms to defend the Jewish community from several accusations with which it has been charged for a long time. We have followed the authors who have written about the colony, without imposing upon ourselves any obligation to copy them to the letter or to believe them on their word. On the contrary, we have acknowledged the errors which we have found there, leaving to the reader the task of judging them. The information which we have from our archives, together with what we have heard from our fathers, as well as some curious notes which are to be found among the old Jewish families, has put us in a position to set down our findings in this weak essay. And as for its results, we flatter ourselves that an impartial man will perceive that the Jews, despite their privileges, despite the constant protection which they have received on the part of the Lords Proprietors, and whatever their merit, their care, and their zeal for the colony in general have been, are nonetheless disdained and regarded by their fellow-inhabitants as a class of men whose connections, good intelligence and friendship are always useless or dangerous for all who profess another religion.

This prejudice, which does as much harm to the philosophy of this century as to politics and which serves only to bury all the good that an ethnic group can have done, has placed us under the necessity of speaking openly with regard to the Jewish community, and to compare it with that under which it lives in Surinam. In accordance with this method, we have brought the history of that which concerns it up to the epoch of the decline which took place in 1770, and since these funereal events have greatly increased these same prejudices, extended the contempt, given birth to calumnies and invectives to its disadvantage, and since, thanks to the philosophy of the present chief who governs us and of those who have the honor to be associated with him on more familiar terms, the hideous object of blind prejudice is beginning to change its face, we judge it necessary, as much for the purpose of cutting off the last head of the hydra that menaces us as in order to lay more stable foundations for this happy change, to make a corollary to everything we have said.

With the exception of what happened with Governor Scherpenhuysen, after the departure of Monsieur Samuel Nassy for Holland, the Jews had reason to be chagrined only about little things which, although susceptible of bringing evil consequences in their train, were nevertheless not real evils; and despite several blows which they suffered in regard to their privileges, and the contempt which the other inhabitants showed them from time to time, all this was, so to speak, made up for by the well-being which they enjoyed at that time and which lasted more or less up to the time of the government of Monsieur Mauritius. But as soon as the Jews lost their well-being, and poverty made itself felt, all resources were closed to them, and only continual contempt and estrangement from all that interested them, and the insulting word *Smous* was applied in abundance to Portuguese and German Jews without distinction, until it later became the favorite word employed by the slaves themselves to designate with contempt any Jew whatsoever: the unfortunate results of the habits of children in the houses of their fathers, and of slaves in those of their masters.

In consequence, the houses of the Jews were no longer frequented by the Christians, and they were never invited to their homes on any festival or on any private or public occasion of rejoicing. They were even spoken to with arrogance, and several times the Jews experienced (almost to juridical condemnation) what *Candide* said when he came to Surinam. Later on this estrangement gave birth to an indifference which was just as remarkable, and which was transmitted from father to son; the bulk of the Christians attached a sort of baseness to having familiarity with the Jews. Forgotten, then, by their fellow-inhabitants, they resumed among themselves in their households a manner of living which, though far removed from ostentation and from minute and forced tidiness, is perhaps more natural and more moral in the eyes of a good philosophic observer than that which is done elsewhere. This indifference which, giving vent to prejudice, produced hatred, was the reason why at the least fault committed by one of its members, the whole Jewish community was blamed for it. Never had "such and such a Jew" committed such and such a crime; but, *the Jews committed it,* and although several wrongs done to the Jewish community were constantly redressed by the always uniform conduct of the Lords Proprietors, prejudice followed its course.

When these misfortunes were generally felt, the nature of the human spirit which attributes its disasters to the slim attachment to its religion, and which often casts men into the gulfs of bigotry, produced

HISTORY OF SURINAM 105

in consequence a striking effect upon the Jewish community in Surinam. In the earliest period of the colony, the first Jews, although otherwise very estimable by reason of their behavior, brought from Portugal that spirit of intolerance which inflicts penalties for the least religious mistake. Everything at that time was judged by the regents with the greatest rigor. Those who had escaped from the flames of the frightful tribunal of the Inquisition were then the richest, the most learned, and in consequence the most powerful of all, and the religious despotism which went forth therefrom as from its first source, in accord with the baneful ideas of superstition, led to the birth of faulty ordinances which prevail until now in the Jewish community. If one compares the persecutions which the Jews of Holland caused Spinoza and Uriel da Costa to suffer before their atheism had been discovered, and the date of the first ecclesiastical institutions of the Jews in Cayenne and in Surinam, one will find that approximately in the same epoch the spirit of fanaticism was prevalent everywhere. This dangerous passion, joined to the meager education which the inhabitants of the colony in general received, gave birth among the Jews to continual discussions which several times gave their antagonists an excuse against them. The renewal of the ecclesiastical institutions approved by Her Royal Highness in the year 1754, which closely imitated old customs and to which the confusion of the questions in which the Jewish community found itself at that time had not permitted giving another form and another spirit, put the seal on everything which was dangerous. Resentment over past quarrels soon set into motion persecutions for the least fault; finally, the misfortunes and the disasters, as it seemed, were bound to be made up for by the force of bigotry. This innocent system, common to all religions in general and which gave birth at all times to superstitious ceremonies which disfigure the foundation of the divine religion, as Monsieur de Toussaint observes in his immortal work on morals, was followed in the Jewish community in Surinam from 1756 on.

Plunged, then, into these lugubrious ideas, and taking whatever happened to them as chastisements from heaven, the Jews did not seek at all to secure redress for the several wrongs commited against their privileges and their franchises. Several small posts which they had had in other times were taken away from them, while half-breeds and mulattoes, both bastards and legitimate, have lucrative posts to the detriment of these unfortunate whites, who count among the mothers of these mulattoes many of their slaves who had been manumitted by them themselves.[94] Their tribunal of civil justice at the Savane felt blows several times; the Citizens' Company, in public exercises, experienced the most extreme contempt, as can be seen from a decision of the Lords Proprietors with regard to the German Jews (Document No. 16). Things were carried so far that the attempt was even made to establish in the city of Paramaribo a quarter for the Jews, with a prohibition of their living elsewhere, and this would have been completely effected if the Lords of the colony had not ordered the contrary on February 18, 1767, in accordance with a certain decree, the execution of which (according to a resolution of May 14 of the same year) was suspended until May 1 of the following year. It was again resolved, despite a vigorous remonstrance on the part of Governor Monsieur Crommelin, made to the Council on May 1, 1767, not to permit the Negroes of the Jews to stay in Paramaribo, under the pretext that they had their Savane where they ought to make their domicile, etc., according to a letter addressed to the Lords Proprietors under date of August 17, 1767, which was rendered null and void by the reply to it which they received under date of November 18 of the same year.

Besides this, the Jews could not be bakers, or grease-merchants, known in Holland under the name of *Smokkelaar* or *vette Warier;* and if, on the remonstrance which Monsieur Is. de Pinto, of The Hague, made in the name of the Jewish community to several members of the directors of the Lords Proprietors, this benevolent tribunal had not at all given its orders on this subject, no Jew at the present time would be a baker or a *vette Warier*. The post of notary public of the Jewish community, known since the time of Governor Sommelsdyk under the name of Jurator, which the Society granted in Holland in 1754 to Monsieur Is. Nassy, when he was there for the lawsuit of the Jewish community against Monsieur Carilho, was created expressly for the accommodation of the Jewish community. This was because of the enormous expenses which the Jews had to pay for the translation of certain acts into Dutch, because a large part of the Jewish community does not know thoroughly [enough] the genius or the tricky points of this language, to protect itself from several prejudices very common in the judicial actions. [This post] has become at present almost useless, because the Jurators who occupied this post after the death of Monsieur Nassy were forbidden by a prohibition against their passing any act at all at Paramaribo, because the secretaries, in order not to lose proceeds of four or five hundred florins which would accrue annually to the Jurator, to the disadvantage of the emoluments of the secretariat, opposed the contents of their act of admission and opposed that which Monsieur Nassy obtained from the directors and which he had exercised without dispute until his death during a period of more than twenty years.

And this [took place], although the Jews had nothing at all to complain about as regards Governor Nepveu, who was very fond of the Jewish community, but who nevertheless did not want to compromise himself by openly taking up its defense in every case. Matters progressed to the point where they would have imperceptibly lost the most favorable articles of their privileges, if the Jewish community had not addressed itself in Holland on matters of great importance; but for other wrongs often palliated with specious reasons, it could not always be a burden to the Proprietors. Besides, with the strongest reasons one cannot complain continually and incessantly demand the reparation of wrongs. Would it not increase the cares of our masters, to keep them incessantly busy and to compromise the Jewish community with its fellow-inhabitants who, being much nearer to it, could still do it much harm, independently of the laws of the country? This reason and many others persuaded the Jewish community to resign itself to its lot until a favorable occasion should present itself spontaneously. Would that it please God that it will never happen, and that the Jewish community, forgetting its past wrongs, will content itself with a future happiness which the present gives it reason to expect! However, no one will take it amiss that we have placed its rights and the apology for it before the eyes of the public and of those who have always protected it and who have the power to remedy things therein in one way or another. They will know with satisfaction, we flatter ourselves at least, that it was not to an ungrateful Jewish community that they accorded their benevolence, and that in their capacity of regents and proprietors of the colony they will find many things which perhaps they do not know.

Ah, great God! in what circumstances have the Jews failed in their duty as citizens? Contributing to the taxes without murmuring, they have always adhered to the governors without any other profit than that of declaring themselves thankful to these august principals, since the death of Governors Nepveu and Texier. Despite a thousand little things which have happened, have they failed in their system? Did not Monsieur Beeldsnyder himself receive the homage which was due to him in his capacity of governor both at Paramaribo and at the Savane? In all the pressing needs of the colony, did not the Jewish community take up arms equally? At the time of the unfortunate success of Tempaty in 1757, were not its citizens employed under the command of the captains of the Christian citizenry in the very place of the revolt, and similarly after that up to the peace with the runaway slaves? In these circumstances were they not seen to sacrifice the Sabbath rest or the religious holidays in favor of the defense of the colony? Is it not known by everybody that at the time of the late war for the independence of North America, at the least suspicion of the movements of the runaway slaves of Boni, the Jews took up posts in the Savane and mounted guard on Saturdays and on holidays of the month of September, 1782, without distinction? Did not the Jewish community take the same interest in this war as did the other inhabitants? (See the order for the fast,[95] translated from the Portuguese.) In consequence, did it deserve, by reason of the pretended fault of several Jewish citizens under arms at the time of the interment of Governor Texier, a resolution of the council which was as dishonoring for the Jewish community as illegal in the eyes of the public? (See Document No. 19, of which we shall speak in greater detail.)

Besides all these reasons, does not policy at all prescribe that the Jews of Surinam are to be regarded with more favorable eyes? Do not Jews, rich or poor, always remain in the places in which they have once settled? Does not the contrary happen every day with the individuals of other groups? The latter, as soon as they find themselves a little better off, go to spend their money in their fatherland; consequently, there is neither profit nor currency for the locality, and everything is lost for the place which furnished them the occasion and the facility of becoming rich. And since there are among them many foreigners, the mother country itself derives very little advantage from them. How many examples of this nature could be cited on this subject in order to prove incontestably that it is only the Jews who are indeed the true citizens and inhabitants of Surinam?

We have seen up to the present only things more contrary than favorable as touching the interests of the Jewish community. May the hope of good fortune to come console it!

After the death in 1778 of Governor Nepveu, regretted generally by the Jewish community, Monsieur the Commander Texier, who succeeded him in the government, whose goodness of heart made him beloved by all who knew him, treated the Jewish community with more mildness. Seconded in his views by the wisdom and the integrity of the public prosecutor, Monsieur Wichers, he never consented to anything which could impair the privileges of the Jews. These two gentlemen, equally respectable by reason of their personal qualities as through their attachment to the cultivation of letters, in agreement with several other beneficent persons whom it will bring us glory to name in its place, conceived an affection for several individual members of the Jewish community, whose (according to what they had the goodness to say) reading and judgment were not at all to be despised, and they began to encourage them. The continual visits which they made to the Savane, accompanied by large retinues by reason of the work on the cordon, which took place ordinarily on the Jewish holidays of September and of October; the receptions which the Jewish community gave them in general, together with the information which they constantly received from the military officers posted at the Savane and at the cordon, about the cordiality, kindness, and hospitality towards them and their subordinates, brought about a happy revolution for the Jewish community, and these gentlemen recognized how greatly prejudice and mistrust can suffocate the reputation of a people in general, and the particular merit of some of its individuals.

It was at this time that Prosecutor Wichers and some of his friends, founding at Paramaribo a society of natural history, had the Jews admitted without any discrimination as both active and honorary members. The eulogy which he delivered there on the physician d'Anavia, a member of the said society who died in 1781, did as much honor to the philosophy of Monsieur Wichers as to the memory of the late Jewish physician.

This fact compensated the Jewish community advantageously for the prohibition which a company of amateurs made that the Jews were not to be spectators at a Dutch theater which they established in 1775, a prohibition unheard of in any place in the world where Jews have permission to live. Let it not be thought that this theater is a society theater; it is anything but that. Everyone provided with a ticket can enter, and there are among the actors women who are granted pensions as actresses. The Jews concerned themselves very little with this insult, and were able, in reprisal, to found the following year another Dutch theater which, in the judgment of connoisseurs, had much more merit than that of the Christians and possessed better actors, although composed of young people of the Portuguese and German Jewish communities who had never seen Europe. (Consult on this subject what Monsieur Sansini, of Naples, said in his remarks on the *Tableau de Surinam,* page 61; he saw the best theaters in Europe, and is therefore in a position to judge.) This theater of the Jews, frequented by persons of the highest distinction, was completely remodeled in 1784,[96] both in regard to a beautiful building made expressly for this purpose, and in regard to the scenery and costumes. Above all, it had good actors who were already at home in the theater [and] skill owed in every sense to themselves and to the effects which competition produces. To the playhouse of the Jews were admitted, without distinction, all the inhabitants of the colony who were provided with tickets which are distributed gratis by the contributors, with the exception only of the actors and directors of the Dutch theater, to whom entry is forbidden. There are, in addition, special seats made expressly for the governor and the administrative councillors, who have free admission, and several of whom generously give recompense for this gift.

The departure of Prosecutor Wichers for Holland in May, 1783, and the death of Governor Texier, which took place in September of the same year, led the Jewish community to fear some unfortunate revolution; and as there were other faults and irregularities in its [the community's] establishment, and much disagreement as regards the meaning which was given to the privileges, to its disadvantage, the means of reconciling opinions in this regard were not known at all. The changing of the two principal magistrates of the colony rendered the matter still more doubtful, the more so as Monsieur Beeldsnyder, who provisionally succeeded the governor, and Monsieur Karsseboom, who succeeded to the office of prosecutor, were not at all versed in the economic affairs of the Jewish community.

These observations led one of the present regents of the Jewish community, who at all times poured out his heart to a person who honored him with his protection, to address to him in Holland in 1783 a letter in which he detailed to him, as forcefully as he could, the state of the Jewish community, both as regards its respective individuals and as regards the other inhabitants of the colony. And since this letter and the ardent care which this friend had to protect the Jewish community in Holland brought about the change in its government which took place in 1785, we shall transcribe its contents together with those of another letter written on this subject to Colonel . . . which had the good fortune to be brought, through the care of Monsieur Is. de Pinto, of The Hague, to the attention of Rendorp, former burgomaster of the City of Amsterdam and president of the council of the Lords Proprietors. We are taking the liberty of adding to, and abridging from, these two letters what is necessary in order to avoid repetitions of many things which are mentioned in this work.

After the exposition of several matters which are not at all germane to our subject, he says there: "These crushing truths, joined to the general misfortunes of the Jewish community, which suffocates in it the germ of all knowledge, make the pains that I suffer increase all the more for me as an individual.

"Whatever were the efforts which I made, seconded by the principal members of the Jewish community, to undeceive some respectable colonists who honor us with their friendship on the subject of the general body of the Jewish community, all was in vain. Each one speaks as a philosopher, each one preaches morality, and nevertheless, despite the fine discourses, ethnic hatred and the prejudices of infancy operate without obstacle. Your absence and the deplorable state of the health of Monsieur le. . . , presage many troubles for us. I have therefore turned my sights in another direction. I have thought that if some petty faults and several ancient customs in the Jewish community could be corrected, internal and mutual tranquillity between Jew and Jew would greatly make up, with a large part of the good of private individuals, for what it has lost with the general public.

"I have therefore studied the genius, the character, the vices, and the virtues of my community, and although a Jew, I do not delude myself about it. Nevertheless, in dispassionate calm, I am borne to the conclusion that estrangement from good company, its ancient customs joined to the meager education which is unfortunately very defective in the colony in general, produced and maintain in it reprehensible pettinesses which influence its manners and make it unjustly contemptible in the eyes of all those who have not thoroughly examined its morality, or calculated the great weight of the good and of the bad in it, and who therefore blindly conceive prejudice against its individuals in general.

"In accordance with these principles, I have told myself a thousand times: a community whose members are, by religious principle (except for some individuals, as everywhere else), good husbands, good fathers, friends of the poor,[97] and hospitable both towards its other brethren as well as towards strangers; a community whose women, setting the example of integrity, are strongly attached to their husbands, despise finery, and devote all their care to their households; a community, furthermore, in which one finds societies composed of true and faithful friends,[98] which has never revolted against its sovereigns, but which knows how to obey the laws of the country, to contribute to the taxes, and which, at the least sign of affection or of equity on the part of the magistrates towards it, is flattered to the point of believing itself loved, is not at all a community whose petty faults are incorrigible. No, sir, the Jews are men, and also extremely sensible men. They have the same organs, the same passions as the Christians. Sensuality works and operates on all men in general; each one seeks only his own welfare; if there are vices there, there are also virtues there, and their mixture is only the appanage of humanity. Therefore to abhor the Jews by reason of their faith, to despise them because they do not observe in every respect the rules of that specious urbanity with which one deceives the universe—this is the height of folly and of wickedness. *The advantages of a nation* (says Monsieur de Zimmerman [the Swiss philosopher Johann Georg von Zimmermann] in his work on national pride [*Vom Nationalstolz*, 1758] *are either real or chimerical; it is presumptuous when it attributes to itself that which does not belong to it, and haughty when it is too convinced of its merit.*"

After a short exposition of the early history of the Jews, compared with their present political and moral condition, the writer adds, "It would be desirable that instead of privileges, they [the Jews] should have the affection of the people among whom they live, and that those of its individuals who deserve to be distinguished from the crowd should be able to enjoy the recompense which the law of nature gives to the individuals of the human species. Frequented, honored by the leading colonists, the entire Jewish community, striving to attain thereto, will have emulation, even envy, to raise itself to the level of some of its brethren. Once this distinction which separates them from the Christians is dissipated, the privileges, the immunities (except for those with reference to worshipping God in their own manner) would become useless and burdensome even in the eyes of the Jews. But while this inequality of condition exists beyond equitable bounds, the Jews will regard their privileges as a supreme good and will shed their blood to preserve them intact. Can a colony whose population is divided into two communities, half Jewish, half Christian, forced to look obliquely upon one another, promise itself many advantages?[99]

"Besides, what are the reasons which cause the Jews, in their state of poverty, to lose the advantages which they had when they were better off? The reason for this is entirely unknown to me, yet I flatter myself that no one will be in a position to maintain, and still less to prove, that their infidelity or their incapacity is the cause thereof, for there is perhaps no community which is more attached to its [political] master and which makes more efforts to oblige him, than the Jewish. And it is for this same reason that there is almost no countinghouse in the colony which does not have Jews as clerks. And in order to convince yourself that their subsistence and the support of their families does not come from anything other than their industry, calculate, sir, the immense sum of money that is expended annually in the colony on appointments and other benefices, of which the Jews are wholly deprived. Advocates, attorneys, sworn clerks of the secretariat, and of the various bureaus of the colony and of the government: the posts of the garrison, the officers of justice, or writ-servers, etc., etc. Add to this the advantages of the prodigious number of managers on the plantations, and a thousand other objects of this nature. Examine, besides, with your natural equity, the manner of living and the means of the greatest part of the Christian colonists, and subtract from the general number a deduction made for the directors and white officers on the plantations, 150 or 200 persons who, like the Jews, derive their subsistence from the work of their hands and from their industry; and then tell me if the support and well-being of all the others does not at all proceed from the advantages of their offices and from their ministrations.

"If there exists such a prodigious difference between the means of the Jews and those of the Christians, if the easy circumstances of some and the necessity of others bring it about that their means do not at all have the same force, or that they do not tend at all to produce the same effects, why, then, will there be demanded of the Jews so many precautions, so many scruples in their commerce, their manners, and the order in their houses? And more of that in supposing of them little pilferings. Is it not true and incontestable that *shame* (as a very sensible author says)[100] *is nothing where unjust contempt precedes the crime? Does it level the road* (he continues) *to cover with opprobrium those who have not rendered themselves culpable of this?* Thus the irregularities of a people which finds itself in this condition, its faults even—could they not be attributed with justice to those who are the cause thereof?

"Thus to alleviate the wounds of the Jewish community, the Jews ought, through an absolute necessity, to be sufficient for themselves and, so to speak, to concentrate on themselves. In order to arrive at this goal, it is necessary to purge our ecclesiastical institutions of their faults, to root out our old habits, and to cast away our prejudices, as the origin of all our divisions.

"And in order to place yourself, sir, in a position to use your good offices towards us with our illustrious masters in Europe, I shall have the honor of making my observations to you on the general economy of the Jewish community, according as my memory will suggest them to me.

"It is known that among all the civilized peoples of the universe laws were made according to the manners, the prejudices, and the circumstances of the epoch which saw them born. Past revolutions teach men both their errors and their future duties. No people, no government has preserved its code without alterations. Let us leave aside what is reported to us about the Chinese and other ancient peoples. These pretended eternal laws are still the basis of a thousand barbarous practices."

After an exact statement and very just observations on the good and the bad, the useful and the harmful in the constitution of the Jews in Surinam, with regard to the present state of the Jewish community, he concludes this article by adding thereto:

"Here, sir, is the faithful account of our condition, of our errors, and of the defects of our politico-ecclesiastical institutions. I have spoken to you with sincerity, and I have opened to you the last recess of my heart. In consequence, I beg you to tell me if it is possible for a collegium of regents, whose members must be changed every six months, and who, besides, are limited in their faculties, despite the extent of the privileges, exposed to the murmurs of the people, and obliged, upon the least complaint, to defend themselves before the governor and the council, continually in dispute about the meaning which it is wished to give to the privileges of the Jewish community,[101] besides having always to work with new members, and consequently with new ideas and new caprices—is it possible for them to be in a position to straighten out the institutions and to put order into the government of the Jewish community and of its members, without the willingness of the legislative power, which gives laws to the entire colony, to cooperate and to authorize the regents, or the most capable men of the Jewish community, to draw up the institutions, under the approbation of Their High Powers and of the Lords Proprietors? I do not at all doubt the controversies which we shall have to suffer on the part of our members; but all that is nothing; the respect due to the Sovereigns will impose silence. But, alas! permit me again ... a small observation: you are at the present time close to our masters, you are a philosopher, you know us. Can we hope that fortune will once be propitious to us? It is a question of the condition of the Jews at the present time, generally speaking in regard to the means of gaining their livelihood.

"In fulfilling the views which I have proposed about the changing of the government of the Jewish community mentioned above, in calming the passions and, furthermore, in attaining the goal of concentrating the Jewish community upon itself, we shall be able to flatter ourselves that we are going to make it happy the while the resources given to the other fellow-inhabitants of the colony are closed to its individuals. If the benevolence of our Sovereigns and the continuous goodness of our masters do not cooperate in rendering the Jews susceptible to all these profits destined for the inhabitants of the colony in general, in accordance with the meaning of their privileges, shall we be able to promise ourselves the happy effects of emulation taken within proper bounds of ambition and even of self-love? If you wish, are not literature, knowledge of jurisprudence, the fine arts, agriculture, and commerce all lost for them? Besides, where is the being sufficiently moral who works, who wishes to acquire knowledge, without counting on the benefits and the advantages that he will derive therefrom? Thus, totally divine as is the morality of J[esus]. Christ who prescribes one's own satisfaction for all sorts of recompenses, and completely excellent as are the maxims of Socrates, of Plato, and of Jean Jacques Rousseau in this respect, does this satisfaction, then, completely divine as it can be, give bread? Does it make those who possess it safe from contempt? On the contrary, the more sensitive one is, the more one consults the right of man based on nature itself, and the more one feels the incompatibility of these lessons in morality."

Fortunately, Monsieur Wichers, Major General in the service of Their High Powers (a title with which no other governor of the colony was endowed before him) arrived in Surinam on December 23, 1784, in the quality of governor general of the colony. His arrival formed the consummation of the wishes of the Jewish community, all the more so because at this same time, by reason of several irregularities of which two individuals of the Jewish community, who were under arms, had rendered themselves culpable, at the time of the interment of Governor Texier, the administrative council, without entering into the reasons which were to serve as an excuse for the Jews, found it good to decree that in the future the Jews were not to appear under arms at the reception of a new governor.[102] And although this resolution was modified in their favor by another one promulgated in the time of Monsieur Wichers, this latter one not having at all redressed their grievances in all respects, they addressed themselves anew to the Lords Proprietors, in the expectation of a more favorable decision. It could be wished that it should be terminated, in order to avoid the bad consequences which this resolution of the council, made in the time of the ad-interim governor, Monsieur Beeldsnyder, and the alleged reparation made on February 15, 1785, in the time of Monsieur Wichers can have, to the detriment of the Jewish community.

The principal members of the Jewish community, conceiving much hope with the government of Monsieur Wichers, whose kindnesses became well known at the time when he still exercised the position of first prosecutor of the colony, adopted the resolution to establish a college of literature under the title of "Docendo Docemur" in the house of Monsieur de Montel, an old man as beloved for his virtues as he was unfortunate in his kindnesses. Upon a prospectus which they made, and the protection which they received from the governor, the college had happy results, since it had, besides, the honor of having as active and honorary members the governor, Lieutenant Colonel Frederici, Monsieur van de Poll, the physician Schilling very highly esteemed in Europe for his works and principally for that on leprosy, Monsieur J. Caucanars, councillor of civil justice, military officers, and several others.[103]

The regents of the Jewish community, as the result of the requests made to Monsieur Wichers at the time of his departure for Holland and in accordance with the contents of two letters of which we have given an extract in this work, after mature deliberations, resolved, in their general assembly, composed of the regents and adjuncts, to turn over the affairs of the Jewish community concerning the reform of their institutions and their regency to the care and equitable judgment of the governor, in order that he might judge of them according to his wisdom. And upon a remonstrance which was addressed to him on March 8, 1785, the governor disposed of everything in accordance with the contents of Documents No. 23, parts 1 and 2, which characterize Monsieur Wicher's wisdom and his love for the public good.[104]

The new regents, by virtue of the commission with which the governor was indeed pleased to charge them concerning the drawing up of the new laws on the economic government of the Jewish community, devoted their attention to preparing the minds of its members, and little by little they achieved their goal of drawing up new institutions or *Ascamoth,* which were presented to the general assembly of the Jewish community to be examined and after that approved. This having been done in orderly fashion and under the required circumstances, this body of general and economic laws of the Portuguese Jewish community is ready to be presented to the governor, in order then to be sent to the Lords Proprietors in Holland, so that they may examine them and give their approval, and then to have that of Their High Powers the States General.

The first year of the government of the new regents named by the governor is marked by the period of the hundred-year anniversary of the synagogue of the Portuguese Jews at the Savane, built under the governorship of Monsieur de Sommelsdyk in 1685. It was celebrated, with all the pomp of which the Jewish community was capable, on October 12, 1785.[105]

During this interval, Monsieur M. P. de Leon, at present co-regent of the Jewish community, a postulant solicitor for fifteen years before the commissioners of petty cases, relying on his capacity for the bar, and, in addition, encouraged by several persons of distinction, requested the council of civil justice to admit him thereto as postulant attorney. This request so alarmed the corps of advocates and attorneys that, upon a counterpetition which they presented, the request was refused "for the present." This obliged the regents to address a request to the Lords Proprietors accompanied by very favorable recommendations. The advocates and attorneys, not doubting that the regents and Monsieur de Leon would not fail to oppose their opinions, without having observed the respect due to the gentlemen directors or awaiting their decision before then addressing themselves to the Sovereign, in accordance with what has always been observed when it is a question of several disagreements or requests which concern the internal government of the colony—this respectable body of the children of Themis [the goddess of justice] addressed itself eagerly to Their High Powers with a very long request, filled less with good sense than with traits of avarice and of prejudices. For, according to the reasons which they alleged there, they do not base their opposition at all on any dishonesty or lack of capacity of the requester, but on the fact that there is no example at all in Holland of a Jew's being admitted as a postulant attorney before the respective courts of the United Provinces. In addition, they complain of the loss which they were going to incur in their judiciary affairs. At the time when the papers of the regents arrived in Holland, the Lords Proprietors received from Their High Powers the remonstrance of the said advocates, in order that they might consider them. In consequence, the gentlemen directors gave their opinion in a writing replete with that noble equity which characterizes just souls and which at the same time places the seal on all the marks of benevolence which the Jewish community has received. We await, from the protection of our Sovereigns, a favorable issue to this affair.[106]

We were forced to add to this *Historical Essay* facts and detached events which are nevertheless germane to our subject. By the result of all that we have here brought forward, one will see that the Jewish community, in its decline, receives at intervals little blows of contempt which deject it and discourage it perceptibly, despite the goodness and the benevolence of the chief who governs us and of those who imitate him in his sentiments. In composing this essay, we have not at all hidden either the defects or the irregularities of the Jewish community. On the contrary, we have depicted it in very vivid colors which do not omit any nuance which could hide its distinctive character, a character susceptible of advantageous amelioration, if the means of their subsistence, the very state of the colony in general, were equally ameliorated. But while things remain on the same footing, the Jewish community cannot promise itself any good fortune whatsoever with regard to its subsistence, for the state of poverty in which its members in general are found is worthy of pity.[107] The little which they earn in the countinghouses of the managers of the plantations, etc., as clerks and bookkeepers, etc., is not sufficient for their maintenance and still less for that of their families. The considerable competition of large shops which the merchants of Holland maintain in the colony, by means of a certain profit which accrues to the factors or shopkeepers, renders burdensome those which the Jews can have. The purchases which they make at auction and which they sell afterwards at retail were their only resources, and it is principally the Portuguese [Sephardim] who support whatever is done in the colony. But this petty commerce, the profit which accrues to them from it, perceptibly declines by reason of the great expenses which one pays there and the small market which one finds in selling this merchandise on the streets, especially when one cannot give this job to the slaves, provided with bills, to run through the streets and to retail the goods while the master is otherwise occupied with making his little speculations.

At St. Eustatius [in the Dutch West Indies] and in the other colonies, both French and English, the colonists are allowed to display their wares before the gate and to sell all sorts of commodities which are not at all forbidden by law, without exception, through themselves and through their slaves on the streets and wherever it seems good to them, without fear of being arrested by the policemen or of being sentenced by the prosecutor. These obstacles, which are detrimental to the poor, accompanied by other vicissitudes which are generally suffered, increase the pain of seeing oneself deprived of every kind of lucrative occupation, either on the plantations or elsewhere. Plurality of means, diversity of ways of earning a livelihood, produces a traffic and a commerce which is advantageous in proportion to the means which one employs therein. But can it be of any advantage to a number of almost 150 poor families of Portuguese and German Jews, in a city where the population is so small, all of whom devote themselves to one sole traffic, to one sole speculation, especially when most of the women of the country, even the most distinguished ones, carry on all this business through their Negresses both in the city and on the plantations, thus taking away the means of subsistence from those who have absolutely no other resources than their industry in the matter of the little commerce which they carry on there? In consequence, therefore, of these hindrances, and of so many other disadvantages which the Jewish community experiences every instant, do not the little pilferings, the cheating, necessarily become indispensable?

Nevertheless, let the archives of the colony be perused, let the nature and the gravity of the crimes which were laid before the council be examined, and it will be seen whether the Jews deserve to be more accused, more ill-regarded, than the members of the other nations who are inhabitants of the colony. On this article, we already hear the voice of criticism and of prejudice tell us that our allegation is weak and very specious, since the regents have charge of exiling from the colony, by virtue of their privileges, those of the Jewish community who have committed some crimes, in order to remove them from the hands of justice. But, despite these observers, we are in a position to prove, by means of the archives of the Jewish community, that since the time that the colony has existed under the power of the Dutch up to the present, which makes a period of 120 years, the regents have invoked the article of their privileges dealing with their right of ostracism, or *Politique Verzending*, against only nine individuals without families, and against two families composed of seven persons, which makes altogether sixteen subjects, of whom eight suffered this penalty because of religion and of disobedience to the established authorities, and not for offenses and crimes. Let researches be made in the archives of the government (for without the governor, this ostracism cannot take place), and let it be denied if it can be; but the contrary will be the result. In making these researches, one will find that in the case of two persons whom the regents wished to banish from the colony on well-founded suspicions that they were forgers, several Christian creditors opposed it, so that their resolutions were rendered useless and these two bad subjects, to the despite and the shame of the Jewish community and of the regents, perambulate the streets of Paramaribo at the present time without fear or remorse.

After having shown, in the most suitable fashion, and with all the force and judgment of which we are capable, the summary of the history of the Colony of Surinam from 1650 up to our days, and having demonstrated its progress and its decline, together with the events which were the cause thereof, and after having presented the history of the Portuguese and German Jews settled there, and having compared their former condition with their modern condition, as regards their privileges, franchises and immunities, as well as that which concerns their political and moral state, their manner of living, their subsistence, their felicity and their sufferings—giving by means of these details a precise and exact answer to the questions which Monsieur Dohm has deigned to ask in the letter with which he was pleased to honor the regents of the Portuguese Jewish community, dated January 29, 1787[108]—it seems to us necessary to add to this work the description of the Colony of Surinam, the state of its culture, its habitations, its population, and its revenues, together with the description of the City of Paramaribo [and] the Savane of the Jews, the manners of its inhabitants, its political and military government, medicine, literature, etc., without, however, permitting ourselves to touch upon anything which concerns its present political government, which we defer with pleasure to those who are in a better position to know, by their capacity and connections, the forces which give movement now to the art of governing, a knowledge incompatible with the state of the Jews in general, who, for the contemporary politics of the place in which they live, must be what in Latin grammar is the neuter gender.

And in order to fulfil our purpose, we shall transcribe here the sketch which Monsieur de Raynal made in his *Histoire Politique,* and the authors whose works we have cited in this essay. In retracing what they wrote about the colony, we shall permit ourselves the liberty of suppressing, adding, recasting, and correcting what is there found to be exaggerated or defective, in accordance with the authority which truth devoid of all prejudice gives. This sketch of its present state, which knowledge of the locality puts us within closer reach of knowing than are the authors who write in their studies and on the basis of information which is garbled and therefore not very truthful, together with what we have presented in this work in the preceding concerning the origin of the founding and the political and moral revolutions of the colony, will form, briefly, its complete history from its beginning up to the year 1788.

End of the First Part

PART II

HISTORICAL ESSAY
ON THE
COLONY OF SURINAM

Its founding, its revolutions, its progress, from its origin up to our days, as well as the reasons which, for several years, have arrested the course of its prosperity; with the description and the present status of the colony, as well as its annual revenues, the taxes and imposts which are paid there, as also several other civil and political matters; as well as a picture of the manners of its inhabitants in general,

WITH

The history of the Jewish Portuguese and German community established there; their privileges, immunities and exemptions; their political and moral status, both ancient and modern; the part which they had in the defense and in the progress of the colony.

The whole edited on the basis of authentic documents joined thereto, and placed in order by the regents and representatives of the said Portuguese Jewish community.

SECOND PART

At Paramaribo
1788

HISTORICAL ESSAY ON THE COLONY OF SURINAM

The colonies which the Dutch possess in the New World are today the principal source of their commerce and of their opulence. To hold onto them, to increase them, to encourage the industry of their inhabitants, their agriculture, and to aid them in their needs, is the duty of equitable sovereigns, and the sole means of enlarging their states in general.

To intend to draw a parallel between the nature of modern colonies and those of Egypt, Sparta, and the Romans is to prepare the bases for the exercise of tyranny and of disorders; consequently, to consider their inhabitants as having fewer rights, fewer immunities, and as being of a class inferior to that of the inhabitants and the citizens of the mother country, is the height of turpitude. This truth was felt by several authors of equitable judgment, but no one perhaps brought it to light more beautifully than the eloquent author of the preface inserted in the first volume of the *Letters of Aristodemus and Sincerus*, on the colonies of Demmerary and Essequibo, which we have cited in this work; a preface worthy of appearing at the head of the immortal productions of the Montesquieus, of the Rousseaus, and of the Raynals, and not of a work where confusion and disorder in ten volumes suffocate and render unrecognizable what there is of truth, of utility, and even of sentimentality.

In one part, then, of this vast territory, bathed on the east by the sea, on the south by the Amazon, on the north by the Orinoco, and on the west by the Rio Negro, which joins these two rivers, the largest in South America, known under the name of Guiana, there was formed the colony of Surinam. In the middle of a country covered partly with woods and marshes laden with nitre, or which otherwise presents only vast arid plains from which sulphurous fumes are unceasingly exhaled, there is found the most important Dutch settlement in America, susceptible, because of its extent, its fertility and the convenience which is afforded to it by its various wide and deep rivers, of becoming the most powerful and the richest of all the colonies of the New World.

The river which gives the name to the whole colony is the most beautiful of the cultivated part. Two leagues from its mouth (not counting a sort of redoubt formed on the Mot Creek, which gives the first warning, by means of a cannon shot, of the approach of some ship) there are two forts, one on each side of the river, which defend this passage in times of war. These forts confront vessels which would wish to sail up this river, and with their batteries well provided with artillery, they second the efforts which Fort New Amsterdam, situated half a league upstream, is in a position to make for the defense of the colony. This fortress, begun in 1733 and finished in 1747, as we have already noted, is situated at the confluence of the Surinam and Commowine rivers, and in the middle of a little marsh which forms a sort of round isthmus. Between these two rivers, it is accessible only by two narrow roads where the artillery prevents all approach, and despite the considerable width of the Surinam river at the place where the fortress is situated, no vessel can pass without approaching it, because of the large sand banks mixed with mud which are found opposite it for more than half the width of the river.

Two leagues upstream there is a concealed battery, intended to cover the port and the city of Paramaribo. It is called Zeeland. This fortress encloses within its precincts the storehouse of provisions and of munitions, materials of the Lords Proprietors, and ordinarily a battalion of infantry which forms the garrison of the city.

The colony has as its defenders a goodly number of troops consisting of three battalions of infantry, two companies of artillery, one corps of engineers, one corps of mountain infantry, and 200 freed Negroes, who perform the service of the light troops. Each battalion has its colonel or its lieutenant colonel, or a major who commands it, subject to the orders and to the commands of the governor, in his quality of major general in the service of Their High Powers the States General, and colonel in chief of all the militia of the country. The colonel commandant of the second battalion is at present Monsieur van Baarle; and the lieutenant colonel, Monsieur Frederici, commandant of the last, has, besides the department of the cordon in his quality of inspector general, the company of the mountain infantry, in his quality of lieutenant colonel, and also that of the corps of freed Negroes, as chief. This corps was formed since 1772 from the best slaves drawn from all the plantations of the colony, and bought at an exorbitant price. This company of freed Negroes is at present at the number of 200, not counting the military officers, their guides, and the others employed in this service. Without detracting from the merit of the several corps which constitute the garrison of the country, this corps, subordinated to the command of a chief who is capable and enterprising, is the most beneficial militia of the colony. They are posted everywhere, and these Negroes, in exchange for their small wages and for other benefits, well-trained, besides, in the profession of arms, under a well-regulated discipline, make continual expeditions against the runaway slaves, and always with more or less success. It would be desirable for the welfare of the colony that this corps should be in a position to be expanded both for the common tranquillity and for the extirpation of the runaway slaves of Boni, those behind Para, and to stand up to the inhabitants of the villages of Juca and of Saramaca in case of some outbreak.

In addition, the colony has for its defense the body of civilian militia divided into eleven companies which form as many divisions (of which the four of Paramaribo are the first), and among this number is the company of Portuguese Jewish citizens. Each has its captain, two lieutenants, and one ensign. Those of Paramaribo mount guard continually every evening near the city hall, which is at the same time the church of the [Calvinist Dutch] Reformed religion and the place where the administrative council meets. The others do nothing except in case of pressing need. But the military troops are divided among the fortresses, the redoubts, the cordon, and in various posts of the colony which surround the plantations in general. These troops are better maintained at Surinam than elsewhere; the soldiers lack nothing which they need.

All the settlements of the colony in general are situated on the Surinam river, the creeks of Para, Paulus and others which empty into it, on the Commowine, its tributaries Cottica and Perica, and other creeks, forming altogether at the present time 591 plantations in number, including 139 for timber and for foodstuffs. Thus the number of those which are under cultivation amounts to only 452 settlements, that is to say: on the Commowine, Cottica, Perica, and on all the other rivers and creeks which empty into them, 331 for sugar, coffee, cacao, and cotton. Together with thirty settlements for wood and for foodstuffs, this Commowine river contains the number of 361 settlements. Of this number, fourteen belong to the Jews, eight are in timber, and six are in coffee and cotton. There are on [the] Surinam, including Para creek and all the others which empty into it, together with the establishments behind the city of Paramaribo, the number of 121 sugar, coffee, cotton, and cacao plantations and 109 for wood and for foodstuffs. This makes a total of 230 settlements enclosed by this Surinam river; of these, thirty-two belong to the Jews, of which twenty-two are for timber and ten for coffee. Thus from the total of these settlements under cultivation, the number of which, as we have said above, amounts to 452, it is necessary to subtract the number of sixteen which belong to the Jews; hence there remain 436 settlements belonging to the other inhabitants, and of this number, 350 have their proprietors in Holland, and eighty-six here.

Thus the present number of its settlements in general exceeds that of 1730 and of 1735 by 150 plantations, an increase due to the rivers Commowine, Cottica, Matapica, Perica, etc. For instead of 177 settlements which there were in 1730 and 1735, there are at present the number of 351 in sugar, coffee, cotton, and cacao, together with water mills (except for several situated along the upper reaches of the rivers which still have mills turned by animals), where there are thirty plantations maintained at the source of the creeks, which produce only timber to provide for the needs of the buildings of the plantations in general. The contrary took place as regards the Surinam river, since in the years 1730 to 1735 there were to be found there, from its mouth as far as forty miles upstream, the number of 224 coffee and sugar plantations, together with mills turned by animals, and today, including therein all its creeks, and those which were formed behind the city of

Paramaribo, with the exception of 109 very small ones which produce only wood and foodstuffs, there are altogether a total of only 121 settlements under cultivation. This makes a reduction of 103 plantations, of the number of which the Portuguese and German Jewish community own fourteen plantations on the Commowine and its other tributaries and creeks, and thirty-two on the Surinam, which make a total of forty-six settlements. Of these, sixteen are in sugar and in coffee, instead of the 115 which they owned up to 1760. We have, in several passages of this work, given the reason for the decline of the Jewish community.

One will perhaps not find, in all America, without excepting any colony, plantations more regular, more beautiful, and more replete with superb buildings and with gardens of a sumptuosity far beyond exploitable limits, than in Surinam. The places of debarkation, the neatness of the paved roads which surround the buildings, the hedges of lemon-trees, and the large number of fruit trees which frame the roads, give one of the most agreeable vistas which it is possible to see. There are storehouses for coffee, which have cost more than 80,000 florins. We have said enough about the immoderate luxury of these settlements to have any need of speaking more about it.

The annual revenue of these settlements, notably of those which produce exportable commodities, has been calculated with much exactitude by Monsieur Fermin in his *Tableau de Surinam*, pages 369-76. The sum of the value of all these products during the space of twenty-six years from 1750 to 1775, in coffee, sugar, cotton, and cacao, amounted to 265,400,000 florins, which makes an annual sum of 10,207,692 florins, six sous, and several deniers.

The revenue produced therefrom in the ten years thereafter, from 1776 to 1786, amounts altogether to 160,000 barrels of sugar, 120,000,000 pounds of coffee, 7,500,000 pounds of cotton, and 6,000,000 pounds of cacao, which makes a yearly average of 16,000 barrels of sugar, 12,000,000 pounds of coffee, 750,000 pounds of cotton,[1] and 600,000 pounds of cacao. The last year, 1787, which was very bad, produced only 11,289,725 pounds of whole coffee and 840,031 pounds of broken coffee, 838,641 pounds of fine cotton, and 114,326 pounds of inferior quality, 802,724 pounds of cacao, and 15,744 barrels of sugar. The result of the ten preceding years, joined to the product of the last year, renders an exact calculation of the net products of the colony, year by year, as 15,782 barrels of sugar, at 1,000 pounds per barrel; 12,064,878 pounds of coffee; 851,483½ pounds of cotton; and 701,326 pounds of cacao.

These commodities, estimated according to the price which they met with in Holland, alternately the last six years, without counting any expenses whatsoever, give for sugar a result of 2¼ sous per pound or 112.10 florins per barrel of 1,000 pounds; for coffee, 10½ sous per pound; for cotton, 21 sous per pound; for cacao, five sous per pound. This makes, altogether, a sum of 9,289,109 florins, two sous and eight Dutch deniers, producing thereby a decrease of 918,583 florins, four sous and several deniers less than the result of the twenty-six years according to Monsieur Fermin, and that, again, on account of the price of commodities which has risen much more in the past six to eight years than in the twenty-six years altogether, according to his calculation.[2] And in order to recognize more easily the decrease in the products of Surinam, caused as much by the present sterility of the lands as on account of the few slaves who are transported there, and on account of the meager credit for procuring the means of supplying them on the plantations, the number of whom is considerably diminished by reason of flights, of deaths, and of those who have grown old in the course of the work, one can consult the parallel of the products which we note here below.[3] From it one will see that from 1777 to the end of 1787 the colony produced less than from 1750 to 1776: 6,255½ barrels of sugar, 8,507,244 pounds of coffee, and 665,307 pounds of cacao, and that, to counterbalance these reductions, cotton surpassed the result of these twenty-six years by only 279,269½ more pounds.

Let there now be deducted from the sum of 9,289,109.2.8, which is the result of the annual production of the colony, the freight of fifty vessels designated for the navigation of Surinam, which grows annually (according to the calculation which will be found at the end of this work and notably in the article "Population, Navigation, Commerce, etc.") at 16,000 florins per vessel, a total of 800,000 florins, and the commissions, unloadings, insurance, sales, warehouses, charges, purchases, etc., at the rate of 12 percent, which amounts to almost 1,114,693 florins, and it will be seen that the inhabitants of the Republic profit annually from the commodities of the colony by nearly 2,000,000 florins, without counting the other benefits which will be found in the article which we have mentioned in this work. Thus it is incontestable that the more means in Holland are sought and the more efforts are made there to ameliorate the conditions of cultivation in Surinam, the more the mother country will derive an advantageous profit for its individuals in general. In order to arrive at this goal, nothing is lacking but encouragement. The cultivated lands of the colony, despite their present exhaustion, are susceptible to amelioration; besides, the lands on the rivers of Saramaca are begging, so to speak, to be cleared, in order to be made equal to those of the Commowine, etc. Credit, vigorous arms for work, population in general—these are what the colony needs in order to increase its cultivation and the number of its settlements.[4]

The greatest number of proprietors of these settlements live in Europe, and their plantations are administered by their agents, whom the mediocrity of their fortune keeps in Surinam. However, there are a small number of proprietors who are in easy circumstances, and about sixty others in a lesser condition, who themselves manage their holdings. The various consumptions of similar inhabitants and the rest of the individuals of the colony, despite what Abbé Raynal says, are not so totally limited as he thinks, and the seafarers of the metropolis who come to seek the products cultivated in this part of the New World, to the number of fifty or sixty large vessels a year, bring in many things of prime necessity, as well as objects of luxury. And if the Anglo-Americans make a profit in their commerce with Surinam (which these authors suppose to be due solely to the indirect routes), from which they derive molasses, etc., it is only because of the objects of pure necessity which they bring in for the maintenance of the slaves on the plantations and of the settlements in general, objects which do not at all come from the Republic in such great quantity or of the same quality, such as salted fish, leaf tobacco, whale oil, flour, horses, mules, etc. These American seafarers carry away in payment molasses, rum, etc.[5]

The city of Paramaribo, the capital of the country, situated several hundred paces higher than Fort Zeelandia, and to the right of the river Surinam as one sails up it, was formerly, as we have noted, only a hamlet inhabited by the Indians. The English began to enlarge it, but when the Zeelanders became masters of the colony, and even at the time of the arrival of Governor Sommelsdyk in 1683, it had a total of at most only 100 to 120 houses. Since that epoch it has become large, principally during the administration of Monsieur Nepveu, by means of various concessions of lands which he made to the Mulattoes and to the freed Negroes, and to the whites who were in poor situation, to the point where it is today the most beautiful and, because of its climate, the most healthful in America. Its spacious and beautiful houses (except four or five which are of brick) are all built of wood. None are not encompassed by beautiful, wide windows, most of them adorned with square window panes.[6] This city is built on a foundation of sand and gravel, filled to the depth of five to eight feet with shells of different kinds and colors,[7] so that paving stones are everywhere very handy, and although, to make up for it, during the great heat spells, this same gravel heats up the shoes prodigiously and casts upon one's face reflections of light which are very annoying, a wind from the northeast blows continually and tempers the heat of the sun, although it raises dust in such great quantity that it sometimes causes stubborn ophthalmias. During the rainy seasons which commence ordinarily in mid-November, and sometimes later, up to May and June, the streets are nevertheless so dry that one can walk without even *soiling* one's shoes.

With the exception of three or four cross streets, all the others are very beautiful, wide, and straight as a string, lined with beautiful tamarind and orange trees. When these last-mentioned trees bloom, which is ordinarily from December to May, they exude the most exquisite perfume mornings and evenings. There are to be counted at present in the city 1,119 houses, both large and small, a large number of which are two-story buildings. There are to be found in the number of these houses five classes of buildings, according to their value. There are probably, for example, four to six which cost from 50,000 to 70,000 or 80,000 florins, twenty from 30,000 to 50,000, a hundred from 15,000 to 30,000, and another hundred from 8,000 to 15,000; the rest always cost from 2,500 to 5,000, 6,000, and 8,000 florins. Of the total of these houses, the Portuguese Jews possess, in full ownership, the number of 127 houses of all qualities and degrees (except those of the first class), and the German Jews similarly have eighty-six, which makes a total of 213 houses, with the exception of six which these two Jewish communities have designated as residences for the poor, donated free of charge by individual persons.

The seat of government is a house built of brick (finished in the administration of Monsieur de Gooyer, at the beginning of this century), to which each governor took pains to add something to embellish it. But as its first construction is defective, neither the form nor the appearance of a château or of some seignorial mansion can be attributed to it. Nonetheless, since it is built on the parade-ground which is called the *Plein,* and since it is accessible by two splendid avenues of beautiful tamarind trees, surrounded by hedges of lemon trees, it has a very majestic aspect. Next to Government House and these two avenues of tamarinds, widened and rendered neat and beautiful by Governor Wichers, there is at present the place reserved for the teaching of military drill to the soldiers, under continual shade, without exposing them to the heat of the sun for two or three hours in succession, as was the case before his arrival. From these avenues one may promenade to Fort Zeelandia, passing over a drawbridge which spans the moat surrounding the fortress. All the houses of Paramaribo which are to be found on the side of the street where that of Government House begins have beautiful gardens which are so artistically laid out and some of them so sumptuous, such as that of the former administrative councilor, Monsieur de Graaf, that of the late Monsieur Benelle, and several others, that they yield in no respect to those of Europe. The rest of all the houses situated in the other streets have each one, to a greater or lesser degree, its kitchen garden for the needs of the household; this makes the dwellings in general useful, pleasant, and commodious.

In this same street there is to be found also a military hospital built by Governor Crommelin in 1758 or 1760. This building, for its purpose, yields to none in America: large, spacious, provided, besides, with a copious pharmacy, with beautiful and wide apartments for the sick, cared for by the physician W. Schilling (whom we have had the pleasure to mention in this work), by surgeon majors, and by other people of the profession, in number sufficient to permit no grounds for complaint to suffering humanity.

The church of the Reformed Protestants (which is the dominant one of the country) is situated almost in the middle of the city, having in front of it a square plaza planted with orange-trees, where the dead used to be buried. This was later prohibited. However, anyone who wishes to have a deceased person buried there is obliged to pay a fine of 500 florins. This church—built of square stones which are quarried from under the ground in the city itself, are only shells and petrified sand, and are called, unsuitably, in Surinam, *Klipsteen,* which means stone cut from the rocks—has still a second story made of wood. Considering the architecture of this building, one would be tempted to assign to it a very remote age, so massive and heavy it is. However that may be, this church, which is at the same time the city hall, where the sessions of the administrative council take place, and where the political archives and the Chamber of Orphans, etc., are located, does not correspond at all to the great objects for which this building is intended. In the second story, where the church which occupies the entire length of the building is located, there is a superb organ, ornamented with fine wooden sculpture and gilded. Besides this church, the Reformed people have another one in Commowine, and another in Perica, where the directors of the plantations assemble on Sundays. For the divine service, each has its minister, and that of Paramaribo has two. There was formerly one who preached in French for the refugees of this nation, who were numerous and did not understand Dutch at all; but since at present everybody knows how to speak it fairly well, all preaching is done only in this language. However, from time to time some sermons are in French.

The Lutherans have their church, built of brick and arched, where they have an organ and a pulpit with very fine and very well executed sculpture. It has been only half a century since the Lutherans obtained permission to build a church and to practice their religion openly. In recompense for this permission, they paid annually the sum of 600 florins for the benefit of the poorhouse of the Reformed religion; however, some years ago they redeemed this annual contribution by means of a lump sum, one-time, equivalent payment.

The Portuguese and the German Jews each have their synagogue, very well built of wood and very neat. The Germans [Ashkenazim] follow the customs of the Portuguese [Sephardim], from whom they obtain two cantors for the services in their synagogue.[8] The Moravian Brethren also have their church; this [Protestant] brotherhood exists in Surinam as elsewhere. They have tried there to present the principles of religion to the Indians, and recently to the freed Negroes and slaves, who ran there in crowds, more for the love of novelty than for any religious enthusiasm, to listen to the lessons of their new priests. But no good effect was produced by the latter, for they only added to their natural spitefulness dissimulation and hypocrisy, as they still pursue their ancient pagan customs and superstitions. At the beginning, when these brethren catechized the Negroes, it was a very curious thing to hear the sermons which the minister of this confraternity delivered there in Negro-English [*Nègre-anglois*], the jargon of the country, which has neither rules nor order whatsover. However, the efforts which he made to translate into this jargon passages from the Bible, the explanation of the eucharist, the dogma of the transubstantiation, etc., were worthy of admiration. Several psalms are likewise translated into this jargon, and they are sung to the accompaniment of a harpsichord, which for them takes the place of an organ. It was in 1779 that this religious attempt had its beginning. It lasted only four or five years, for at present the new proselytes very seldom attend their church, and they no longer boast of their new faith.

The Roman Catholics, despite their efforts, never were able to obtain freedom to practice their religion in Surinam (we have spoken, in the course of this work, of the opposition which they experienced there even in the time of Governor Sommelsdyk). However, in 1785 they obtained, with the consent of the States General and the Directors, permission to have a public church, and at the beginning of the year 1787 two Catholic priests came from Holland who, after having gathered together their flock who had strayed away on the plantations and elsewhere, without pastor or communion for so many years, found it possible to purchase a fine, two-story house, of which the first story is intended as the residence of the priests, and the second as the church. All the non-Catholic inhabitants, Protestants and Jews, contributed to the collection which they made to provide for the needs of their enterprise. In consequence, they outfitted their church with everything that they needed to practice their faith, with much order and propriety. They dedicated it on April 1, 1707, celebrating there for the first time a high mass, accompanied by a band of musicians.

The governor, the administrative council, and the council of civil justice were asked to be present. They paid them their respects, after having expressed their thanks to Their High Powers and to the Lords Proprietors. The influx of people was so great then that it was feared that some damage might happen to the house, so much does novelty impel people; but this was indeed most excusable, for those who were born in the country and who had never seen Europe and who know nothing about Catholicism were astonished to see ceremonies so unlike the faith which they professed. The Jews, especially those who had some knowledge of their ancient ritual, were astonished to see many parallels to the religion of Jerusalem in priestly times. This church will probably not make much progress, because the small number of Catholics is neither sufficient nor in a position to provide the means even to pay the debts contracted for the purchase of the church. This will no doubt disgust those who still remain hidden. Besides, one of the priests returned to Europe, and the other died in November, 1787. Nevertheless, they are waiting for another one.

There is perhaps no other place in the world where religious tolerance is more extensive and more strictly observed, without there ever having been any discussion or controversy whatsoever, than in Surinam. Each one there prays to God in his own manner, and each one there does what seems to him most efficacious for the salvation of his soul. We shall relate in this connection a witticism of a French plantation manager; he stated to one of his compatriots at Lyon (whither he made a journey recently), who had boasted too much of the tolerance of France, that in Surinam he had eaten in a house the family of which was composed of pagans, Jews, Roman Catholics, Greek schismatics, and Calvinists. They were, he added, all at the table, gay and contented and living, besides, in perfect union.[9] Amiable philosophers join together to implore the Supreme Being for the welfare of a government which, without losing from sight the regard due to its own established church, knew how to make fashionable and to protect the opposite of that which has made streams of blood to be shed in Europe. May it prove possible to banish civil intolerance and national prejudice forever from the earth!

The council of civil justice formerly assembled in the same place as the administrative council; when the two had to meet at the same time, the church was taken as the place of assembly. However, since the year 1774 the colony purchased a fine house situated opposite the "Plein" of the government. It was built (besides its first floor) in two stories; the second floor is the place where the council meets, with a large and spacious vestibule; on the third floor there meets the petty civil judica-

HISTORY OF SURINAM 137

ture, known under the name of the commissioners of small cases, and the medical collegium. On the first floor is the civil secretariat, very properly maintained and in good order; we shall speak of all these tribunals more in detail.[10] Besides these public buildings, there are two almonries, the one Reformed and the other Lutheran, where indigent orphans, old people, and those who are not in a position to earn their livelihood are received. The Jews have no special house at all in which to maintain their poor, but each family has an annual allowance proportionate to its needs. As a result, one never sees mendicants in the streets as in most of the cities of Europe. The Reformed religion, besides this, has a public school for the instruction of the children of the almonry.

Political and Civil Government of the Colony

The political government is chosen from among the inhabitants, named for life by the free domiciled inhabitants who, in addition, receive incomes, without distinction as to religion or color. These nominations are made in a double number, and the governor has the right of election among those who have the most votes, which is done by means of tickets read aloud by the secretary, in the presence of the council and the voters.

The governor exercises a supreme authority in the entire colony, in the name of the States General and the Directors; this applies both to the administrative council and in military affairs, for the troops are under his orders in his quality of colonel-in-chief. However, in political affairs of importance, he is obliged to convoke and to consult the council, of which he is the president, as well as of the council of civil justice and of all the collegia of the colony. He has only one vote there, but this is decisive in each tribunal when they are equally divided. He names *ad interim* all the political and military offices which are vacant, except that of the prosecutor, that of the comptroller, and that of the pre-advisor [lieutenant governor], until they are disposed of otherwise by the Directors. In general, he orders everything that he believes necessary for the maintenance and the security of the colony, and although the governor is obliged to convoke the administrative council on matters of importance, he can nevertheless order or establish the contrary of that which has been decided by a plurality of the votes, by declaring himself responsible for the event, until the Lords of the colony dispose thereof otherwise. And, following this authority, no edict can be published without the consent of the governor in his quality of representative of the Lords. The governor there has also the right of pardon in criminal offenses, both civil and military, a right which was conceded to him by the Sovereign.

The political and criminal justice council, which meets four times a year, is composed of the first prosecutor (who has a second one to replace him in his absence or in case of illness), the latter without a decisive vote; of nine councillors; of a comptroller general, who has the department of all the bureaus of the colony, but without a vote in the council except on that which concerns finances; and of a secretary. Everything that concerns criminal affairs, politics, finances, and the general administration of the country is the province of this tribunal, and all its sentences are subject to revisions before Their High Powers, unless they follow an extraordinary criminal case.

The council of civil justice, independent of the first council, also meets four times a year, and judges only civil affairs in general; and one may appeal from its sentences above 600 florins before Their High Powers. It is composed of the governor; of ten councillors who are named by the administrative council to serve in this capacity for four years; of a pre-advisor named by the Lords of the colony, who disposes of all civil matters in the absence of the governor; and of a secretary. This office of advisor was created in 1782. Ordinarily the second prosecutor is vested therewith, and no one can occupy it unless he has been admitted to the bar in Holland. It is on the basis of his advice that civil proceedings are most often judged. Monsieur Karsseboom, who was the second prosecutor, and auditor general or military prosecutor, was the first who held this office. After he became first prosecutor (after the arrival of Monsieur Wichers, in his capacity of governor general), the advocate Meurs was vested therewith, together with that of second prosecutor and of auditor. But on his death, which took place in November, 1787, to the regret of all those who had known him, the position remained vacant until it was entrusted by the Lords of the colony to the advocate Sichterman.

There is also a third subordinate council which deals with pecuniary matters of little consequence which arise among the citizens; it is called the "commission for small cases," the amounts of whose procedures range only from one to 250 florins. It is composed of a vice-president, who is always a veteran of the council of civil justice; of nine commissioners; and of a secretary. Cases above fifty florins can be appealed to the council of justice. The advocates and attorneys who plead before this council plead also before the commissioners; but meanwhile they have solicitors for procedures up to 100 florins, and among the latter only two Jews have been admitted in all this time.

The Portuguese Jewish community has also its council of civil procedure, where are settled the differences which arise among the members. All cases are argued there according to the jurisprudence of the country, where there are observed, as much as the situation of the Savane permits, the ways and the orders of the council of civil justice of the colony, to which the sentences in proceedings of more than 100 florins can be appealed. There are solicitors admitted under oath by the regents to argue cases, but each individual has permission to make his own defense, or to authorize another person, independently of the solicitor, to argue the case for him. The costs of the proceedings and the fees of the Jewish secretariat are very moderate, and the cases are settled with all possible speed, according to the contents and spirit of the privilege in virtue of which this civil tribunal is constituted. The regents, in addition to what concerns civil affairs, dispose of whatever concerns the ecclesiastical and economic affairs of the Jewish community; but when matters of great importance are to be considered in regard to politics or finances, they must take the advice of the assistants [officers] who are the veterans and have already served as regents.

It is about this city of Paramaribo, and in particular about the Jewish inhabitants of Surinam in general, that Abbé Raynal, in the next to the last edition of his *Histoire Philosophique et Politique,* printed at The Hague in 1774, declared:[11] "There is perhaps" (he said) "no empire on earth where this unfortunate community (the Jewish) is so well treated. Not only has it been granted the freedom of professing its religion, of having lands in full ownership, and of itself settling the differences that arise among its members; it enjoys also the right, common to all citizens, of participating in the general government, and of competing in the elections of the public magistrates. Such is the progress of the spirit of commerce that it silences all national or religious prejudices in the face of the general interest which should bind men together. What are" (he continues) "these empty labels: Jews, Lutherans, French, Dutch? Unfortunate inhabitants of a land so troublesome to cultivate, are you not all men, etc.?" This piece, worthy in all respects of the heart of the philosopher who wrote it, is struck from the coin of truth. The impartial philosophy which prevails there is felt by the true Christian and equally by all virtuous men, of whatever religion they may be.

And from what we have reported in this work, and from what one will perceive by consulting the justificatory documents added to it, it is proved incontestably that, with the exception of participating in the general government, as Monsieur Raynal said, based on the contents of the privilege of the Jewish community, the Jews of Surinam, thanks to the kind acts of the Sovereign and of the Lords Proprietors, enjoy all these religious and political advantages. What, then, could have been the reason, what could have motivated Monsieur Raynal, to suppress this article, which refers particularly to the Jews, in the last edition of his work?[12] Was it probably in order not to inspire other powers by the example of the tolerance of the Republic of Holland, exclusively towards the Jews of Surinam? Was it probably in order not to ascribe to the Jews distinguished merits which procured for them all these protections? No, certainly, the heart of the philosopher, who merited from the [English novelist Laurence Sterne's] *divine Elisa Draper,* and from all sensible and just men, the beautiful title, the glorious epithet of "Defender of humanity, of truth, and of liberty,"[13] cannot have conceived such objectionable ideas. And it is only bad information, which prejudices and hate had perhaps directed to him, that could have made him conceive the necessity of suppressing this piece as being useless or contrary to the truth, and to cause him to add in his new edition several very unfriendly expressions towards the Jews which will effect more evil than he himself thinks, and from which his heart will perhaps again have to suffer. Because as a true philosopher he should support the tolerance of Holland, report the immunities of the Jews in Surinam which are owing to the benevolence of their Sovereigns and of the Lords of the colony, and rise up, at the same time, against the little effect which this same benevolence produces towards their fellow inhabitants, and say, with a celebrated author: *It is not the whole thing not to burn people as in the Inquisition; one can burn with the pen and with contempt, and this fire is all the more cruel as its effect passes over to future generations.*

In addition to the political and civil superior and inferior magistracies which we have just described, there are commissioners, of whom we shall speak later, for the city, for the roads, and for the public works (*Gemeene Weide*), and two committees, whose members are appointed for life, for the Chamber of the Orphans, both to manage the property of minors who do not have guardians as well as to receive the inheritances of those who die intestate. There are, in addition, sworn land-surveyors, an assayer of sugars, a gauger for molasses or syrup, and many other employees, both military and civil, about whom we lack space to present information in detail.

In 1782, a collegium of medicine was created, composed of a president, who is always a member of the administrative council; two physicians; an apothecary; and a surgeon, named by the administrative council. This collegium serves to examine the diplomas of those who wish to practice the art of healing in the colony, and to tax the accounts of the physicians, apothecaries, surgeons, male-midwives, etc.

POPULATION BOTH OF THE CITY OF PARAMARIBO AND OF THE WHOLE COLONY IN GENERAL, NAVIGATION, AND COMMERCE

According to the most exact calculation, the number of the [white] inhabitants of the city amounts to two thousand souls, without counting the garrison of the country and those employed in the military service; and included in this number are 615 Portuguese Jews and 430 German Jews, altogether 1,045 persons, who are thus more than half the white population of the city. Besides this, there probably are (not counting the militia of the free Negroes) 650 Mulattoes and free Negroes; this makes a total of 2,650 free persons. The slaves who are kept there, both to work as house servants and to be hired out by their masters according to their capabilities—among whom [slaves] there are a large number of carpenters, masons, locksmiths, etc., etc.—can be reckoned at the number of 6,000 to 8,000. Thus the population of the city in general amounts to above nine or ten thousand souls.

The expenses which they have annually for merchandise coming from Europe and America are inconceivable. In proportion to its population, no city in America spends as much as that of Paramaribo. There is at the present time an immoderate luxury [even] among the slaves, who have formed among themselves a sort of order, which they call "Dou," for example, "Dou D'or," "Bigie Dou," "Dou de Diamant," that is, "made of gold," "made of diamond," "made large." This will probably render it necessary to suppress at least the excesses which are already very noticeable both because of the thefts which must necessarily result therefrom, and because of the little that the whites can impose upon them in this respect. This makes them assume an intolerable pride and a decided contempt for the ladies of the country.

The general population of the colony, including the two thousand whites whom we estimate the city of Paramaribo to have, will probably amount altogether, blacks and whites, free persons and slaves, to from 50,000 to 55,000 souls. In the colony there is a total number of 591 settlements in general, large and small; from this number it is necessary to deduct forty-six belonging to the Jews, which we are not counting here at all because we are taking their population separately, with the result that there remain 545 plantations. On these plantations there are from one to four whites, including managers, clerks, and commanders. Some of them have only two, and the greatest number have only one white; so that, taking an average of two whites for each settlement in general, the number of 545 settlements will produce a total of 1,090 persons. The population of the Portuguese Jews in general, including those who live in Paramaribo, in the Savane, and on the plantations, amounts to 834, and the German Jews to 477, which makes altogether 1,311 persons, in addition to the number of almost 100 free Jewish Mulattoes, of these two Jewish communities. Add to the number of these 1,090 persons of the settlements the number of 955 whites in the city of Paramaribo—after subtracting 1,045 Jews who make altogether the number of 2,000 souls in the city—with 1,311 Jews, and the population of the whites in general will be found to amount to 3,356 souls.[14] Add further to this number 650 Mulattoes and free Negroes, including the 100 who have been counted among the Jews, and the general population of the free persons in the colony will amount to 4,006 souls, so that in the total number of 3,356 whites in the colony, there are found there the number of 1,311 Jews, which makes above a third of the white population in general.

The number of the slaves has been greatly diminishing for several years. Mortality, flights, the small number of them brought in from the Guinea coasts [of West Africa], the number of those who have been freed for the service of the colony (known under the name of the corps of free Negroes, of which we have spoken), and of those who have attained the goal of achieving their liberty, are the causes of this diminution. Nevertheless, the number of the slaves in general, according to the most exact calculation derived from the assembling of several pieces of information which we have received from various persons, amounts to from 45,000 to 50,000 souls. When one considers this number in connection with those of the population of the free people of the colony, and the annual product or revenue of all its settlements, and when one compares them then with the immense number of the Negroes and the white population in St. Domingue [Hispaniola], and the revenue of this island, one will find that, in proportion, Surinam produces much more revenue than St. Domingue and the other [Caribbean] islands of America. And if one adds to this observation the prodigious quantity of foodstuffs, merchandise, and hardware brought in by the vessels which arrive from Europe and which are consumed in the city and on the plantations, one will find, again, that no colony of America furnishes as advantageous a market for the mother country as does Surinam. These advantages, joined to the profit which the Republic derives from the freight of fifty or sixty large vessels which sail there every year on the average, and the thousand other benefits which result therefrom for the merchants of Holland, to the disadvantage of the colonists, will convince one of the right which the colonists have to expect equity from Their High Powers, from the Lords of the colony, and especially from the merchants and "Geldschieters," advancers of money, in Holland, for the[ir—the colonists'] generous sacrifices to free the colony from the burden of its debts and from the cancerous plague of its interest payments.

The freight of the merchandise which is brought into the colony for the consumption of the settlements and for the shops of private individuals can be calculated on a yearly average as being between five and six thousand florins; and that for several years already, since before the credit of the colony had fallen, the freight of each vessel amounted to more than 9,000 florins.

The freight for the return of the commodities can equally be valued at 16,000 florins[15] for each vessel, which, added to the freight of 5,000 florins for the importation, makes 21,000 florins. Multiplying this by the fifty vessels which sail there gives the sum, from these profits, of 1,050,000 florins, without including therein that for the transportation of passengers, or even the bricks which are sold at a high price and which the vessels can hardly help carrying, since they serve them as ballast. To these profits add further the annual expenses of all the plantations in general for merchandise which is brought in directly from correspondents in Holland, and in order to determine these expenses through a most natural and most exact calculation, we have divided the total number of 591 settlements which the colony has into nine classes, from 200 florins up to 4,000 florins, both for the clothing of the Negroes, for the iron [*ferrures*—shackles?], and for utensils of every sort, as well as for supplies for the directors. And we have found that on the average a settlement cannot spend less than 1,486 florins a year; this makes for all of them together a matter of 878,226 florins. Subtract from this sum a fourth for the planters, both Christians and Jews, who buy what they need from the merchants of the country, and there will nonetheless remain 658,679½ florins which the merchant proprietors, or the correspondents in Holland, send to the planters, from which they derive a considerable profit, without further counting the immense amount of merchandise and of fine furniture which the merchants of Holland send to the colony annually for their own account, for that of private individuals, and for the shops (of which there is an excessive number), which altogether, without exaggeration, can be calculated at almost 1,500,000 florins a year.

These profits, added to those which the captains of the vessels derive for the drygoods and foodstuffs brought in by them for the account of the merchants of Holland; the profits of other considerable markets; the freight of the vessels; and the enormous expenses incurred in the sale of the products of the colony in Holland, with insurance at an excessive rate to the advantage of the mother country, will form, on a revenue of almost 9,000,000 florins per year which the colony in general makes, an annual profit of 5,000,000 to 6,000,000. [This is] without counting the interest on the money borrowed by the colonists and inhabitants of the colony in general, which can also be regarded as a real profit.

The commerce of the colony in general, both with regard to that which has a direct connection with the mother country, and with regard to that with the English Americans, and between colonists and colonists respectively, consists in the purchase and sale of drygoods and foodstuffs, such as iron, cloth, broadcloth, linen-cloth, hardware, clothes, hats, copper utensils, crockery, fine porcelain, wines, beer, brandies, and, finally, everything of the most exquisite kinds which luxury of clothing and good living can devise: flour, salt, meats, refined sugars, etc., etc. For the sale thereof, there was formed a prodigious number of shops, most of them situated on the bank of the river; and food stores and stores for most of the things brought in by the Americans for the provisioning of the Negroes of the plantations. And if the interests of the Republic could permit making Surinam a free port, and if the colonists themselves had permission to sell their products, the colony would no doubt experience a happy change, without, however, causing any damage to the mother country. But in order to realize this idea and to make it possible and profitable at the same time, it would be necessary for great geniuses to meet together once, to reconcile the interests of the colonists with those of the mother country, and then, perhaps, this great truth, of which we perceive only a sketch still surrounded by clouds, would appear in full daylight.

Every kind of specie is current in Surinam; but, unfortunately, scarcely anything is to be found but paper money printed in the country; this takes the place of current money.[16] There are also Danish shillings [escalins] introduced into Surinam in great numbers since 1768 or 1769, particularly by a grease-merchant[17]; these are current in Holland at only three and a half to four sous; they pass here for five sous, and there is a further profit of 5 percent when they are exchanged for the paper money of the colony.

Establishment, and Purpose, of the Offices of the Colony, and the Taxes Which the Colonists and Inhabitants Pay

We shall be very concise on this matter, and in order not to expose ourselves to uncertain information, we shall say only what everyone knows in Surinam.

By virtue of the grant of Their High Powers accorded to the West India Company under date of September, 1682, which forms the basis of the municipal law of the colony, the Lords Proprietors receive a right of a capitation-tax, which consists in the annual payment, after the first ten years of residence of the inhabitants, of fifty sous a head for those over twelve years of age and twenty-five for those between the ages of three and twelve years, not only for whites, but also for free Negroes and free Mulattoes and for slaves without distinction; this is paid to the capitation-tax office, called *Hoofdgeld.*

All Dutch vessels are subject to the fees of entry and departure, the same as English-American boats; the former pay three florins per 4,000 pounds, and the latter double that rate, with the exception of 5 percent for each cargo which they bring into the colony, and for the molasses which they export, together with other fees which they pay to various other agencies. Coffee which is exported to the mother country pays fifteen sous for each 100 pounds, cotton thirty-five sous, and a barrel of sugar a florin.

These fees are collected by another office known under the name of *in-en-uitgaande Rechten,* import and export.

The office of public sales receives a fee of 5 percent on everything which is sold there, charged to the purchaser, with the exception of the sales of Negroes newly brought in from the coasts of Africa, which pay only 2½ percent. Aside from this, those who make the sales pay 3 percent on everything that is sold there.

The net yield of these three offices belongs to the Lords Proprietors, the yield of the first two by virtue of the beneficial domain which they have over the colony, and the yield of the third by the favor of an agreement with the administrative council, confirmed by Their High Powers.

Besides these contributions, the inhabitants pay various taxes which are collected by various offices to provide for the expenses which are charged to the inhabitants, in accordance with agreements made on different dates with the Lords Proprietors and subsequently approved by Their High Powers, as we have noted in its place. Thus in order to meet the expenses of the detachments against the Negro runaway slaves, the defense of the colony, and the maintenance of the cordon, that is to say, for the portion which is charged to the inhabitants, there was established an office [to take action] against the runaway slaves, known under the name of *Cassa tegens de Wegloopers.* There, each inhabitant and merchant declares, under oath before two commissioners of the political council and the receiver, the profits which they make in their trade, their business, the yield of their capital, and of the sum which they declare, they pay from 4 to 9 percent, according to a certain division which was made in various classes. The planters pay for the products of their settlements in the following manner: the price of each pound of coffee is calculated according to the latest placard published in December, 1787, at the rate of seven and a half sous, cacao at three and a half sous, cotton at nineteen sous, and each barrel of sugar at seventy florins; and of the total of that which forms the commodities produced on each settlement, 5 percent is paid to the said agency. Besides this, for each cession or transfer of land which one inhabitant makes to another, one pays 3 percent of the amount of the purchase each time this land passes to new owners. This agency is for the purpose of providing for the expenses necessary for the defense of the country, and to pay the collector, who draws as his wages a certain percent of the amount which he collects each year.

To the agency of the community, or *Gemeene Weide,* there is paid the tax on houses according to the value which is estimated on the basis of their annual rent, at 2 percent a year, the same as for the apportionment of animals; twenty florins for a carriage, ten for a chaise, and the same amount for a riding horse. Each square foot of wood unloaded in the city to be sold there pays, according to quality and size, from four duttes to 1 sou, and each plank of fifteen-foot length and an inch thickness pays thirteen duttes, and for each of twenty-foot length and one-and-a-half inch thickness five sous. The yield of this office is intended for the maintenance of the roads, of the ports, of the lanes of trees planted on the streets, and for other works necessary and continuous for the embellishment of the city.

The agency of moderate charges, *modique lasten,* collects three florins ten sous for each barrel of beer; twenty florins for a barrel of wine; four florins for a case of fifteen bottles of brandy or of gin; two sous for each bottle of wine of any sort imported into the colony; 500 florins a year for each large inn; and 250 florins for every other tavern, for the privilege of being permitted to operate these public houses. Besides these taxes, this office collects the post office fees, which form a considerable amount. Their yield is intended for the payment of the ecclesiastical ministers of the Reformed religion, the wages of the first prosecutor, and various other needs of the colony which are charged to the inhabitants. Besides these fees, this agency receives also, for the benefit of its treasury, the net income of the agency of the exempt officers of the colony, known under the name of *exploicteurs,* for the expenses imposed upon the inhabitants in the name of civil justice, both for the seizure of the property of private persons in litigation, as well as for the sale thereof at auction, according to the law; this causes as much expense as its net revenue, after the payments made to the employees, etc. Besides, this constitutes the most substantial part of the receipts of the said agency of moderate charges.

Description of the Savane and of the Cordon, Climate of the Colony in General, the Diseases, Character of the Creoles, etc.

Eight or ten leagues from Paramaribo, on the left bank of the Surinam river, as one sails up it, is to be found the village of the Jews called the Savane (a Spanish name, accepted generally in America, to designate a prairie, or a treeless extent of plain), because of the large prairies which surround it. It belongs in full ownership to the Portuguese Jewish community, according to a formal concession to the community by Samuel Nassy in September, 1682, to which he added, further, in August, 1691, twenty-five acres of adjacent land, according to short notes of these dates which are to be found in the archives of the community. This land was at once enlarged by the gift of 100 acres of land which was made by Governor van Scherpenhuysen in the name of the Lords of the colony in Holland, according to the *Warand,* which is found in the collection of the privileges, Title 8, dated September 12, 1691. This Savane is situated on a mountain which rises thirty to thirty-six feet above the level of the river, having on each side a deep valley, which gives the Savane the complete shape of an isthmus. The inhabited ground is formed of a very firm, clayey soil, mixed with stones of a reddish color which inclines a little to black.

Monsieur Renaud, a French botanist, who resided for several years in Surinam and who is at present in France, claims to have found there the lava of an ancient volcano, but the large quantity of white sand which is found 200 paces from this mountain renders this idea very doubtful and equivocal. The place where regularly built houses are to be found forms a rectangle 450 feet long by 300 wide, divided by four cross streets. The houses built at the corners of the rectangle are large and commodious, although of a mediocre architecture which still savors of the thrift of our ancestors; but some of them are tolerably handsome. The houses whose rears face the two valleys of the mountain and the river bank, each one of which has its little garden shaped in the form of a slope, planted with shrubbery and with pot-herbs for the house, present a view that is very agreeable as one approaches from the place of debarkation. In the middle of this rectangle is to be found the synagogue, built of brick in the year 1685, ninety feet long, forty feet wide, and thirty-three feet high, supported by large wooden columns with a properly constructed vault which covers the roof of the building. On one side is the section for the women; situated higher, and opposite it, in the section for the men, is a large ark of beautiful cedar, where the Scrolls of the Law are kept; it is of a beautiful architecture, and ornamented with very well executed sculptures which reflect much honor (considering the infancy of the colony [when it was made]) upon the one who fashioned it.

This church [*Cette Eglise*] has as its other ornaments the crowns of silver with which the Scrolls of the Law are decorated, and other necessary furnishings of the same metal, large candlesticks of yellow copper with several branches, and chandeliers of several kinds which cost the individuals who donated them a considerable sum. Below the synagogue or [more precisely below] the women's gallery there is a chamber where the regents hold their meetings, having next to it the archives of the Jewish community kept in very good order. Everything there is so properly built and the synagogue has such an indescribable majesty, that although its size is quite ordinary, it elicits the admiration of those who see it for the first time. On one side of the Savane there is a military post, and the warehouse of foodstuffs for the cordon, which starts from one of the corners of the Savane, opposite the synagogue, where the great prairie begins, which on one side encloses the cemetery of the community. In its center there is a sunken place more than 200 feet in circumference and filled with sand as white as snow, which is used for various purposes; it is transported to Paramaribo in great quantity, both for the service of the hospital as well as for that of individual persons, etc.

After passing this sunken place, one encounters the beginning of the two valleys which, if they were filled with water, would form the shape of two gulfs around the mountain. These two valleys are of the same extent and of the same depth; in their center, on white sandy soil, rise two small springs of water as cold as snow, whose somewhat reddish color indicates some ferruginous matter in the midst of the mountain. At the height of one of these valleys there is another spring of water of a very agreeable taste and of the most beautiful crystalline color. This spring comes from the summit of the mountain and, winding to its very middle, it makes a passage for itself and flows in regular manner between small shrubbery. It seems that nature, in making this mass of water flow in the prescribed manner, has joined together its various small canals into one single tube, which has flowed as from a faucet ever since the Savane has been known. Never, whether in winter or in summer, and even in periods of intense heat, have this spring and the two ponds of water been seen to dry up, to be diminished, or to be increased. The physician Stuyvesant, who lived for a long time in Surinam (at present he resides in Utrecht), made several tests on the water which flows from the top of the mountain, and he found it very deobstruent [laxative] and diuretic, and the experience which we have had with it a thousand times confirms this truth. For when one takes some of this water in summer, or at a time when one can be sure that it is not at all mixed with rainwater and drinks it with Rhine wine and sugar, one finds the same effervescence and the same effect as if it were seltzer or spa water, with the exception of the odor and of the saline taste which these waters have, from which this water is in every way free. The Jews make use of it in treating tertian fevers and constipation.

A little in front of the mountain there commences the cordon or line of defense of the colony (of which we have spoken), formed alternatively by a captain's post, a picket, a sergeant's post, etc., up to the major's great post called Mauritzburg, where there is the hospital to which the sick of the other posts are brought to be cared for. Beside this post is the economic residence [*l'habitation oeconomique*—headquarters?] of the cordon, known, following the government of Monsieur Beeldsnyder, under the name of *"Gouverneurs Lust,"* and before that under that of "Rehobot" (a Hebrew word meaning "rest" [*sic*—actually, it means "spaciousness"]). This residence encloses in its precincts beautiful gardens planted with herbs, with fruit-bearing and kitchen-garden shrubs, with large meadows where a sufficient number of cattle are kept. [The herbs and shrubs are] for the service of the hospital of Mauritzburg and also for the horses and mules necessary for the transport of foodstuffs for the Savane and for the various posts that are found on the road. Everything there is so solidly and regularly constructed and maintained that, without lapsing into any luxury whatsoever, or having anything there which is not indispensable and necessary, the habitation has a very agreeable look. It is there that criminals, both whites and Negroes and in chains, go to work in order to expiate their crimes, and it may be called the *Rasphuis* [house of correction] of Surinam. From the major's post at Mauritzburg, one arrives at the source of the river Commowine by a four-hour march; upon crossing it, one finds the beginning of the second cordon, which ends almost at the sea.

The road of the first cordon which begins at the Savane, of the width of 150 to 200 feet on a foundation of white sand, with one side lined with posts and others with a thick grove, forms, whether by carriage or on horseback or even on foot, the most beautiful promenade that one could desire.

There were formerly at the Savane seventy-five to eighty houses, occupied by fifty to sixty families, each of them with four to six slaves and foodstuffs which they got gratis from the adjacent plantations. They made planks and beams for the neighborhood, from which they derived their subsistence. At the present time, since the Jewish community has lost the greatest part of its plantations, and since five-eighths of its members reside in the city of Paramaribo, this village is almost deserted, to the point where there are only twenty-two poor families living there and forty-nine houses. All the others have fallen into ruins, because of the inability of the owners to repair them. These poor people, to the number of 100 to 120 persons who live there, before this time derived their maintenance from the trade which they carried on with the soldiers and officers of the cordon, to whom they furnished everything they needed at the prices current in Paramaribo. But since, unfortunately, there are at present many competitors who do business with the soldiers, the poor inhabitants of the Savane find themselves in such a deplorable condition that one day or another this village is necessarily going to be abandoned. Nevertheless, since the synagogue and the freedom which are to be found there attach the Jews to this place, people are never lacking, in the month of September of each year, for the celebration of the Feast of Tabernacles, sometimes to the number of 200 to 250 persons who come from Paramaribo and the plantations, and then fill all the houses. In this month there never fails to be also a large number of Christians, who likewise come to visit the place and to promenade on the cordon. And despite the deplorable condition of the Jewish community in general, nonetheless little parties for dancing and rejoicing are given there, and these make the place, for the period of four weeks, an agreeable sojourn; and since the air which is breathed there is, by constant experience, the healthiest in the entire colony, and since the Savane is, besides, the sole place of retreat where one can sojourn and conduct one's household with all imaginable liberty, it never fails to be frequented during the festival, but after that time, everything becomes sad and dismal.

The whole place, considered carefully, offers in its own manner simple beauties of nature, worthy of notice. The mixture of the verdure of the grasses on the meadows and of shrubs of various kinds, which bear flowers and small fruits of various colors, scattered over a base of white sand; the two valleys which run along the mountain and which disclose on both sides two other mountains white as snow; to the west, the view of the synagogue and of the village; to the east, the beautiful road of the cordon drawn in a straight line up to five hours' march [;] to the north the descent of the mountains and the view of the river; and to the south, the verdure of a vast forest—these form a view so pleasing that strangers, among others the Ordonnateur [Governor] General of Cayenne, Monsieur de Malouet, who considered it attentively in 1776, were impressed at seeing how nature, in its economy, yet was able to embellish the place which it had rendered sterile. We were compelled to dwell, perhaps at too great a length, on the description of the Savane because we have noticed that of all the authors who have written on Surinam, none has deigned to say something about it. It was enough that it was a small village of Jews in order, as it were, to speak of it only in passing.

As regards the climate of the colony in general, it has been, since the great clearing of the land made on the settlements, and since the rivers, which have been enlarged considerably, gave the winds free passage, the healthiest of the entire Guiana coast. The heat there would be excessive from August until mid-November if it were not tempered by a northwest wind, which prevails almost continually from July up to November. There are many clouds which moderate the burning heat of the sun, and which yield frequent and abundant rains, and it is then that the winds sometimes change to the southeast. The days and the nights are almost equal all year around; it is only in the month of July up to mid-August that one notes that the days are twenty-five to thirty minutes longer than the nights. The four seasons of the year which are observed in Europe are not felt in Surinam; we reckon our winter from January, which varies continually until March; spring from April until June; summer from July up to August; and autumn from September up to November and sometimes up to December, when the rains begin; but they are so mingled with heat, with cold in the mornings, with rains, with winds, and with a burning sun that the seasons become all mixed up, without having anything perceptible whereby to distinguish them.

The sicknesses which most frequently prevail there are catarrhs and the whooping cough, which cause many ravages among children; fevers of all sorts, principally the bilious ones; dropsy, inflammation of the spleen, dysentery, and all those which produce venereal diseases, which are perhaps the cause of a type of elephantiasis which, unfortunately, is beginning to prevail in Surinam among the whites and the Negroes. Children suffer a great deal from attacks of worms, and newborn children of the Negroes from tetanus, which carries off a prodigious number on the plantations, despite all imaginable attempts to cure them. Nevertheless, despite these maladies, there is no epidemic whatsoever there, except sometimes of dysentery on the plantations, but this causes very little ravage compared to the other places of America, where this malady has once appeared. On the contrary, all illnesses are cured very favorably, and more quickly than in any other place; but, to make up for this, convalescence there requires much care and trouble, and perhaps this is also only because of the scanty diet that is commonly observed there. The inhabitants are active, vigorous, and impetuous. They sometimes become ill as the result of the excesses which they commit, and they do not have the patience to adhere to their diet, or to take advantage of the rest periods which they need in order not to languish in the period following their illnesses. Among the Christians, the great use of strong drinks, the little knowledge which they generally have of having recourse, for the cure of their diseases, to the simple and exotic medications of the country before they go to the physicians or to the Negroes, make them succumb more quickly to the least inflammatory or bilious attack than do the Jews, who follow their own method constantly, drink only very little wine and liqueurs, and eat at noon much fruit and confections, although they make much more use of oil, fat, spices, and pepper in large quantity than do their other fellow inhabitants.

Those who are born in the colony are, in general, of tall and advantageous figure. The colors of their faces still preserve, with some modifications, the colors of the country where their ancestors were born. There is never any hunchback or lame person born there, or anyone afflicted with the deformities which are often met with in Europe. The fair sex especially distinguishes itself advantageously, principally among the Jews, of whom the German women, both by that lively and animated coloring which forms the radiancy of their sex, as well as by their alluring eyes, must hold the first rank. These women lack only education and the knowledge of the great world for them to have in any respect to yield to the most distinguished European women. But [they suffer] the lack of everything needed to form the soul of a society, ignorance of languages which deprives them of a lively conversation, of that agreeable tittle-tattle so natural to the sex; besides, continually chattering in Negro-English and surrounded by Negresses, the women and their daughters, generally speaking, despite their beauty, are so timid and embarrassed when they find themselves in a company composed of several strangers, that one can almost say that they pretty much approximate the inanimate portraits which decorate the partitions of their apartments. Yet they do not at all forget the penchant, natural to women, for finery, or for whatever can augment their natural beauty.

The men there are about the same as everywhere, with the difference that at the age of twelve or fourteen years, they know the art of reproduction, which is at once cultivated with the most ardent zeal. This disorder comes only from communication with the Negroes, and from the little care which relatives take at home to restrain themselves in the presence of the children. The cause thereof is the free talk which is capable of stimulating desires. Nevertheless, we must say with pleasure that this fault is not so common among the Portuguese Jews, generally speaking, principally when it is a question of the least conversation, no matter how little free it is, before the daughters of the house; for it is the first care of the mothers not to leave their daughters with the Negresses, and never to go out of the house without having them at their sides. And it is further, because of this constant care and these assiduous efforts, that the Portuguese Jewish children in Surinam are more attached to their parents than in any other place.

"A vivacity of spirit, a singular penetration, a promptitude to grasp all ideas, and to convey them with fire; the power of combining, jointly with the talent of observing, a happy mixture of all the qualities of the mind and of character which render man capable of the greatest things," make up the distinctive character of the Creoles in general, according to Abbé Raynal, Volume 6, page 168. And this definition, a little modified, is especially applicable to the Surinamese in general. But this hot imagination which he further notes there, which cannot suffer any restraint—if we may correct Abbé Raynal—does not make them incapable of all the exact sciences, and of everything which can be acquired only through much study and meditation! Even music, this divine art that strikes and touches the sensibility of man, was never learned by any Creole to the extent that he was able to call himself a musician; for, rebuffed from the very beginning by the accord of the notes and the analogy of the sounds to form proper melodies from them, they quit their lessons and then come back to them after a time, and always by leaps and bounds. The dance and all exercises of the body are those which interest them for a longer time. In poetry and in bellettristic diversions, which ought in consequence to amuse their lively and sparkling spirits, they only make continual leaps like birds on a tree who jump without ceasing from one branch to another.

Thus, in consequence of these faults of inconstancy in their minds, would not one be tempted to believe that Creoles in general do not know friendship, and that they know how to appreciate only that which can impress their tastes, and that even when rebuffed at the beginning of various enterprises, they must be vain and inconstant? Yet it is incontestable that they are constantly hospitable and generous. They love gold; but they do not adore it, and it is only to spend it and even to make gifts of it that they love to possess money.[18]

Medicine. Empiricism. Deceit of the Negroes in General

Medicine is practiced there in the same manner, and with the same method, as everywhere else, and although it is necessary to follow there the dispensary of Amsterdam or of The Hague, there are filled in the pharmacies all sorts of prescriptions, according to the dispensaries of the various places of Europe, to comply with the views and even the caprices of the physicians. And it is for this reason that the pharmacies of Surinam are enriched by an immense number of medicaments of every sort, besides being adorned by everything that can flatter the eye. The children of Aesculapius [physicians] at present number eight: four Christians and four German Jews; a number of surgeons; and eight apothecaries: six Christians and two Jews, one Portuguese and one German; three accoucheurs: one Christian, one a Spanish Jew, and one a German Jew, who are included in the number of physicians and surgeons.

The art of healing in Surinam, even generally supposing that all those who profess it have the necessary talent and experience, will never make any perceptible progress there as regards the art; nor will it contribute much to the fortune of those who practice it; because the best remedy, the most exact observation, becomes useless by reason of the mixture that is generally made there with the cures of the Negroes, who play the greatest role with their herbs and their pretended cures, both among Christians and among Jews. For despite the deceit of these empiricists, despite their frightful ceremonies unworthy of all those who profess a religion, they are regarded as prophets in Surinam. Never was any miracle so boasted about as those of these Negroes, or respect paid to the assurances and to the faith which men, and, above all, the white women of the country, join thereto to praise their singular merits. If a sick person happens to die under the hands of these empiricists, the most stupid and the most foolish that one can imagine, it is not at all their ignorance or their medicaments, employed without any order or method whatsoever, that have contributed to his death; but it is the poison which was given to the sick person, according to the report of the pretended physician. And, adding faith to these false assurances, one has the misfortune to lapse sometimes into injustice against those who were accused or suspected by these Negroes, themselves rather poisoners than physicians.

Yet we do not disagree that some sick people have been cured under their ministrations, especially those who were attacked by strong delirium after or during very strong illness, or after childbirth. But these cures are most often effected by the antidotes which they know how to employ against various kinds of poisons and which they know how to administer to the sick from the information they receive from the Negresses of the house. Most frequently a person who has been cured by them of a delirium or of some strong abdominal tension is at first suspected of having been poisoned. This truth, which experience has many times confirmed, is still the reason why, when a sick person dies of a known illness, one that the physician of the house himself has predicted, his death is at first attributed vaguely to poison. This might go on to infinity, if we wished to expose the abuses that have taken place in this regard. Nevertheless, we shall give a short exposition of the ordinary manner in which these Negroes effect their cures.

When a sick person wishes to put himself in the hands of one of these empiricists, of whom there is an immense number of both sexes, he has him summoned. The latter never comes at once, but ordinarily one, two, or three days later, apparently in order to provide himself with sufficient knowledge of all that takes place in the house of the sick person, and for that they always have someone there in a position to give them this information.

Having arrived at the home of the sick person, he asks him what pains he has, for instance, in what part of his body? Is your head affected, or is it a fever, or inflammation of the stomach, etc.? Do you feel these indispositions strongly, or are they moderate, etc.? The Aesculapius, without informing himself more thoroughly, always makes signs of wonder. Well, he is asked, will you cure him?—All is in the hands of God. I shall see him, but . . . one must have patience, but . . . it is necessary to give something to God in order to help me with His lights. This demand, which is already known, always brings, according to the means of the sick person, two, three, ten, or twenty florins.

The physician goes off well content, and returns the same day, the next day, or three days later according to the condition and the need of the sick person. After coming back, he asks for a little brandy; he casts into it some pounded India pepper, known under the name of grana paradici, or *Malagueta scepre,* Malacca pepper. Then he drinks a little of it, and gives some of it also to the sick person, and throws the rest out of the window, the while muttering a few words. After that he asks for the most faithful Negress in the house. When she comes, he gives her a piece of root or of herbs, etc., to cook and give to the sick person; and from that day on, everything must pass through the hands of this Negress. If the sickness is feverish, it is India pepper mixed with herbs that is applied. If the head is affected, it is moistened with this decoction and with pepper. If the stomach is inflamed, or if it is a case of dropsy, the most irritating emetics and more pepper for rubbing him are applied. If there are pains, incisions are made like those for applying cupping-glasses, and on top of them are put more pepper mixed with ashes, which causes the sharpest pains to the sick person, and the stains of which, blackened by the ashes which penetrate into the incisions, are never effaced.

For all light illness, those sicknesses which appear externally, from whatever cause they originate, these they always pretend to cure with these same remedies. Some (whose disposition or nature, as Monsieur [Joseph?] Lietaud says, mocks the sickness and the physician) escape; others die or, more often, languish. A thousand deceitful tricks are employed for the cure of sick Negroes. We have seen them suck, from a pipe in a wound, pieces of scorpions or of other insects which they claim had been drawn out of them and which those present simply believed to be the truth. Yet when one examines them before they make the operation, one discovers their deceit. A Negress was ill after a miscarriage, and she asked her master to have her cured by one of these Negroes. He came, gave her some beverages, and said in advance that in three days the Negress would expel the bones of a second foetus which she still had in her womb. When the day had arrived, he made his grimaces and told the Negress to look in the chamber-pot after she had urinated into it. She did so, and to the astonishment of the women, little bones were seen in the bottom of the chamber-pot. This was acclaimed as a miracle, but they were only the bones of small birds which had been picked up and thrown into the pot at the moment when the

Negress went to it. A woman was sick, and it was said that she had been poisoned; the physician appeared, and said to the woman: You will vomit up the poison. Then, the next day, he gave her an emetic; the sick person threw up some bile, and after she had vomited, the Negro poured out the water and showed those present little balls of cotton and little bits of hair. How was this introduced into the body of the sick person? How conceive the possibility of poison wrapped up in cotton and hairs? But those present did not attempt to unravel this mystery; they praised his success and spread abroad everywhere the pretended miracle that had been effected.

This is, in general, the manner in which most of the Negroes cure sicknesses in Surinam, and the basis which one has there for giving credence to their pretended miracles. Yet despite all these deceits and the disturbances which their barbarous methods cause to the health and the minds of most of the women of the country, and even of the men, we admit that there have always been in the colony, and [are] even at the present time, some Negroes who have a special knowledge of the medicinal plants of the country, by means of which they have effected cures, to the astonishment of the physicians. We know some persons, white and Negro, who have escaped death through them; but it is not to these Negroes, whose number is very small, to whom people often have recourse, but rather to those whom one Negress or another who wishes to favor them gives assurance that they are good physicians. It is enough that one is colored black to be in a position to do more than all the physicians together. This blind confidence most often causes some women to fall into a credulity which is reproachable in many respects.

Everyone knows the Negro dance which is commonly called "Mama," which goes on until they fall into a faint and which can be compared, with very little modification, to the "St. Vitus dance" which Monsieur Lieutaud describes in his treatise on practical medicine. The most renowned priestess is a Negress called Dasina; she has in her house a secret chamber, to which her initiates have free entry. This chamber is surrounded by little idols in human and animal shapes, crudely made of earth. In a corner there is a large earthen pot filled with water in which she keeps some small adders.[19] And before taking on some sick person to cure, she consults her pot and her figures which are her oracles, and she gives the sick persons some water that is in the pot to drink. Despite a number of false cures and of false prognostications which this Negress often makes, her word is nonetheless believed. Although no one fails to take a white physician for sick persons, she very often deceives him by clandestinely adding her remedies to the remedies which he prescribes if the sick person is in danger, or by suppressing them completely if he gives hope of a cure.

Yet it is the greatest pity that no efforts at all are made in Surinam to buy from these same Negroes the quantity of medicinal plants which they know, so as to make a happy use of them. Only sacrifices of money are necessary to get everything from them, which would be a great good fortune for the colony in general, and especially for the plantations. For how many roots and herbs do we not have here which surpass the Quassy wood, discovered by the Negro of this name and which caused such talk in Europe? Thus it is not necessary to believe that, because these Negroes practice deceptions in their cures, they do not know the plants that are suitable for some illnesses. Their simple report is worth more in these cases than all that they perform themselves, for they do not at all know the sicknesses so as to be able to apply them successfully, nor do they know how to diagnose the causes that have produced them, to increase or diminish the doses, or to mix them with some corrective in proportion to the illness. But these medicaments, well known and distinguished with exact notes of the illnesses to which they are applicable, according to the definition of these Negroes, would be sufficient to make of them a treasure for humanity, as soon as they were directed by experienced physicians.

The Negro Quassy, who gave his name to the wood which he discovered and made himself famous in Surinam through his pretended witchcraft, engaged for a long period of years the minds of most of the colonists. He was often employed to go to the plantations to discover the poisoners among the Negroes; he was consulted on all sorts of illnesses, even to give remedies for the sterility of women. The acuteness of his intellect, the considerable knowledge which he was able to acquire from the Indians among whom he was almost continually, an austere and majestic tone (accompanied by a colossal figure) which he knew how to employ when he spoke to the Negroes, procured for him so great an influence among them that they respected him as a priest to whom God deigned to reveal His orders. He was attacked, from his youth on, by elephantiasis, which he himself was able to cure totally, and despite the loss of four fingers of one hand and almost all his toes which were eaten away by the sickness, no mark at all remained of it; his face and all his body were so smooth and so clean that no one would venture to believe that he had been attacked by this baneful disease.[20] This cure procured for him great credit, and even sufficient influence among the whites, so that no one refused to consult him clearly for all one's needs. But such excessive confidence caused him to abuse the kindness of the whites and led to many false accusations against the Negroes. For, relying too greatly on his knowledge, he did not make sufficiently accurate researches, nor did he observe the appearances and the operation of an accused conscience, which often reveals itself upon the countenance. For it is only by this method, accompanied by good information on the part of the Negroes which he knew how to acquire at once, that he was able in some cases to find out things which appeared to be most hidden.

In order to undeceive those who, blinded by the actions of the Negro Quassy, attributed everything to supernatural knowledge, a certain Monsieur Pichot took it upon himself to try an experiment. In order to achieve his purpose, he took from his house four or six silver forks and carefully laid them away somewhere without communicating his procedure to anyone. The forks having been missed, he threatened the Negresses of the house with a dreadful punishment if the thief were not revealed to him. The Negresses, being innocent of this theft, unanimously asked for the *Loacouman* Quassy, that is to say, the Diviner. The master had him called, and offered him a double payment if he discovered the thief. Therefore he commenced his ceremonies, and after having made the women slaves pass before him according to the custom, he called them back a second time. The lot fell on one of them. The poor accused woman, confused and trembling, denied the deed, contradicted herself, stammered, and finally the imposing tone of the diviner wrested a confession from her. "Where are the forks?" he is asked. He makes no reply. "You must tell me," said the master to Quassy. "Monsieur, put this Negress under the rods, and she herself will tell you." Monsieur Pichot, with an air of satisfaction and in the presence of a number of people whom he had in his house to witness this scene, had the chest in which he kept his papers brought to him and closed the door of the house. He opened his chest as though to pay the diviner, and drew out the six forks which he himself had put there, and said to the diviner, "Liar, scoundrel, behold your lies and your crime committed against an innocent person." The diviner, completely confused, did not know what to answer, and a good shower of blows with the cane which Monsieur Pichot gave him caused him to leave the house ashamed and troubled.

The same thing happened with another one in regard to a gold ring which the women are accustomed to wear when they sew. Six months after a poor Negress had been cruelly whipped as the thief of this ring, following the divination of Quassy, the master of the house received from his correspondent in Holland, to whom he had sent a case of several small bottles of the jams of the country, a letter of thanks, conveying his respects to his wife because she had prepared the jams with her own hands, because he was sending back to her her gold ring which he had found in one of the small bottles. A thousand frauds of this nature occurred in the case of this pretended sorcerer, who otherwise had much knowledge and who died in 1787 without anyone's having extracted from him any secret at all.

Yet, despite these facts and several others known to the entire colony, the inhabitants still love to lend faith, without reflection, to the deceits of the other Negroes, who possess neither the capacity nor the genius of the said Quassy. In order to recognize still more clearly the ignorance of these Negroes, one has only to consult the apothecaries of the colony, and then one will know that the greatest part of the Negroes, not having the least knowledge of the medicinal plants of the country, come to buy medical drugs of whose virtues and often even of whose names they are ignorant, so that it is necessary to conjecture or guess in order to supply them. Besides, there is another disadvantage aside from that which we have just reported. Even surgery (although the Negroes almost never intermeddle at all in this line) sustains harm, because the surgeons who maintain infirmaries in their homes for Negroes who are afflicted with sores cannot make any progress, because their patients, in order to escape from the labors of the plantations, always have means which these empiricists furnish them to keep their sores for a long time, in order not to be handed over to their masters in a state of health.

We shall perhaps be accused of having spoken at too great length

HISTORY OF SURINAM 163

with regard to the deceits of the Negroes of the colony. Yet, if one carefully considers the disadvantages which the talents so gratuitously attributed to them cause to the colony in general, we flatter ourselves that we will be excused for the details which we have given about them, in favor of our good intention which envisages only the welfare of the colony in general and the remedy of the disorders which take place very often. Besides, if Father [Benito Gerónimo] Feijoo [Feyjoo y Montenegro], a Spanish Jesuit, wrote in his *Théâtre Critique* [*Theatro Critico Universal* (1733)] several treatises on spectres and on ghosts with the intention of correcting his nation on these blind beliefs, it seems to us equally permitted to try at least the most proper means to cure our amiable colonists of a blind belief which causes them, without their thinking of it, an infinity of evils.

LITERATURE IN GENERAL. LITERARY SOCIETIES, LIBRARIES, ETC.

It has been seen, from all that which we have said in the course of this work, that education in Surinam has at all times been too limited. Only writing is learned there, a few rules of arithmetic, a little grammar, the elements of the language of the country, and those of French. As soon as a child of the age of twelve to fourteen years knows how to write well, he is placed with some person or other, at the secretariat or elsewhere, to learn the art of copying. And when he knows how to write well, the parents are satisfied and regard their child as capable of advancing in all the sciences. Consequently literature could make no progress in Surinam. Before the time of Monsieur Mauritius, in general nothing of what concerned letters was known; he himself said this in several places of his work of poetry, printed at Amsterdam by Schouten in 1753, page 166. After this time people began little by little to procure Dutch, French, and Spanish books, and with the aid of several European Frenchmen who came here from time to time, the taste for literature began to grow; but no literary society was formed until the time of Governor Texier. [Such a society was formed then] through his efforts and those of the Prosecutor Wichers, who was the first to establish a college for researches into nature, of which we have spoken.[21]

Many years before this time, Monsieur de Montel, a Portuguese Jew, a great lover of French literature, had begun a steady correspondence with Monsieur Marc Michel Rey, librarian in Amsterdam, and he furnished works to all the booklovers of Surinam. The late Governor Texier, Monsieur Wichers, Lieutenant Colonel Frederici, the physician van Wiert, the late Monsieur de Meinertshagen, the physician Schilling, the late Monsieur van Dam, and several other Christian and Jewish booklovers created at Surinam a library that was so large and so filled with works on all subjects that it yields in no respect to any other in all America and equals several of the large libraries of Europe. The taste for literature having been formed by reason of the ease of procuring works in the libraries of private persons, which they voluntarily lent to those who asked for them, created there several years ago the taste for forming literary societies in imitation of that for researches in nature; but on other subjects. We have spoken of that of the Portuguese Jews, and even inserted the prospectus in the justificatory document No. 21. Besides that one, there are two where the members meet once a month to communicate to one another the contents of the works which they receive from Holland for their society, and to sell the same works among themselves. Another one, under the name of "Surinaamse Lettervrienden," was established in 1786; there essays are written on Dutch poetry and on the purity of the language, and each member furnishes the best that his intelligence and talent suggest to him. This is then corrected jointly, and one or two volumes of poetic productions that have come out of this college are printed annually at Paramaribo.

Yet despite this fine appearance, literature there makes very little progress, since the majority of the inhabitants, and even several members of these societies, take few pains to entertain themselves with a book, or to hear lectures on literary subjects. As a result, often on evenings when meetings take place, the colleges are almost without a sufficient number of members, even to encourage those who take the trouble to compose some literary work. We Surinam Creoles, who have never seen Europe, or any other place in the world than the country of Guiana which we now occupy, ought to thank these gentlemen for the taste for literature which several of them have given us. The vast collection of instruments of physics, of medicine, of optics, and of several other curiosities, of the physician Schilling, has made us comprehend a thousand particulars of nature and has caused us to perceive various objects impossible to conceive of when one does not have an

HISTORY OF SURINAM

education formed by the necessary steps. And if someone there has some general notions, it is only the incisive intelligence of the Creoles, and their natural genius, that give them in general the power to grasp the consequences, without the help or the assiduity of a master. They make more progress from a simple instruction than is made otherwise in two years of school; but this instruction should not be confined to the theory of a science, where the most luminous logic is capable of giving sufficient notions to any European on any subject at all. It is always necessary that practice accompany it at the same time; the visible objects, and their eyes, so to speak, enlighten their intelligence more than elsewhere, and cause them to understand the progress and the analogy of what they see more easily than the Europeans themselves. For example, let there be explained to a Creole that the air which we breathe can be pumped out of us mechanically and that thus we can be entirely deprived of it, and he will comprehend nothing of this; but show him the pneumatic machine, make some little experiment in his presence, and immediately he understands the possibility and the truth, and will even be capable of reasoning very correctly about it, and so on.

If our knowledge were not so limited as it is, or if we were capable of entering into that which concerns the metaphysics of the human spirit, perhaps our modest observations, though disconnected [and] apparently incompatible, would be able to furnish material for several philosophical researches, the basis of which would be the mind and the genius of the Creoles of America and especially of Surinam.

The language which is generally spoken in the country is Dutch, and among the Portuguese Jews also Portuguese and Spanish. And although the French language is known by a large part of the inhabitants, it is not at all of such familiar usage as it is in Europe.

With the exception of the collection of insects known to everybody and which Madame [Maria Sibylla] Merian made in Surinam, no one since 1690 has ever thought of following her method in other branches, or to enrich her collection by new discoveries made in the place itself. Some observations and even discoveries made at random by various persons of the colony united together to form a body would be a very curious work; but where could the patience be found to assemble the details scattered in this home or in that one, and still more where to find the means or the designer to execute them and to put them in order? This dearth of knowledge forces us to refer our readers to the work of Madame Merian and to the details which are given in the *Histoire Générale des Voyages,* Volume 21, on the best-known insects and plants of Surinam.

The Life Led in Surinam, Amusements, Theatres, etc.

The inhabitants of the colony of Surinam are revolted by the description which the author of the *Tegenswoordige Staat van America* ["Present Condition of America"], which we have cited several times, has given of the life which is generally led here. Nothing is more false or more calumnious than everything which this author sets forth. The Surinamese would deserve to be regarded as the most debauched and despicable people in the universe if the least part of all that he says were true. The inhabitants in general are industrious, quick in their affairs, and very zealous to fulfil their duties to the advantage of those whom they serve. It is true that they love strong drink, and that in general they make much use of gin and of rum; but despite this they are neither drunkards, nor do they ever display any shameful spectacle. It is only in the small cabarets that are frequented until nine o'clock in the evening by sailors and by people of the lowest class that one sometimes hears the noise common among those who are affected by drunkenness. But the rest of the inhabitants always maintain a modesty and a wisdom so praiseworthy that one will perhaps find very few examples thereof in the other colonies. Never [is there] anything that can disturb the social order, no tumult in the streets, no company of giddy-headed young people during the night. Finally, it is very rare that anyone has to complain of his neighbor, or that any fracas happens in the streets. On the contrary, the most even life that one could imagine is led here. If news of Europe is lacking, all [life] is dull there [in Surinam]; there is simply no subject with which to entertain oneself; and lacking news or some new matters, one speaks ordinarily only about the general affairs of the country. Each one chats at his own will and with full liberty on politics, the economic government [policy], court trials, and the advantageous or disadvantageous seasons for the harvesting of the coffee, cotton, etc., on the plantations. Those who love reading entertain themselves with some other booklover, but as soon as some people come, one quits this party to amuse oneself with bagatelles of little consequence. One enters the home of another when it seems good to him and with the license of a good friend, seats himself at the table, stays, chatters, and leaves without ceremony or embarrassment. And it is everywhere the same, with the difference that the [various] classes of the inhabitants, despite their universal freedom, do not mix at all.

Several lodges of Freemasons constituted in the requisite order, both of Jews and of Christians, who visit mutually; some dance parties, most often made up of individuals who share the expenses; a private card game for the evenings; several cabarets where one goes to take refreshments before dinner; circles formed among the people of the first distinction each week or every two weeks at one another's homes; two theatres for Dutch comedy, one of the Christians and the other of the Jews, of which we have spoken, where twelve plays are presented in that of the Jews and six to eight plays in that of the Christians annually; promenades in the afternoon on horseback or in a carriage indulged in by the people who can afford this expense, etc.—such in general are all the amusements which there are in the entire colony. Again, most people entertain each other only in their own homes, and make use of all these public places only from time to time; so that one can say that the life which is led in Surinam, although the saddest and the most somber of any other place in the world, is yet the most salutary. Everything that the richest man can have, the poor man can equally have; and with the exception of high living, of a numerous cohort of slaves for the service of the home, and some ostentatious furniture, a man with a modest income does as much as a millionaire with his income in the thousands.

On the plantations, generally speaking, the managers get up at dawn, examine the surroundings, go to the gardens, and return to the house to take their coffee or tea, go off once again to inspect the jobs which the Negroes have done there, and return ordinarily at 10 o'clock. Then they breakfast very quickly, receive the mutual visits of their friends the other managers, and, if they are alone, they go to take a rest until two or three o'clock in the afternoon, return to the places of their work, and take their dinner and their supper together, ordinarily at six o'clock in the evening. In this fashion, and with this uniformity, they pass their lives delightfully. If there are some among them who get drunk and make an uproar with their neighbors, this is no reason at all to accuse the managers in general of all sorts of punishable irregularities, as the author of a letter inserted in the *Post van den Neder-Rhyn*, a Dutch periodical, No. 525, maliciously imputed to them.

We have completed the task which we imposed upon ourself to the extent to which it depended upon ourself, and to which considerations of politics and of conventions in several respects have permitted us to do. We do not doubt at all that in this work we have left out many things which are to be desired, many articles which are susceptible of great reflections which could be developed both in regard to the Jews in particular and in regard to the colony, its physical, moral, and political condition, in general. But if this work, despite its faults, is worthy of attracting the attention of the public and of effecting in some manner a change favorable to a community that has been unfortunate for so many centuries, then we shall consider ourselves happy.

The State of the Exports of the Colony of Surinam, from the Beginning of This Century until the Year 1788

Years	Barrels of Sugar	Pounds of Coffee	Pounds of Cacao	Pounds of Cotton	Pounds of Tobacco	Pounds of Roucou
1700	10,500					
1701	10,550					
1702	10,572					
1703	10,700					
1704	12,100					
1705	12,860					
1706	1,468¼		900	600		100
1707	18,499¾		925	325		925
1708	12,125¾					300
1709	18,401			743		600
1710	15,661			1,543		
1711	21,546¼					
1712	22,695½			2,587		
1713	14,568½			2,765	1,215	1,712
1714	22,028½			2,030		6,865
1715	19,532¼		400	1,780		4,429
1716	17,639¼		800	900		4,700
1717	14,552½			708		1,875
1718	12,435½		1,200	1,488		2,100
1719	17,316¼			760		2,169
1720	19,480¾			1,550		1,000
1721	25,848½			2,180		230
1722	29,866½			2,242		650
1723	20,734			1,540		200
1724	25,818	5,627		974		

Years	Barrels of Sugar	Pounds of Coffee	Pounds of Cacao	Pounds of Cotton	Pounds of Tobacco	Pounds of Roucou
1725	22,190¾	46,086	390	865		
1726	24,833¼	142,702	3,249	300		300
1727	26,660½	207,373	4,659	350		965
1728	25,836	230,162	1,372			220
1729	26,248½	272,165	339	156	10,464	315
1730	27,100	503,667				
1731	23,241½	530,032		1,230		783
1732	27,356	1,101,147	3,168	191		714
1733	20,756½	789,097	2,694	82		81
1734	22,488	1,257,006	355	66		
1735	17,169¾	1,376,335	3,875	316		
1736	25,525¾	1,620,365	14,550	533		
1737	21,560¾	3,256,472	16,933	437	302	
1738	20,648¾	2,401,260	30,315	1,677		
1739	19,131	3,184,933	56,951	2,206		
1740	24,228	4,971,246	77,853	3,334		
1741	25,362½	4,863,447	164,011	1,307		
1742	30,693¼	2,765,702	125,058	1,119		
1743	19,738¼	3,007,014	256,892	876		392
1744	22,342¾	3,497,121	407,021	1,025		238
1745	22,853¼	2,392,776	674,749	528		565
1746	19,691½	2,577,864	547,235	557		
1747	18,134½	4,100,001		510		
1748	20,069	1,407,547	320,861	581		
1749	22,741¾	3,167,021	287,896	300	29,945	

Years	Barrels of Sugar	Pounds of Coffee	Pounds of Cacao	Pounds of Cotton	Pounds of Tobacco
1750	30,754¾	3,536,339	338,882	114	1,988
1751	28,153½	4,331,298	205,307	3,572	2,168
1752	28,324	5,356,480	313,218	5,217	2,575
1753	15,280	2,888,650	140,319	8,392	2,730
1754	19,284	6,350,745	145,392	4,959	5,627
1755	16,417½	2,872,572	85,332	1,803	1,420
1756	22,501	6,763,627	163,712	1,449	
1757	18,169	8,696,486	107,404	1,838	
1758	14,998	6,789,286	123,842	785	
1759	18,737¾	10,859,313	102,012	2,078	
1760	21,014	10,206,487	128,482	1,292	
1761	22,173½	10,899,749	142,724	1,134	
1762	21,961	12,239,001	113,228	6,116	
1763	21,869½	13,712,281	119,108	8,701	4,630
1764	20,630	9,454,390	131,050	34,341	
1765	20,121	13,809,000	160,530	50,780	
1766	19,820	14,200,200	230,300	138,119	
1767	21,019	13,780,400	295,132	208,315	
1768	21,763	10,906,000	410,532	257,302	
1769	20,915	14,706,015	271,320	227,967	
1770	14,730	9,860,750	230,547	168,260	
1771	20,314	11,971,000	465,714	213,985	
1772	19,780	12,680,125	390,945	93,985	
1773	16,981	16,315,138	381,909	185,457	
1774	13,313	12,016,117	516,630	125,128	

HISTORY OF SURINAM

Years	Barrels of Sugar	Pounds of Coffee	Pounds of Cacao	Pounds of Cotton	Ships Leaving Surinam for Holland
1775	20,255	13,300,000	733,338	144,428	We have not
1776	17,350	11,750,000	650,155	330,127	been able to
1777	16,300	12,950,500	720,430	310,125	ascertain the
1778	15,975	11,150,300	630,170	280,000	number of ships
1779	14,795	13,100,800	530,430	430,175	leaving from
1780	15,700	11,750,000	570,350	650,800	Surinam from
1781	16,980	11,971,116	571,150	840,200	1774 up to
1782	17,327	10,812,814	580,345	975,546	today.
1783	15,673	12,587,535	490,855	1,125,454	
1784	14,324	12,913,465	560,194	1,020,587	
1785	16,176	9,787,300	670,136	930,413	
1786	16,750	12,976,170	675,940	936,700	
1787	15,744	12,129,756	802,724	925,967	

Years	Pounds of Indigo	Pounds of Beechwood	Pounds of Raw Wax	Pounds of Dyewood	Gallons of Copaiba Gum	Ounces of Gold	Vessels Leaving Surinam for Holland
1700							
1701		2,300					
1702		3,100					
1703		1,350					
1704		4,700					
1705		6,800					
1706		8,700					
1707		10,600					16
1708		10,800					20
1709		4,500					14
1710		7,758					13
1711	150	20,000			80		17
1712	138	30,920			161		21
1713		46,645			46		29
1714	1,328	18,695					17
1715	532	9,424					22
1716	109	65,611					24
1717	100	56,049					23
1718	1,100	18,602	600		13		17
1719					80		24 [22]
1720	180	1,500		2,700	36		20
1721		1,000					27
1722	505	82,385					32
1723		111,782					25
1724		157,908					29

HISTORY OF SURINAM 173

Years	Pounds of Indigo	Pounds of Beechwood	Pounds of Raw Wax	Pounds of Dyewood	Gallons of Copaiba Gum	Ounces of Gold	Vessels Leaving Surinam for Holland
1725		17,864					24
1726		17,000					29
1727		5,250			100		28
1728							27
1729							27
1730							29
1731							26
1732							32
1733							26
1734							30
1735							28
1736	14					5	35
1737		6,830					34
1738		9,250					33
1739							36
1740		17,621		35,537			44
1741							50
1742				4,056			50
1743							47
1744	270	11,200					46
1745				5,700			48
1746		6,903					43
1747							38
1748							40
1749							40

Years	Pounds of Beechwood	Pounds of Dyewood	Pounds of Simarouba Bark	Ships Leaving Surinam for Holland
1750				49
1751				49
1752				59
1753		2,000		39
1754	11,643	1,475		56
1755	9,897			38
1756	43,921		2,179	52
1757	4,861			55
1758	7,110			46
1759				53
1760				50
1761				55
1762				62
1763				72
1764				46
1765				64
1766				69
1767				68
1768				54
1769				65
1770				52
1771				65
1772				53
1773				57
1774				46

LIST OF THE EMPLOYEES OF THE COLONY GOVERNORS GENERAL

After we have finished our history, it seems to us that no one will be displeased at finding here the list of the governors who have successively ruled the Colony of Surinam under different masters in Europe; as well as the account of the commanders, prosecutors, and of other principal employees of the colony from its founding up to our own days.

Under English Rule

The Year 1665 . . . Francis Lord Willoughby of Parham, alone until the year 1662. Under the aforesaid Lord Willoughby and Laurence Hyde, by virtue of the charter of Charles II, King of England, dated June 2, 1662.

GOVERNOR

1662 to 1667. Monsieur Biam

Under the Province of Zeeland

February 27, 1667: Abraham Crynssen, Vice-Admiral, conquered the colony, and he left there as governor,

June, 1667: Captain Maurice de Rame, Governor General, named by the States [Legislature] of Zeeland without the concurrence of the [Dutch] States General.

December, 1668, to 1678: Phillippus Julius Lichtenberg, whose successor, named by commission of Their High Powers, and the Prince of Orange, by virtue of the sovereignty which they have always maintained over the colony, was, from

April, 1678, to 1680: Johannes Heinsius, who died at the end of April, 1680. From this time on and up to 1682, it appears from a remonstrance dated May 6, 1680, that the colonists desired that, instead of a governor, there be named an administrative council of twelve, instead of the seven which they had there. Of these, each one would have precedence for one month in the capacity of governor. And after debates with the members of the council whom they had at that time, it was decided to add to their number the following five persons:

1. Nicolaas Bruynings Wilderlandt
2. Isak van Muldert
3. Gerrit Wobma
4. Philip Bregt
5. Adriaan Hoogenkamp.

This arrangement (at least in regard to the presidency) had no effect for, according to the privileges of the Portuguese Jewish community, it is clear that Monsieur Laurens Verboom, commander under the administration of Monsieur Heinsius mentioned above, governed the colony, after his [Heinsius'] death, in the capacity of governor *ad interim,* although he had taken only the title of commander. Thus he can be regarded as the successor of the late Monsieur Heinsius, from May, 1680, up to the arrival of Monsieur van Sommelsdyk, as will be seen in the continuation of this list.

May, 1680, to November, 1683: Commander Laurens Verboom.

Under the Directors

The States of Zeeland, ceding the colony to the West India Company, and this latter to the three co-proprietors known then under the name of the Chartered Society of Surinam, Cornelis van Aarssens, Lord of Sommelsdyk, one of the co-proprietors, was named, by virtue of their agreement, governor general of the colony.

November 24, 1683, to July 19, 1688: Cornelis van Aarssens van Sommelsdyk, named above, from November 24 [1683], when he arrived in Surinam, until July 19, 1688, when he was assassinated, who was provisionally succeeded, from

July 19, 1688, until the 25th of the same month and of the same year: by Laurens Verboom.

July 25, 1688, to March 8, 1689: The administrative council, with Commander Abraham van Vreedenburg, until the arrival of

HISTORY OF SURINAM 177

1689 to 1695: Jan van Scherpenhuysen, March 8, 1689, and dismissed in 1695.
1695-1706: Paul van der Veen, October 20, 1695; dismissed in 1706.
1706-1707: Willem de Gruyter, October 23, 1706, and died in 1707.
1707-1715: Jan de G[o]oyer, April 15, 1707, and died in 1715.
1716-1717: Johan Mahoni, January 22, 1716, and died in 1717.
1718-1721: Jean Coutier, March 2, 1718, and died in 1721.
1721-1727: Henri Temminck, October 1, 1721, and died in 1727.
1728-1734: Charles Emilius de Cheusses, July 26, 1728, and died in 1734.
1734-1734: J. F. C. de Vries, then commander, provisionally from February, 1734, until July 9 of the same year, when there arrived there
1734-1735: Jacob Alexandre Henri de Cheusses, July 9, 1734, and died in February, 1735.
1735-1737: Jean Ray, July 6, 1735, and died in 1737.
1737-1741: Gerard van den Schepper, September 11, 1737, and died on November 1, 1741.
1742-1751: Jan Jacob Mauritius, February 7, 1742. In May, 1751, he was sent to Holland by the commissioners of the Prince, saving his honor and his wages. A month afterwards he was provisionally succeeded by the president of the commissioners of the Prince,
1751-1752: Baron de Sporcke, in May, 1751, and died on September 7, 1752, and was succeeded provisionally by the commander,
1752-1754: Wigbold Crommelin, in September, 1752, until March 6, 1754, when there arrived the effective governor,
1754-1756: Pieter Albert van der Meer, March 6, 1754, and died in August, 1756, and was succeeded provisionally, because of the absence of Monsieur Crommelin, by the above-mentioned
1756-1757: Jean Nepveu, then prosecutor and secretary of the administrative council of the country, after having passed through all the grades. Hence one can say that Nepveu had the same career in Surinam as did Abraham Patras, governor of the East Indies; and what is still more remarkable, Nepveu commenced his career there approximately at the same time as Patras finished his in the Great Indies, that is to say, in 1734.[22]

Nepveu, therefore, served as governor until the arrival of the effective governor,

1757-1769: Wigbold Crommelin, March 2, 1757. He resigned his position, with the consent of the directors, on October 27, 1769, in favor of

1769-1779: J[e]an Nepveu, mentioned above, October 27, 1769, and died on February 27, 1779.

1779-1783: Bernard Texier, at first provisionally, and after that effectively. Died on September 25, 1783.

1783-1784: Wolfert Jacob Beeldsnyder Matroos, provisionally through the departure of the first prosecutor, J. G. Wichers, for Holland before the death of Texier, September 25, 1783, to December 23, 1784, when the effective governor general of the colony arrived there, with the title of general major in the service of Their High Powers.

1784-: Jan Gerard Wichers, who is living at the present time.

COMMANDERS

We do not know those who held this position or its equivalent under English rule, or in the time of Governors J. Lichtenberg and Johan Heinsius. Under the Zeelanders, there was as commander

1678 to 1679: Monsieur . . . Versture, appointed on the . . . , and died or left for Europe on the . . . . He was succeeded, still under the Zeelanders until 1683, by

1679-1688: Laurens Verboom, who became governor *ad interim* through the death of Heinsius in 1680 until the arrival of Governor van Zommelsdyks [*sic*], when Verboom resumed his position as commander under the directors; he died on July 25, 1688.

Under the Directors

1683: The above-mentioned L. Verboom, who added to his position as commander that of the first administrative councillor, besides replacing the governor in all the affairs of the colony during his absence or in case of sickness. The successor of the said Verboom, in all his positions, was

1688-1703: Abraham van Vreedenburg, on September 3, 1688; he left for Holland in 1703.

1703-1725: François Antoine de Raineval, November 3, 1703; dismissed on October 3, 1725.

1725-1728: Johannes Bley, October 3, 1725, to September 16, 1728; he became commander emeritus; died on March 8, 1731.

1730-1735: Joh. Franc. Corn. de Vries, April 12, 1730; died on March 4, 1735.

1735-1737: Gerard van de Schepper, July 6, 1735; became governor on September 11, 1737.

1737-1742: Marcellus Brouwer, December 4, 1737; died on December 13, 1742.

1742-1746: Philippe Chambrier, May 30, 1742; dismissed on December 30, 1746.

1746-1748: Jean Louis Larcher van Kenenburg, October 22, 1746; died on May 10, 1748.

1748-1756: Wigbold Crommelin, October 9, 1748; he became governor *ad interim,* through the death of Baron de Sporcke, in 1752, and effective governor through the death of Governor van der Meer in August, 1756.

1756-1771: Charles Egon Delanges de Beauveser, May 4, 1757; died on April 1, 1771.

1771-1772: Arend de Jager, July 3, 1771; died on January 30 of the following year.

1772-1783: Bernard Texier, May 6, 1772; he became governor through the death of Jean Nepveu; he died in this capacity on September 25, 1783.

Since Texier, the office of commander and consequently of first administrative councillor was abolished, and in its place there is only a colonel commandant for the militia (at present, van Baerle), who does not interfere in anything that concerns the policy of the country.

FISCALS [Prosecutors]

1650-1683: We do not know those who held this office from the time of the English and the Zeelanders. But we do know that under the government of the Directors, there served as prosecutor of the colony, which, then and up to the year 1745, during the prosecutorship of

J. H. van Werven, included the office of first constable of the colony with reference to civil affairs:

1683-1683: C. Glimmer.
1683-1702: P. Mumi.
1702-1703: H. Muilman.
1703-1708: C. de Hubert.
1708-1727: Samuel Althusius.
1727-1735: Adriaan Wiltens.
1735-1745: Willem Gerard van Meel.
1741-1746: Jacob Halewyn van Werven. It was in his time that the position of constable of the colony for the civil division was separated from that of prosecutor.
1746-1749: Nicolas Antony Kohl.
1749-1749: Jacob van Baerle.
1749-1749: Jan Bavius de Vries, provisionally.
1749-1751: Samuel Paul Pichot, named by the commissioners of the Prince on the affairs of Governor Mauritius and never recognized as such by the Directors.
1751-1754: George Cortius, prosecutor. During his prosecutorship, there were established two prosecutors, and the position of auditor or military prosecutor was added to that of the second prosecutor, which [already] existed.
1754-1764: Jean Nepveu, second prosecutor; he became the first through the death of Cortius.
1764-1772: Bernard Texier, second prosecutor, and through the promotion of Nepveu to the office of effective governor, he was made the first prosecutor in 1769, and became commander in 1772.
1772-1780: J. G. Wichers, first prosecutor. J. H. van Heemskerk, second prosecutor. The latter became controller of the office of the pay chest against the runaway slaves. He was succeeded, in
1780-1785: by Cornelis Karsseboom, living at the present time, who became first prosecutor through the promotion of J. G. Wichers to the office of governor in 1784. He had as second prosecutor
1785-November, 1787: Monsieur van Meurs, who died in November, 1787. His positions, as second prosecutor, as auditor, and as pre-adviser of the council of civil justice, of which we shall speak later, are vacant.

CONTROLLERS GENERAL, OR MASTERS OF THE FINANCES OF THE COLONY

1766: This office was created by the Directors during the prosecutorship of Jean Nepveu in 1765 or in 1766, and was entrusted to him. It was, at that time, not regarded as of very great importance, and his wages were only 1,200 florins, at the request of Nepveu. This office passed to the second prosecutor, Texier, his successor, with many changes, both as regards the power and the extent of this office, and his wages.

F. E. Becker, who declined it sometime later and was then reappointed with an extension of his powers and an increase in wages.

W. J. Beeldsnyder Matroos, who became governor *ad interim* in 1783, desiring, after the arrival of the effective governor Wichers in 1784, to be appointed to the office of controller of the office of importation and exportation of the colony. He had as successor in the office of controller [general] Frans Gomarus, who is alive at present.

PREADVISER OF THE COUNCIL OF CIVIL JUSTICE

This office was created by the Directors, during the governorship of B. Texier. The first to be vested therewith was

1781: Cornelis Karsseboom, the second prosecutor of the colony and auditor. He became the first prosecutor in 1784. He had as his successor

1785: C. Meurs, who died in 1787. This position is vacant at present.

SECRETARIES OF THE TWO COUNCILS

UNDER THE ENGLISH GOVERNMENT

1662-1667: Jan Pary [John Parry].

UNDER THE ZEELANDERS

1680: A. van Gheluive.

UNDER THE DIRECTORS

From a certain period on, there were two secretaries at the same time, one for the administrative council, and the other for the civil [government]; they served both courts without distinction.

1684: Marcus Broa.
1688: Adriaan de Graaf.
1703: Abraham Kinkhuyzen.
1717: N. Strauch, Abm. Grommé, appointed together.
1717: Willem van der Waaijen.
1726: Abraham Bols.
1726: Pieter Brand.
1734: Willem Gerard van Meel, who became prosecutor in 1735.
1735: Ephraims Comans Scherping.
1737: Cornelis Graafland Jacobszoon.
1746: Jacob van Baerle, who became prosecutor in 1749.
1749: Jacob Fredrik du Fay.
1751: Jean Nepveu, who became second prosecutor in 1754. In the meanwhile, he served as secretary, until the arrival of
1755: Willem van Stamhorst, Junior.
1757: Anth. Voerst van Aversberg.

Secretaries

1759: François Ewoud Becker.
1764: Amadeus Constantinus Valencyn.
1768: Albert de Milly, who became controller of the office of importations and exportations in 1780 and was repatriated in 1784.
1773: W. J. Beeldsnyder, until his departure for Holland, and during his [Beeldsnyder's] absence, the first sworn clerk of the secretariat,
1776: J. E. Vieira, occupied his position; Beeldsnyder returning from Holland with the position of controlle. [general], [Vieira] came in for secretary.
1780: A. Gootenaar.
1780: C. Graafland, repatriated in November of the same year.
1780: C. Rappardt, who died in December, 1781.
1780: A. J. Halloy, who quit his position in 1783.
1783: J. J. Wohlfahrt, at present in office.
1786: Griethuysen, in place of Gootenaar, who died in this year, for the civil administration. The two last named [Wohlfahrt and Griethuysen] are at present in office.

JUSTIFICATORY DOCUMENTS for the CLARIFICATION of the WORK with REFERENCE to the HISTORY of the JEWISH COMMUNITY ESTABLISHED in SURINAM.*

No. 1.

Privilege or exemption, accorded and agreed upon by the Directors of the Chartered West India Company at the Council of the Nineteen, to David Nassy and Associates, as patron [*patroon*] or patrons of a colony to be established on the island of Cajana [Cayenne] or other places on the Wild Coast of the West Indies.

Article 1.

The aforesaid David Nassy and Associates are granted and permitted to establish a colony of four or five miles of land on the island and rivers of Cajana, consisting of as many pieces of landed property as shall be cultivated by the colonists, yet remaining so far from the [already established] colony on Cajana that they shall not be troublesome to the inhabitants there. They shall further agree to plant and to occupy the aforesaid colony within the first four years beginning at the latest on the first of September, 1660, under penalty that if this does not take place within that time, the uncultivated, unworked, uninhabited, and unpossessed land shall revert to the Company at that time and that it may deal with it as it sees fit.

Article 2.

The aforesaid David Nassy and his Associates shall have and enjoy jurisdiction over the bays that are found in the colony established by them and over half of the rivers situated on both sides of the aforesaid colony by near indications; provided that the Company for here and

---

* These documents—except for Nos. XVIII, XXI, and XXII, which appear in the *Essai* in French—have been translated into English from the Dutch versions supplied by the author of the *Essai Historique*.

there, in its own name, shall declare that free navigation and trade in the aforesaid bays and up the aforesaid rivers, as well as travel to and from there, shall be maintained.

Article 3.

The aforesaid David Nassy and his Associates are further granted free and allodial [rent-free] ownership in perpetuity of the aforesaid colony with its appendages and dependencies, for as much as his Associates shall have, in the period of four years, populated, worked, ruled, utilized, and cultivated; following this they shall have the right to dispose of it forever by will, contract, agreement, or any other way, such as one may do with one's own property, except that such a will or contract shall not be valid in case the colony shall be cut off from this state and Company and conveyed to other countries.

Article 4.

The aforesaid colony is likewise granted and permitted to have jurisdiction over high, middle, and low justice, which shall be observed in the manner expressed in Article 14.

Article 5.

The aforesaid colony shall be possessed by David Nassy and his Associates in the form of a fief [*leen*], appointing for this purpose a suitable person or several persons, who assent to this fief, with the payment of a fixed vassal's gift, to the amount of sixty gulden.

Article 6.

All this has no effect to diminish the sovereignty and supreme control, with all that is implied thereby, of Their High Powers and of the Company, as far as the latter is allowed by its charter.

Article 7.

The Jews shall also enjoy such freedom of conscience and right of public worship [*vryheid van conscientie met publique excercitie*], synagogue, and school, as is granted to their brethren in the city of Amsterdam. They may follow the teachings of their ancestors, without any hindrance, in the district of the colony as well as in all other places of our dominion, and this with all the exemptions and privileges which our native citizens enjoy. For we obligate the people and the aforesaid patron and his Associates to maintain the aforesaid freedom of conscience among all their colonists, of whatever nation the same may be, and that with the exercise and public religious observances of the [Calvinist Dutch] Reformed Religion, as may be the case in this land.

Article 8.

The Company grants to the aforesaid David Nassy and his Associates freedom from tithes [*tienden*] for a period of twenty years, of which he shall be empowered to grant freedom to his colonists for so many years as shall seem advisable to him, together with freedom from all poll-taxes [*hoofdgeld*] and other imposts, which shall be received at the expiration of the ten or twenty years, and shall be used for the discharge of the common burdens, the building of public works or fortifications, and, at the expiration of the twenty years, both tithe and poll-tax are to be collected in behalf of the Company.

Article 9.

If any of the colonists, either by themselves or their servants, shall discover any minerals such as gold, silver, crystals, marble, saltpetre, or pearl fisheries, of whatsoever nature these may be, they may own and possess them as their own property, but they shall pay certain costs and recognitions for a period of ten years; after the expiration of these ten years, they shall be obligated to pay a tenth of any revenue coming from these to the Company.

Article 10.

The colonists in general, for a period of ten consecutive years, shall also be free from the Company's taxes on materials for service in agriculture, working minerals, maintenance of men, building of houses, lodges, fisheries, and all that is needed for this.

Article 11.

Likewise these, for a period of five years, shall be free of all the Company's taxes on gums, dyestuffs, balsams, crops, and other wares, without exception, that are found in the colony, or are produced by their industry, or are noted and brought to this country; after that time they shall pay no more to the Company than is paid by others who are obligated in places where the Company has possession.

Article 12.

The colonists are permitted to transport their goods from this country in their own hired or chartered ships, or in those of the Company, if any are available, and shall be obligated to land their equipment at the aforesaid colony, to make places where there are chambers of commerce, to the end that, before they begin to load, they shall inform the comptoir of the size, fittings, and manpower of their ships, and also determine a suitable commission fee for the Company, following and in conformity with the usages of the Company, and also by all others traveling within the limits of the charter of the Company, and it is further granted to keep every such vessel to such use as shall seem good to the people.

Article 13.

The colonists are permitted, as far as the circumstances of the colony will allow, to establish there all sorts of fisheries, for the drying and pickling of fish, and for a period of twenty years may bring them to the West Indies islands of the [Dutch] state and elsewhere, provided that they do not remove, under the cover of this action, minerals, crops, or whatever else there may be, under the penalty that if the contrary be found true, the senders, to the benefit of the Company, shall forfeit the value of all this, and in addition the goods which are apprehended and discovered shall also be forfeited on the same behalf.

Article 14.

The Company shall appoint a sheriff [schout] in the aforesaid colony in order to establish justice and police supervision there, provided that the colony is in condition to have special councils and judges appointed there. The patron or patrons shall be able to nominate double the number [of judges] from the most capable persons living in the colony, who are Dutch Christians and of the true [Dutch] Reformed Religion, [representatives of] whom the sheriff, or anyone upon whom the supreme command is conferred, shall appoint to the positions.

Article 15.

All lawsuits, disputes, and crimes shall be settled by the aforesaid judges, and their sentences shall be executed, provided that in no case shall such sentences exceed the sum of 500 gulden; the aforesaid sentences may be appealed to such courts as shall be given this supreme authority by Their High Powers and the Company.

Article 16.

In regard to the slave trade, the aforesaid colonists, insofar as the needs of the colony may [require], shall have such rights as are granted by the Council of the Nineteen. Their accommodations at all times shall be estimated as those allowed to the colony in [nearby] Essequebo under the Chamber of Zeeland.

Article 17.

They shall also be provided by the Company with such a number of slaves as shall from time to time be needed there, in accordance with the orders and regulations made by the Council of the Nineteen, or to be made in the future; but the slaves who are captured by the colonists on the sea may be brought into the colony, and they may transport them to any place that they see fit, on payment of a tax to the colony of ten gulden per slave, and on the further condition that a fourth of the slaves must remain in the colony, to the advantage of the colony on the Wild Coast.

Article 18.

The Company is empowered, at the expiration of the first ten years, to appoint a receiver of the Company's dues, to whom the heads of the colony and the judges there shall be obligated to extend a helping hand and to maintain in the future the Company's authority.

All this done and confirmed by the shareholders of the Chamber of Amsterdam, September 12, 1659.

No. II.

General Privileges, Title I.*

[* See the English text offered in *Publications of the American Jewish Historical Society,* IX (1901), 144-46.]

Whereas it is good and sound policy to encourage as much as possible whatever may tend to the increase of a new colony, and to invite persons of whatever country and religion to come and reside here and traffic with us; and whereas we have found that the Jews [*de Hebraische Natie*], now already resident here, have, with their persons and property, proved themselves useful and beneficial to this colony; and being desirous further to encourage them to continue their residence and trade here; we have, with the authority of the governor, his council, and assembly, passed the following act:

Every person belonging to the Jewish community [*de Hebreeuwsche Natie*] now resident here, or who may hereafter come to reside and trade here, or in any place or district within the limits of this colony, shall possess and enjoy every privilege and liberty possessed by and granted to the citizens and inhabitants of this colony, and shall be considered as English-born [*Engelschen gebooren*]; and they and their heirs shall in this manner possess their property, whether real or personal. It is also hereby declared, that they shall not be compelled to serve any public office in this colony, and that we receive them under the protection and safeguard of our government, with all the property they now hold, or shall hereafter possess or import from any foreign place or kingdom abroad. We also grant them every privilege and liberty which we ourselves enjoy, whether derived from laws, acts, or customs, either regarding our lands, our persons, or other property, promising them that nothing of what they now possess, or shall hereafter acquire, shall be taken from them or be appropriated among ourselves, by any person of whatsoever rank; but that, on the contrary, they shall have full liberty to plant, trade, and do whatsoever they may consider conducive to their advantage and profit, on condition that they shall be true subjects of our Sovereign Lord the King of England, and shall obey all orders already issued by him, or which he may hereafter promulgate. It is, however, to be well understood that none of these orders shall be contrary to what is herein contained.

It is also hereby granted and permitted, in the most ample manner possible, to the Jewish community to practice and perform all ceremonies and customs of their religion, according to their usages; also those relating to their marriages and last wills or testaments; and that the acts of marriage made according to their rites and customs shall be held valid in every respect. It is also hereby declared that they shall not suffer any let or hindrance in the observance of their Sabbath or festivals, and those who trouble them on that account shall be considered disturbers of the public peace, and shall be punished accordingly. Also that they shall not be bound to appear, on the said days, before any court or magistrate; and that all summonses and citations for the said days shall be null and void. Neither shall their refusal of payment of any claim made against them on these days prejudice them in any way, or diminish any right they may have. The possession of ten acres of land at Thorarica is also hereby granted to them, that they may build thereon places of worship and schools; also for the burial of their dead. They shall, moreover, not be compelled to do personal duty, but shall be permitted to send a substitute, except in case of war, when they also shall be bound to come forward with the other inhabitants. Permission is also hereby granted them to have a tribunal of their own; and that in cases so litigated, the deputies of their community may pronounce sentence in all cases not exceeding the value of ten thousand pounds of sugar. Upon which sentence, pronounced by the said deputies, the judge of our court shall grant execution to issue; and they shall keep registers and records of the same according to custom. When an oath shall be required, it shall be administered in conformity with the customs of the Jewish community, and such an oath shall be deemed valid, and have all the force and effect of a judicial oath, notwithstanding any law to the contrary. That all this may be fully known, I have, by order of his excellency the governor, his council and assembly, signed the present on the 17th of August, 1665.

(signed) JAN PARY [John Parry], SECRETARY.

No. III.

Today, December the third, 1700, there appeared before me, Steven Pelgrom, notary public at the court of Holland, licensed and residing at Amsterdam, the later-mentioned witness *Samuel Nassy*, merchant, for some years past a former resident of the Colony of Surinam, but at present in this town, and known to me as notary. And he has, in his conscience, at the request of the worthy Lord Directors of the Chartered Society of Surinam, witnessed and declared that it was true and certain that he, the attestant, was personally in Cajana [Cayenne] during or about the year 1664, at the time when Monsieur Noël, in behalf of the French, had a fortress built on the Sin[n]amary river, in which the French, under his command, had placed a garrison, and that the aforesaid fortress was later, in the year 1665 or 1666 (but he has forgotten the exact time), taken by the English, before the Colony of Surinam was recaptured from the English by the Province of Zeeland.

Further the attestant declared that according to his best memory he knew well that in the month of November, 1688, when the Colony of Surinam was possessed by or in behalf of Their High Powers the States of Zeeland, there came to Surinam *Anthony le Febure*, Lord de la Bare, councilor of his Royal Highness of France, and also lieutenant general of his forces in America, and that he, the attestant, was present at the very time when the aforesaid lieutenant general dealt and treated with *Abraham Crynssen,* commander over the aforesaid Colony of Surinam, in behalf of the Province of Zeeland, on the subject of boundary lines between Cajana and the aforesaid Surinam, and that the same at that time had arranged and agreed that the aforesaid Sin[n]amary river should constitute the boundary between the French of Cajana and the aforesaid Colony of Surinam, and that this fixed basis should be mutually observed.

He gave as reasons of knowledge and truth that he, the attestant, had resided for more than twenty-seven years in Surinam, that he himself had been present at the making of this agreement and had seen its conclusion at that time. And that at the same time his attestant brother *Joseph Nassy* was in the quality of commander,' according to a commission from the aforesaid Crynssen, and by reason of the aforesaid limits that had been made, in behalf of the aforesaid High Powers the States of Zeeland, and had remained unmolested in the possession, and command of the Eracubo river and the Cananama river, which belonged to the district of Surinam, being the outermost rivers on this side of the Sin[n]amary. In regard to this he is very sure of his knowledge, for he himself dwelt there, and had seen and experienced it, presenting respectively on its behalf the need and request for having it strengthened in the future for all time. This is in the presence of *Pieter van Haps* and *Coenraad van Esterwegen*, as witnesses of this request; (signed) *Samuel Nassy, P. van Haps*, and *K. van Esterwegen*.

The above copy was collated with the original, in the custody of the Secretary of State, from the minutes of the late notary *Stephanus Pelgrom*, and has been found to agree with it, July 5, 1769. By me, the undersigned secretary of the aforesaid city.

(Signed)

J. H. DE HUYBERT.

No. IV.

Extract from the articles granted to the inhabitants of Surinam, by Captain Commander *Abraham Crynssen*, at the capture of Fort Zeelandia from the English, confirmed May 6, 1667, and approved by Their High Powers the States of Zeeland, on April 30.

Article 3.

That all persons, whoever they may be and of whatever nation they may be, whether English, Jews, etc., who at present live in Surinam in person or with their families, shall absolutely be permitted to retain their money, lands, property, and goods, of whatever sort or species they may be, and these are confirmed to them and their heirs, so that for all time they may enjoy and bequeath them, without the least opposition, molestation, or hindrance; and that, on the contrary, all those who do not reside here in Surinam may by no means have property there, notwithstanding that they may have persons here who represent them or their families; they are absolutely excluded from this article, and all their property, of whatever sort or species it may be, is from this hour confiscated by Their High Powers the States.

Article 4.

That all the present inhabitants, of whatever nationality they may be, shall have and enjoy the same privileges as the Dutch, among whom they shall dwell.

Extracted from the original act of approval of Their High Powers, the States of Zeeland, in the custody of the Secretariat of Surinam.

No. xv [sic].

To the Honorable Lord *Philippe Julius Lichtenberg,* Sovereign of the Province, Rivers, and Districts of Surinam.

With proper respect we, the Jewish Community [*de Joodsche Natie*], residing here in Surinam, show that since the time of the English rule, by a special act given to us, and granted by the lord governor, his council and assembly, on August 17, 1665, we have, without any hindrance of sure privileges, mentioned in detail in that act and specified hereunder, been permitted to keep our persons and property, under the aforesaid government, safely at all times, without the least infraction of the same. Accordingly, we also, in view of the manifold troubles that have occurred here in the two past years, have had no opportunity to make a remonstrance to the governor; further, in letters from various regions from many of our coreligionists, who are inclined to come and settle here, inquiry is made as to our conditions here and how we are treated. We desire moreover, for us and our descendants, for our persons and property, further favorable privileges which we look forward to obtaining from Their High Powers the States of Zeeland as before from the English government, to be secured by a special act of Their High Powers.

Therefore we request most humbly that this, our remonstrance of . . . and a few small points, tending to the prejudice of none, but, on the contrary, to the peace and tranquillity of all, be received, and that the same, through your favorable intercession with Their High Powers, should be set forth in a letter under your hand and seal, and thus brought about; and that in the meanwhile, while you are awaiting the decision of Their High Powers, we may see ourselves provisionally benefitted, through a favorable note under your hand and seal, by the enjoyment of the aforesaid privileges, specified hereunder. This done, we shall remain as before, with all zeal and affection, as we are in duty bound, obedient subjects of Their High Powers and your Excellency's humble servants.

(Here is inserted a copy of the Act, i.e., Document No. II.)

Points about which we should like to inquire.

1. That all ecclesiastical affairs that are ordered by those persons chosen by them for the preservation of unity among them shall be in force, and that in case of a lack of obedience, complaint shall be made to the governor, that this may be punished.

2. In case it may happen that any person or persons among them should create a disturbance or be found to be of an evil life, and there should be fear that in the evening or morning they will fall into the hands of justice and so bring about a scandal to the Jewish community, in such a case complaint may be made to the governor through a person or persons who are deputies of the Jewish community, with sufficient reasons, and there shall be no difficulty in preventing a scandal before the Jewish community, by forcing such a person or persons to leave the colony.

3. In case some Jews come to settle here, whose property has perhaps been confiscated by the Inquisition or in any other manner, and that thereby they have fallen into debt, that the same should not be suddenly seized for debt, but dealt with leniently in the courts of justice, following the customs in all colonies; but they shall be obliged to pay something now and then, in order that they may yet subsist.

4. That we may be permitted on Sunday, when both we and our Negroes are allowed to work, to have the privilege of visiting one another, and to that end, when the marshal finds us on the river, laden with nothing else but our own persons or goods, which might give any presumption of work, he shall be bound to allow us to pass to and fro unmolested.

5. That all which is mentioned above shall be confirmed to the good faith of the Jewish community. In the future, it may also happen, to the advantage and benefit of the Jewish community, that the same may be committed, that a request therefor, asked respectfully and with proper reason, may be granted. (Signed) *David Nassy, Isaack Pareyra, Isaac*

Arrias, Henrique de Caseres, Raphael Aboab, Samuel Nassy, Isaac R. de Prado, Aron de Silva, Alans d'Fonseca, Isaak Mezo, Daniel Messiach, Jacob Nunes, Isaac Gabay Cid, Isaak da Costa, Isaac Drago, Bento da Costa.

The request of the Jewish community having been seen, it is provisionally decided to accord them the enjoyment of any of these requests, and that at the first opportunity, as far as it is possible, to try to have Their High Powers pass an act to that effect, confirmed by their hand and seal, in order that the same may be secured in this.

Done at Paramaribo, October 1, 1669. (Signed) *F. Lichtenberg;* provided further with his seal (L. S.). Agrees on collation with his authentic copy shown to me and registered May 28, 1734, to which I certify.

(Signed)

ABRAHAM BOLS, SECRETARY.

No. VI.

Extract from a letter of the Lord Directors of the Chartered Society of the Province of Surinam, to his excellency, the Lord of Sommelsdyk, governor of the aforesaid province, dated December 10, 1685.

Furthermore, having seen and examined the request and the additional answer of the Jewish community, sent to the country by a letter of May 20 of this year, touching a request in regard to the continuation of such privileges and rights such as they, both under the English rule and otherwise, have acquired successively from time to time, we, in consideration of the fact that the same privileges in no sense would bring about a disadvantage or contempt to the colony, or any prejudice which anyone might expect to come, we have found it good to write this to your excellency, that you are to maintain the aforesaid privileges acquired by the Jewish community in Surinam, in the same manner as was formerly the case in the country, and you are to notify them of this fact. Agrees with the aforesaid extract, as I witness. (Signed) *A. de Graaf.* Registered November 30, 1701 (L. S.) and agrees with the registration with the secretariat here in Protocol No. 37, Folio 148 verso, as I witness. (Signed) *N. Strauch,* Secretary.

No. VII.

Extract from a letter from the Lord Directors of the Chartered Society of Surinam, written to his excellency, the Lord of Sommelsdyk, dated August 9, 1686.

Furthermore, it having also passed through our thoughts, for your highness' consideration, in regard to the giving of an order to those of the Jewish community that they should celebrate the Lord's Day as is customary here in the country, we have not found it important to make the least change in this respect, but, on the contrary, to continue according to our instructions made on that subject on December 10 of last year. We have not proceeded in this without a proper consideration, but after mature consultation over the matter; therefore the thing anticipated shall be done so that they shall live there on the Lord's Day in the same manner as in this country, without giving any offense or scandal to our people. (Signed) Agrees with the aforesaid letter, as far as concerns this extract, to which I attest. (Signed) *A. de Graaf*.

No. VIII.

Extract from the minutes of the resolution adopted by the governor and the administrative council of Surinam.

Friday, May 6, 1695.

It was further noted that the regents of the Jewish church [*de Joodsche Kerk*] have taken the title of regents of the Jewish community [*de Joodsche Natie*], and that this has been wrongfully entered in the minutes; accordingly, after previous deliberation it has been found good and agreed to stop them, and to give them no further qualification than that of regents of the church or synagogue, which shall be made known to them, in order that they may obey the decree.

No. IX.

Extract from the minutes of the resolution adopted by his excellency the governor and the administrative council of Surinam.

Wednesday, June 3, 1693 [sic]

There was read to the meeting the request of *Emanuel Baron de Belmonte* and *Samuel C. Nassy,* as authorized by the whole Jewish community of this province, presented to the Lord Directors of the Society of this province of the date of March 19, 1695 [sic], containing complaints about the strict maintenance and observance of Sunday, and that they had been considerably damaged in regard to their privileges. This was deliberated and it was found that the aforesaid poster applied to all the inhabitants of the colony in general, without the intention of doing any particular damage to the Jewish community. It was therefore found good and agreed to order the prosecutor to enforce the aforesaid placard in regard to the Jewish community, in no way except with circumspection and in case there is any public disturbance.

No. x, Part i. 1.

Extract from the register of minutes and resolutions of the council of administration and criminal justice of the Colony of Surinam.

Tuesday, March 10, 1750.

Moses Naar, captain lieutenant of the citizens' company of the Portuguese Jewish community, and in this capacity commanding officer of the commando sent out to Canavinika, to pursue the slaves of the late Mister Thomas, on the request previously made, has made a verbal report of his commando, and has stated that the same has caught or overtaken seven head of Negroes and Negresses, both large and small, that they have already been brought back here, and that through him the necessary orders have been given to patrol for others daily and to hold a watch so that they, being busy in the swamps, may not well escape. He also stated that he was informed that since that time some twenty head from different plantations in Cassaneka had been captured or shot, etc.

All this being heard, and due notice having been made of the report, the aforesaid captain lieutenant, *Moses Naar,* was thanked by the governor, in the name of this council, for showing zeal, vigilance, and good service in this expedition, to the benefit of this country.

No. x, Part 2, 1.

Extract from the register of the minutes and resolutions of the council of administration and criminal justice of the Colony of Surinam.

Wednesday, March 11, 1740.

On the reading of the minutes of yesterday, consideration was taken by the council that by the resolution of the 4th instant to certain superior officers of the commando against the runaways, both in Saramacke, under the command of the captain lieutenant of the militia C. O. Creutz, and against the Negroes of the late Mister A. Thomas, to give a present for duty performed and good leadership out of the fund for runaways, it was found good to present the aforesaid officers, both of the commando behind Paramaribo, as well as that concerning the slaves of A. Thomas, because of having done their common duties, a prize for the ensign of the Hensel Militia, etc.

To the lieutenant of the citizenry of lower Commewyne, Gabriel de Lasatte, etc.

And finally, to the captain lieutenant of the citizenry of the Portuguese Jewish community, *Moses Naar,* with a similar coffee service, to the value of about 150 Dutch gulden, and that on the latter two there should be engraved in remembrance the arms of this colony.

No. xi.

Extract from the letter of the Noble Highly Honored Lord Directors of the Noble Chartered Society of Surinam, written to his excellency, Governor *J. J. Mauritius,* dated July 6, 1747.

At the same time there has come into our hands a missive from the deputies of the Portuguese Jewish community, together with the old regents of the synagogue in Surinam, written at Paramaribo under date of February 2 of this year, containing an account of their dealing with Carrilho, and a request to be further maintained in their privileges.

We have thought it good to make you acquainted with this and to direct you at the same time to inform the deputies of the Portuguese Jewish community, etc., that we are satisfied with their conduct and behavior in this matter, and that you have received an order, such as we have added to this, to maintain this community in all their *properly obtained privileges.*

No. XII.

Items of request, delivered to the Honorable Commissioners of His Illustrious Highness, the Prince, Hereditary Stadholder, by the undersigned planters and inhabitants in the Colony of Surinam, who humbly request that the necessary redress may be granted the undersigned.

ITEMS OF REQUEST
Article 12.

That the Jews of the country may be ordered not to have any participation in the making of nominations to the administrative council, supporting this very humble request by the following reasons:

In the first place, that under no Christian power are the Jews admitted or tolerated to mix in the affairs of government, least of all the nomination of a council and judges; still less to be able to effect an act of judgment in their own courts, as happens here (to great confusions and disputes among the Jews), and that because of pretended privileges, which were never approved by the Sovereign (to whom, as is proper, is granted all such competency), but only by the Society entirely. In the whole collection of their pretended privileges, this is not found.

ANSWER OF HIS ROYAL HIGHNESS TO THE ACCOMPANYING ITEMS OF REQUEST

This request cannot be granted now, but the privileges of the Jewish community shall be seen to and examined.

2nd. They offer their votes to the governor, or the same are extracted from them by promises or threats, which has been seen openly several times, especially under this administration, and is the chief cause of division and hate within the community.

3rd. Whenever a nomination for the council takes place, their communities are forced by their pretended regents to come to Paramaribo, the capital, among which communities are found many shabby persons, fugitives, and bankrupts, who may leave their Siberia for three days before and three days after the nomination, and come to enjoy safely their pretended right, during which time they are free from all prosecution, summonses, writs, executions, apprehension, imprisonment, etc., which freedom is granted to them for no other reason than to be the master of their votes.

Article 23.

That no one should be taken into the secretariat as clerks under the age of twenty-five, and as copyists under the age of twenty; since the younger ones who are now employed think more of play than of their duty.

This article will be referred to the directors of the Society, to provide in consultation with the governor and the councils.

Item, that no Jew may be employed in the secretariat, whether to copy or to act as messenger.

Article 43.

That thus all lucrative offices and posts may be assumed and served by persons, but not like now the secretariat of the chancery court, which is served by a Jew, and the inspection of the cowshed, which is served by another. Since *Hinckeldy* and *Philip Eckhart*, Directors with the governor, cannot vacate the posts with which they are benefitted, your suppliants leave it to the consideration of Your Highness that it would be good if the inspection of the cowshed and the officer of the lands be placed in subordination to that of the community pasturage.

The holding of offices will be determined herewith in person.

No. XIII.

Letter from Her Royal Highness, Madam the Princess *Anne,* Dowager of his late Royal Highness, the Prince of Orange and Nassau, etc., etc., etc., written to the *parnassims* [*sic*—Hebrew for "Regents"] of the Portuguese Jewish community in Surinam, dated May 27, 1754.

Honorable Discreet Beloved Citizens!

When, on July 20 of last year, we presented our final report on Surinam matters to Their High Powers, it was impossible for us to do so in connection with what concerned the Portuguese Jewish community in Surinam, since we had not then received the papers, documents, and answers necessary for an examination of the disputes that arose among the Community.

A portion of these answers have come to us from various quarters, and we have studied and examined the disputes, hearing in regard to this some of the most distinguished of the Jews who live in this country, and among others, the person of *Isaac Nassy*, himself the authorized agent of the parnassims [sic] and deputies of the Portuguese Jewish synagogue and of many distinguished inhabitants and planters of the Portuguese Jewish community in the Colony of Surinam, because of which the aforesaid *Isaac Nassy* has placed in our hand various items of request for the purpose of restoring the tranquillity and peace in the Colony of Surinam among those of the Portuguese Jewish community.

On these items we have taken advice from others, as a result of which we have weighed over and come to an agreement with the deputies of the Society of Surinam, what would be best for us to put into effect for the restoration of harmony and peace; after mature deliberation we have found it good to approve and consent to certain of these requests.

In consequence of this we have decided to undertake the election of the parnassims and treasurer for this time only and without consequence for the future, and we send you our choice signed and sealed, No. 1.

We obligate you to open this up on the first day which is agreed upon for the election of parnassims and treasurer, and afterwards to publish it in your customary manner, and that the persons named therein should be recommended in our name in the most serious manner, putting aside all partisanship, hate, and animosity, and that they should be concerned only with the being and well-being, the restoration and maintenance of quiet, peace, and harmony in the Jewish community, and that further the same should be recognized as parnassims and treasurer and should be properly respected.

We further charge you on the aforesaid day, and later on from year to year, to appoint and constitute one of the Jewish inhabitants of Paramaribo, under the naming of the parnassims, to take upon himself the direction of the house of prayer there, which appointee is made by us for the first election, signed and sealed, No. 2.

We order you to have all the appointed parnassims enjoy all the honors attached to the title, yet without granting the vote to the old regency in the community.

We further order and charge you to restore the person of *Isaac Nassy,* when he shall have returned to Surinam, at once, again, in his office of adjutant gabay or treasurer and adjutant cashier of the church [*Kerk*], on the same footing, salary, and emoluments as he had before he left the colony, and to that end to license the person of *Is. de Britto,* who had been appointed to that post, leaving it for once to your judgment and discretion to say whether the aforesaid *de Britto,* through his zeal, industry, and capacity in assuming the aforesaid office, has made himself worthy to be remunerated for the sake of unanimity; in which case we recommend him to be vested by the Jewish community with the first lucrative post which falls vacant.

And as we, following our comment on Article 12 of the items of request, made to us by certain planters and inhabitants of the Colony of Surinam, that we were ready to examine the privileges which have been granted from time to time to the Jewish community in Surinam, in order to bring them for approval before Their High Powers, we order and charge you to send us all these privileges as speedily as possible.

We expect that you will scrupulously follow and put into effect all our orders as mentioned, and make us a report of what has been done, as well as wholeheartedly to effect our wholesome design, namely, of restoring quiet, peace, and harmony among the Jewish community in Surinam. With this I am,

Worthy Discreet Beloved Citizens!

We commend you to God's holy protection.

The Hague, May 27, 1754.

At the order of Her Royal Highness (Signed)

Your well-wishing friend,
(Signed) ANNE.
J. J. DE BACK

No. XIV.

Honorable Discreet Beloved Citizens!

Now that we have seriously considered the disputes which have arisen for some time among the Jewish community in Surinam, in respect to their ascamoth or ecclesiastical constitutions [*Kerkelyke Institutien*], and further having considered the various articles and reports given for that purpose, we have found it good, for the restoration of harmony within the community, to place the aforesaid ascamoth in the hands of the parnassims of the Portuguese Jewish community of Amsterdam, with orders to examine the same, and to serve us with their advice as to what extent the aforesaid ascamoth are found compatible with the welfare of the community.

In consequence the parnassims mentioned, in the presence of the representatives of the heads of both parties who are still here in this country, have carefully examined the ascamoth, and have made therein as far as possible, and with the approval of both representatives, such changes as they believe capable of providing for the maintenance of quiet, peace, and well-being among the Portuguese Jewish community in Surinam.

We send you herewith the ascamoth with these alterations; we approve them completely, and order you to accept and observe them scrupulously.

With this I am,
Honorable Discreet Beloved Citizens!
We commend you to God's holy protection.

(undermentioned)
At the order of Her Royal Highness.
The Hague, August 22, 1754.
(Signed) J. J. DE BACK.

Your well-wishing friend,
(Signed)
ANNE.

(The address reads)
Honorable Discreet Beloved Citizens!
The parnassims of the Portuguese Jewish community in Surinam.

No. xv.

EXTRACT from the register of the resolutions of Their High Powers the States General of the United Netherlands.

Wednesday, April 24, 1755.

By the Councilor Pensionaris, etc.

That Her Royal Highness has promptly examined the resolution taken by Their High Powers on July 20, 1753, and that the sole remaining point, concerning the disputes among the Portuguese Jewish community in Surinam, could not have been settled before, since the papers, documents, and replies relative to it had not yet come before Their Highnesses.

That Her Royal Highness, on that account, had agreed on certain arrangements with the Directors of the Society, together with the representatives of the Portuguese Jewish community in Surinam, now residing in this country, and has acted to restore quiet and harmony in the colony.

That Her Highness has made certain revisions, and, to the end of satisfying the representatives of the Jewish community, has taken upon herself, for this time only and without consequence for the future, the election of parnassims and treasurer.

That as a result of this, Her Highness, with the representatives of each party, has brought to hand lists of nonpartisans and pacific members of the Jewish community, which lists have been examined by both parties, and Her Royal Highness has made a choice from them.

That Her Highness has also chosen, at the request of the aforesaid representatives, one of the people of the Jewish community at Paramaribo, who, under the name [title] of "parnas," shall have the care of the house of prayer there, together with orders to the parnassims in Surinam to continue to appoint such a person from year to year.

Furthermore, since various complaints have arrived regarding certain defects in the ascamoth, or ecclesiastical constitutions, Her Royal Highness has placed a copy in the hands of the above-mentioned representatives, which has been submitted to the parnassims of the Portuguese Jewish community at Amsterdam, with instructions to give their advice to Her Royal Highness as to which of the aforesaid constitutions are compatible with the quiet, peace, and welfare of the Jewish community in Surinam, and which deviate therefrom, in order that the latter may be abolished and all further dissensions about them may cease.

That the aforesaid parnassims, following the instructions, have carefully examined the ascamoth, and have made the necessary corrections in them, as far as possible, with the approval of the above-mentioned representatives. Her Royal Highness has entirely approved them and has ordered the parnassims of the Portuguese Jewish community in Surinam to consider and observe them scrupulously.

That Her Highness has made various orders and arrangements, in order to prevent all future quarrels and discords among private persons in the Jewish community.

That Her Highness has informed the parnassims in Surinam of all the previous missives, with instructions to put them into execution. Her Highness received, a few days ago, their rescript, dated October 18, 1754, in which, after acknowledgment of their thanks, they have given a report of their arrangements to Her Royal Highness, and at her request have sent her the collection of the privileges which from time to time have been granted to their community in Surinam; which privileges, following the comment of Her Royal Highness on Article 12 of the well-known items of request, approved by Her Royal Highness on July 20, 1753, she has carefully examined.

That Her Royal Highness has placed the aforesaid collection [of privileges] in the hands of the Directors of the Society, and has requested and received their consideration and advice concerning them.

That in consequence it appears to Her Highness that these privileges, insofar as they are demonstrated by Their High Powers to be to the greater stabilization of quiet and peace among the Portuguese Jewish community in Surinam, should be able to be approved, with these few restrictions and changes.

That inasmuch as Her Royal Highness has already, on August 22, 1754, approved the ascamoth of the Portuguese Jewish community in Surinam, all such ascamoth presented to Her Highness, contained in the collection of the privileges, which may be contrary to those already approved, are not to be approved in any other way than with the alterations and modifications in the ascamoth made and inserted by Her Royal Highness on the aforesaid August 22, 1754.

And that in view of the privilege which is found on pages 7 and 99 of the collection, *they may banish from the colony, when such are ac-*

cused by the deputies, all persons of an evil life and those who can bring shame upon the Jewish community.

Her Royal Highness understands that this privilege shall have relation only to poor, shabby people and those who are fugitives from elsewhere, who have not established themselves in the colony, and would like to settle there; but as for those of the colonists who have established themselves in Surinam and have property, Their High Powers order and decree that from this time on the political arrangements, following the privilege, shall not be affected, except through a deliberation of the deputies, together with all the adjuncts or old parnassims of the community, and that nothing shall be decided except by a two-thirds vote.

That, further, the aforesaid parnassims, with their sending of the privileges to Her Royal Highness, have again made requests in favor of the community. The first is that they may be able to bring their wares in Paramaribo to the doors of the inhabitants for purchase. The second is to obtain a recommendation and prohibition to the governor and council of the colony, not to mix in any affairs of the community which, following the privilege of full jurisdiction and all that adheres to it, depend on the parnassims of the synagogue or the deputies of the community.

That Her Royal Highness, in regard to these two requests, has decided to send them to the Directors of the Society, as being the best informed about these things, yet with the recommendation that if they find them useful and reasonable, they should be willing to be favorable to the Jewish community.

That, following the request of Her Royal Highness, it has pleased Their High Powers to approve and confirm all the arrangements made by Her Highness in regard to the Portuguese Jewish community in Surinam.

The matter having been deliberated, Their High Powers thanked Her Royal Highness for her ceaseless zeal and vigilance for the best interests of the aforesaid colony, and this was further found good and approved.

Third, that all the arrangements of Her Royal Highness for the restoration of quiet, peace, and harmony among the Portuguese Jewish community in Surinam should be approved as specified above.

Fourth, that the indicated collection of privileges of the Portuguese

Jewish community in Surinam, with the few additions and restrictions mentioned above, should likewise be approved and are now approved.

And the extract, etc.

> Agrees with the original, as far as this extract is concerned, deposited at the secretariat of the government.
> (Signed)
> H. STENHUYS, First Clerk.

No. XVI.

EXTRACT from the register of the resolutions of the noble, great, honorable Directors of the Chartered Society of Surinam.

Tuesday, April 6, 1768.

The Lord Sheriff Rendorp, following and in discharge of the commissorial resolution of the Lords of this Board, dated August 5, 1767, together with the Lord Sheriffs Dedel and Ploos van Amstel, having verified and examined the request of the regents of the High German Jewish [*Hoogduitsche Joodsche*] synagogue of December 4, 1765, presented to this Society, have given a circumstantial report of their findings and have served this gathering by their consideration and advice.

The matter was deliberated, and the aforesaid Sheriff Rendorp was thanked for the report he made together with the other Commissioners, [and] for the trouble they took. It was found good and agreed, in conformity with this, to write to Governor Crommelin that, without dealing in detail with the merits of the matter in question, it was agreed and was the opinion of this board that he, the governor, should be obligated to permit the High German Jewish community to participate in the citizens' drill, with the same right as that which the Portuguese Jewish community enjoys; that these should not be ranked after all the other companies, but be placed according to the other citizens by their respective districts; and also to let them enjoy the faculties in order to be able to appoint, as approved, any other person in their place at drill or exercise of citizens; and that pending future deliberation by this Society on all procedures of exercises regarding present punishment of those who did not attend, however incurred, already undertaken, or which shall be undertaken in the future, the matter will be held by the Society in status quo, with a temporary suspension ad interim.

(Signed) *Jacob de Petersen.*

Agrees with the aforesaid. (Signed) *Jan Willem Roskamp,*
Acting Secretary.

No. XVII.

EXTRACT from the minutes of resolutions made by the noble, honorable court of administration and criminal justice of this Colony of Surinam, etc., etc., etc.

Thursday, May 14, 1767.

To the court, assembled this day, etc.

There was read a memorandum of the regents of the Portuguese Jewish synagogue and the deputies of that community, containing a request to be released from the prohibition of notification, of the date of February 18, 1767, specially taken in regard to them.

In which regard their Honorable Powers, etc.

The matter was deliberated, and in regard to the aforesaid memorandum it was found good and resolved to declare that the aforesaid resolution and notification of this court, in regard to the Portuguese Jews, although they are not planters, should not take effect before the first of May, 1768.

And the remonstrators shall be given a copy of this.

Agrees with the above resolution.

(Signed) J. E. Vieira, Sworn Clerk.

No. XVIII.

Translation [into French] of the order and exhortation to observe a day of fasting and of solemn prayer, proclaimed by the collegium of the mamad [*mahamad*] of the Portuguese Jewish community at the Savane, April 24, 1781.

The collegium of the *mamad* and deputies of the Portuguese Jewish community, as representing the body of our church [*le corps de notre*

Eglise], grieved to the heart in view of the horrible calamities which war can bring upon unfortunate mortals, calamities by which we are threatened, and which we have all the more reason to fear since we have just learned what disasters, what unforeseen misfortunes [British occupation], have desolated the inhabitants of St. Eustatius [in the Dutch West Indies], and, more particularly, our unfortunate brethren.

In a century that is so enlightened, should we expect to see men deaf to the cries of oppressed nature, and sacrificing to ambition and to resentment those most sacred things—the right of nations and of humanity? May it please God to have less to sigh over the fate of our brethren, for the honor of the civilized peoples, and for the glory of a community long an ally of our august Republic, and of which our predecessors have even been the subjects, that this desolating picture of the surprise of St. Eustatius should have been drawn in this first moment of trouble, where the frightful objects are represented to sensible and virtuous souls, under exaggerated and gigantic points of view; and that if this sad event has been such as the *Gazette de Martinique* has reported to us, may it be the only example in the annals of the nations which future centuries will be able to find!

Woe unto us if Providence abandons us and withdraws its protection from us, and if the British nation has actually caused its laurels to be tarnished at St. Eustatius, and if destiny delivers us into its hands, what have we not to fear? A fate equal to that of our compatriots and of our brethren; our possessions desolated, our houses pillaged, our wives and our daughters delivered over to the brutality and to the caprices of the soldiers—misfortunes more fearful than death itself.

If the least sinister event suffices for us to implore the favors of heaven, how much then ought we, at this time, to raise our voices to the Lord, and to implore His divine mercy in our favor, so that He should deign to remove from us the misfortunes which threaten us!

It is in accordance with these just motives, animated and urged on by the zeal of our congregation, filled with love for and recognition of our sovereigns and of our compatriots, that our church has decreed that there be published that which is being done by this present statement, to set Monday, April 30, of this year, for observing a day of fasting and of solemn prayer; so that every one of our brethren may be able to come with a heart that is contrite and broken, filled with the holy love of God, to implore the Divine Majesty and to pray to the omnipotent God of Israel, Who has so often, by means of glorious miracles, delivered His people from the misfortunes which have assailed them successively during so many centuries; so that He will deign to look with favor upon this Colony of Surinam, and to sustain the patriotic love, courage, and the other martial virtues which are notable among the chiefs who govern us, and among those who defend our fatherland; so that the laurel may be affixed to our ramparts.

You see with what firmness and patriotic courage we must sacrifice ourselves for the defense of the country and pray to the Lord to grant victory to our Republic, whose wise constitution fetters fanaticism by law, lets the standard of tolerance be unfurled, etc., makes Holland the abode of liberty, and the fatherland of all men [*le séjour de la liberté, & la patrie de tous les hommes*].

May the God of our fathers, Who holds the destiny of empires in His hands, deign to hear our prayers on this day of fasting, of penitence, and of supplication; may He come to our aid, and may He protect us and preserve and guard our colony, crowning the wishes of His children, and blessing the universe with perpetual peace!

And in order that each of the members of the church may fulfill such sacred duties, the present exhortation and order will be published, according to usage, praying to all and every one of our brethren to come to one of our synagogues on the day indicated, to join their vows and voices, to exalt the glory of the Lord and to implore His kindness.

And the *mahamad* declares that on this day of fasting every *jahid* (a Hebrew word which means "member") and congregant to whom for any reason whatsoever entrance into the synagogue has been denied may come there freely, without this resulting in any consequence for the future.

No. xix, Part 1. L. °

NOTIFICATION

Complaints have come before the court of administration and criminal justice concerning disorders and irregularities caused and performed by several citizens of the Jewish community who, on the day of the interment of the late honorable governor general of this colony, *B.*

Texier, were on hand under arms together with the other citizens.

As a result it has been found good and resolved by the aforesaid court, in view of the occurrence of these events, to eject the citizens of the abovementioned Jewish community who, on the occasion of several festivities, were accustomed to appear with the citizenry of this town under arms, as militiamen; and that in the future, when such cases arise, through the captains of the respective companies under whom they go forth, it was commanded that this should not be. Nevertheless, there shall be no diminution of citizens' drills and duties, such as up to the present time the aforesaid Jewish community has been obligated to do. In order that there shall be no pretense of ignorance in this case, this resolution, as is customary, shall be published and placarded.

Done at Paramaribo, December 15, 1784. (Signed) by order of the Court. (Signed) *Gootenaar.*

We, Monsieur *Wolphart Jacob Beeldsnyder Matroos,* governor general *ad interim* over the Colony of Surinam, and its rivers and districts, etc., etc., etc.

Having seen and examined the definite notification under date of December 15, 1784, brought to us as governor and by the council, we have, as duly authorized by the Most Noble, Great Lords Directors, Regents of the Colony of Surinam, found it good and agree to approve the same and to ratify it, just as it was approved and ratified by them.

Done at Paramaribo December 21, 1784.
(Signed) *Beeldsnyder Matroos,* at the order of the *ad interim* governor.
(Signed) *H. Schouten,* First Clerk (L. S.).
Agrees with his original. (Signed) *Jb. Dieulesit,* provisional Sworn Clerk.

No. xix, Part 2.

EXTRACT from the register of the minutes and resolutions of the court of administration and criminal justice of this Colony of Surinam.

Tuesday, February 15, 1785.

There was read the request of the regents of the Portuguese Jewish community, as well as of the High German, both containing, after allegations with very extensive arguments and assertions, their complaints about the content of the notification of this court under date of December 15 of last year, by which those of the Jewish community were ejected because they had appeared here in Paramaribo under arms on the occasion of the festivities. They made complaints and grievances on that account, maintaining that they had been considerably injured by the decree, and they further request that the aforesaid notification may be placed without effect, all this further expressed in both requests.

This was deliberated, and it was found good and resolved to declare that the court feels that, in view of certain irregularities perpetrated by several individuals of their community, as well as by the unseemly encounter through one of the regents of their community, in regard to the most noble strict governor *ad interim,* Monsieur *W. J. Beeldsnyder Matroos,* on the occasion of the interment of the noble strict governor general *Bernard Texier,* they have been found guilty of impropriety and disrespect towards the noble strict [governor general], and that therefore the statements contained in their memorandum, that they have never failed in obedience to the good orders of, and proper respect for, the head of the government of a colony, are not in conformity with the truth.

The court, by the resolution which they took and the notification which was given, should be able to insist that their humble supplication should be taken into consideration and their submission in this should be presented with especial deference to the consideration and care of his most noble strict honorable lord governor *J. G. Wichers.* For this reason it is willing to give up the mentioned resolution dated December 15, 1784, and the notification for that purpose, and to nullify it, and thus admit the Jewish citizens to the public exercises and drillings on the old footing, in the firm confidence that the regents of the Jewish community, as worthy chiefs, will take care in the future that the court shall never be given any reason for displeasure, either from them or any of their community.

And that in the unusual case which might happen, that the citizens of the community might be commanded to come under arms on the day on which their Sabbath falls, that they shall make such remonstrances as shall be found necessary in a decent and respectful manner to the most noble strict lord governor.

And authentic copies of the aforesaid resolutions shall be given to the regents of both the Portuguese and the High German Jewish communities, in order to serve as an official decree for their people of both groups, as well as for their own guidance.

No. xx.

EXTRACT from the register of the minutes and resolutions of the court of administration and criminal justice of the Colony of Surinam.

Wednesday, December 15, 1784.

It was finally recommended before the council
That, etc.
Further, with a serious recommendation to the regents of the aforesaid Jewish community to take care that, out of the privileges so graciously granted to them, no wrongful consequences should be drawn or extended, beyond what the plain letter of these will infer.

And that an extract shall be given to the regents of the aforesaid Jewish community, to the end that they may regulate themselves precisely by it.

Agrees with the aforesaid register.

(Signed) *Jb. Dieulesit,* provisional Sworn Clerk.

No. xxi.

PROSPECTUS
OF A COLLEGE OF
LITERATURE
under the Protection of His Excellency
Monseigneur
J. G. Wichers,
Governor General of the Colony of Surinam, etc., etc., etc.
under the title
of

DOCENDO DOCEMUR ["By teaching are we taught"].

Whoever desires to be instructed and seeks the means of attaining to it, does his duty; but he who takes the trouble to find illumination in order to share it with his compatriots is worthy of praise.

We have in this colony, not only in our Jewish community, but equally among the Christians, a number of young people endowed with so fine a perception, and with a skill so surprising in their natural instincts, that it would be easy to make them useful to their country and to refine their manners. Exactly nothing is lacking to them for the attainment of this goal than reflective ideas, to acquire the knowledge which is so useful for the liberal arts and for the sciences, the very soul of society.

Our ancestors in general, despite their riches, neglected to give their children the necessary education. Writing, which they had them taught, produced in general very good scriveners, but the language of the country was neglected. No notions of geography, nothing of commerce, no literature in general. Our youth, in short, endowed more than elsewhere with so admirable a perspicacity of spirit, nonetheless is in a state of the crassest ignorance. The passion for play which, so to speak, seems innate in them, removes them, far away from the desire to learn, and weakens their organs to the point where, if some remedy is not provided for giving them an education and for making them feel where this dissipation is carrying them, frightful consequences must naturally ensue therefrom.

Novelty pleases all persons in general; it will certainly stimulate the curiosity of our youth. The natural intelligence of our fellow citizens, the warmth of the climate, this vivacity of temperament, this happy organization which even Europeans are forced to acknowledge in them, give us the hope of succeeding in our enterprise.

To establish something useful that can serve as an incentive to youth and will at the same time attract their natural curiosity by inspiring them to emulation, is without doubt a great difficulty. This we feel. But what could be a still greater difficulty than to establish public schools? For want of individuals of the requisite capacity who could, furthermore, not be procured except with much trouble and expense; for want of the means of the majority of the fathers and mothers to meet these expenses, no matter how little they may cost; and after all this, what would result? Everyone knows that the majority of public schools conducted by several masters, who aim only at their private interests, are not at all in a position to supply what a college of literature can do, even if it were only the decency and the respect which are necessarily inspired by a society which is willing to sacrifice its moments of leisure for the good of humanity.

Our mutual inclination for literature, the love of one's neighbor, the desire to fulfill the patriotic views of his excellency Monseigneur the Governor *J. G. Wichers,* as a lover of letters, have occupied us a thousand and a thousand times, and, seeking the means to attain to our goal, we have found no others at all than that of employing our feeble lights for the purpose of edifying the youth and of bringing them to virtue.

In consequence we have resolved to establish in our private society, which is known here generally for harmony of sentiments and for sincere amity, a college of literature. Monsieur de Montel, in his declining years, flattered at being able to contribute to the welfare of his compatriots, offered gratis an apartment in his house and the entire use of his library filled with rare and classical books in which there can be found ideas on nearly all subjects.

We have with pleasure accepted an offer which is as honorable as it is disinterested, and we should be greatly flattered if his excellency should be willing to grant us his protection in the above matter, for under such happy auspices, we do not at all doubt that we shall succeed, if not in rooting out the evil, at least in correcting it.

In the expectation, therefore, that his excellency will accord us the honor of his approbation, we propose to open our college on Sundays and Wednesdays, from six o'clock in the afternoon until nine o'clock, and for lack of scholars to guide us in this course, we shall utilize in their place the reading of the following works:

1. The preliminary discourse of Abbé [Claude François Xavier] Millot, which contains an abridgment of ancient history, and which is to be found in the first volume of the elements of his history *[Abrégé de l'Histoire Ancienne* (Paris, 1787)?].

2. *The History of the Kings of Rome* [*Histoire Raisonnée des Premiers Siècles de Rome* (London, 1756)?], by [Charles] Palissot [de Montenoy].

3. [*History of*] *the Revolution*[*s*] *of the Roman Republic, by* [*René Aubert, Abbé de*] Vertot.

4. [*Histories of*] *the Revolution*[*s*] *of the Roman Empire,* by [Simon Nicolas Henri] Linguet.

5. Anecdotes about Rome, to remind us, and to serve us as an index of what we shall have already read.

Then, in conclusion, we shall take up what concerns ancient history.

6. [*Causes of*] *the Grandeur and the Decadence of the Romans,* by [Charles de] Montesquieu.

After having finished this history we shall occupy ourselves with that of the Jewish people, in which [Humphrey] Prideau[x'] *Old and New Testament Connected in the History of the Jews* (1716)] and Gouré [*sic*—Willem Goeree's *Mosaize Historie der Hebreeuwse Kerke* (Amsterdam, 1700)] will have the preference.

Then we shall take up the history of the [Dutch] fatherland, of which the abridgment *[Abrégé de l'Histoire de la Hollande* (Leyden, 1778)] by [L. G. F.] Kerroux appears to us to be the best; and modern history [Part Second of *Elements of General History*] by Abbé Millot.

Then we shall occupy ourselves with commerce, navigation, and agriculture. The [works of the] Abbé [Étienne] de Condillac, [Pierre Daniel] Huet, [Geronimo de] Ustars [*sic*—Ustariz], [Guillaume] Raynal, and the interests of the nations in regard to commerce will be able to serve us as guides.

Then we shall take up philosophy in general, and for this subject we believe that we shall be able to give the preference to:

1. the *History of the Progress of the Human Mind in the Sciences and in the Arts Which Depend on Them,* by Monsieur [Alexandre] Savérien.

2. the *Erudition Complette* of [Jacques Frédéric de] Bielefeld [*sic*—Bielfeld].

3. the philosophy of common sense.

4. the [*Of the*] *Philosophy of Nature,* by Monsieur [Jean] de Lisle [de Sales], etc., etc.

We shall bring in from Holland periodical works on medicine, literature, and politics, to serve us both as instruction and as amusement.

Both sexes of the age of puberty and of all religions without distinction will be eligible for admission to it as amateurs, previously giving notice to the president from one session to the other in order that the members may receive knowledge of them, either to admit them or to reject them by a plurality of the votes.

The lectures will be alternately in French and in Dutch, and if there is in the sessions any person who does not understand these languages at all, the lecturer will interpret them in Spanish or in Portuguese.

During a lecture, it will not be permitted to talk; but after it is finished, every one will be free to make his objections and his reflections, etc. The indulgence of the Society ought necessarily to inspire complete confidence among the emulators, and if even, in the course of a lecture, there is found some difficulty to resolve, one will be able politely to interrupt the lecturer in order to propose one's doubts to the assembly; and supposing that the members are not able to provide solutions to the objections, the company in this case will labor privately to try to clear them up.

Every literary quarrel will be judged provisionally without appeal by the dean, in order to avoid the evil consequences which could ensue.

A new lecturer will be elected every six months, and for each year a president and a treasurer, but the secretary will be perpetual.

No one will be eligible for admission as an actual member of the college without the unanimous consent of the Society in general; honorary members will be obliged to attend the first session in order to be proposed.

The expenses of the college, both for the purchase of books and for other needs, will be calculated at the first session, the same as the admission of the actual members and of the fellows, the first six months payable in advance.

Under the supposition that we shall not be able at all to follow the order of the lectures announced above, whether because of little aptitude on the part of the young people, or because the subjects are too abstract or above their capacity, or, in short, if other branches of science are more agreeable to them, we shall, in such case, seek some other method suitable to their capacity, in order to place them in a position to be able to follow us in the plan which we have proposed for ourselves, promising them (if they encourage us by their attachment to letters) that we shall then occupy ourselves seriously with the choosing of a good person capable of teaching them in the college, by principle, the elements of mythology, geography, mathematics, commerce, agriculture, etc. In the meantime, we shall make every effort, by means of good, well-known authors, to put ourselves in a position to be able to teach them.

May the God of the universe bless our enterprise, and in view of the purity and of the uprightness of our intentions, may He be pleased to inspire the youth with virtue, the taste for work, and the love of letters, so that they may be able to contribute to the general welfare of the colony and thus realize what [the Roman poet] Horace says: *Fructus laboris gloria* ["The fruit of labor is glory"].

Done and signed by us, in the house of Monsieur de Montel, this day, February 16, 1785.

Members according to their age, signed, *de Montel, J. H. de Barrios, Jr., S. G. Soares, Is. de la Parra, Imanuel d'Anaria, S. H. Brandon, D. D. J. C. Nassy, D. N. Monsanto, M. P. de Leon, M. de la Parra*, members of the college. His excellency Governor *Wichers,* Monsieur *W. van de Poll*, Lieutenant Colonel *Frederici*, the physician *G. W. Schelling*, Messieurs *S. H. de la Parra, Samuel Fernandes, J. Moize de Chateleux, S. H. Moron Abenatan, Junior, Jeos. de la Parra, E. Soesman, Abm. de Samuel Robles Demedina, Is. Caucanas, Brown, D. H. Brandon, Daniel Jn. Lobo, Jr., A. Bueno Bibal, Isack de Abraham Bueno Demesquita, M. H. Nahar, Jos. Gabay Fonseca, Abraham Bueno Demesquita, Isak Naar, Meza David Sarruco.*

No. XXII.

Letter from his excellency Governor *J. G. Wichers,* to the members of the college "Docendo Docemur," on the occasion of the prospectus which was presented to him by the commissioners of the said college.

GENTLEMEN!

I have received with much feeling and sentiments of thankfulness your prospectus of a college of literature.

I love the sciences and the arts, I honor them, and shall do all that I possibly can to protect them. Thus, gentlemen, your college not only merits my approval, but I shall be delighted to be able to be of use to you. I take the liberty of communicating to you my observations.

I. First, it is necessary to teach geography.

II. General history, following Abbé Millot, [Jacques Bénigne] Bossuet['s *Discourse on Universal History* (1679)], [Johannes Florentius] Martinet['s] *World History*.

III. Jewish history according to [Humphrey] Prideaux.

IV. The history of Holland, the abridgment of [Jan] Wagenaar['s] *History of the Fatherland*, printed at Utrecht; [and E. M.] Engelbert['s] *Ancient History of the United Netherlands*.

V. Philosophy, or rather, morals, according to Bielfeld['s] *Erudition Complette* [and] [Friedrich Wilhelm] Pestel['s] *Droit Naturel* [*sic:* "Natural Law"—*Fundamenta Jurisprudentiae Naturalis* (?)].

Time will clarify your ideas. You will see the little disadvantages and then your changes will be more appropriate.

It is with much affection and esteem that I have the honor to be,

Your very humble and affectionate servant,

(Signed)
WICHERS.

This February 25, 1785.

No. XXIII [a]

Very Honorable Gentlemen!

The Portuguese Jewish community, consisting of more than a third of the white inhabitants of this colony, has already for a long time been given our attention, in order, as far as possible, to remove the decline which has taken place in this community, and to make such a considerable number of the inhabitants more useful for themselves and more beneficial to society.

Yet we despaired of succeeding in this, for lack of the necessary illumination and power. Then through the able remonstrance of the adjunct treasurer, *David de* [the son of] *Is. C. Nassy,* the first was gained, and by the resolution of the collegium of the mahamad and universal junta, dated March 8, the second was put into effect, and thus there was entrusted to us the power and authority, by such means as would be found useful and necessary, to dispose of the reforms and the redress among the Portuguese community in regard to their privileges, ascamoth, usages, customs, and financing of the synagogues.

Consequently, we have seen and minutely examined the memoir of the representatives of the mahamad and universal junta, dated March 8 of last year, and taking into consideration the necessity of the plan of reform proposed by the deputies of the community for the restoration, rehabilitation, peace, and tranquillity of the community, we have found it good and agreed to it. Before revising the plan proposed, we have decided to lay out certain points of reform and redress. It is highly necessary and even inevitable to increase the number of the regents and to have them serve for a longer time than is fixed by the ascamoth. It is best that they should continue in office, in order to be able to work in it with firmness, care, and diligence, and through a basically acquired knowledge of the affairs, to be put in a position to work out a complete and well-organized plan of reform.

In addition to those already commissioned and chosen, we have chosen others to serve with them for a period of three and a half years, beginning from the day customary for the election, namely, the last day of the Jewish Passover, when it should have taken place (but did not because of our request of March 19), and this will be superseded, and the persons will be announced in the enclosed official letter.

Ordering the aforesaid letter to be published on the first coming Sabbath, and following that, both on the Savane and here in Paramaribo, to choose according to custom the persons already named by us.

We grant herewith to such elected persons, in addition to and besides their customary dignity, power, and authority in their position of functioning regents authorized by the ascamoth, the additional power and authority to put into effect the necessary plan for reforms and redress in the community (following the resolution of the general junta, dated May 8 of last year, and the political demonstration of the adjunct treasurer, *D. J. C. Nassy*). Likewise, following the election of their parnassim, they are to determine whatever concerns the affairs of the community, and to submit to us their plan for examination and approval, in order that, when all this has received the final consent and approbation of Their Noble High Powers, the directors and rulers of the colony, they may be able to attain their purpose.

We further order all the members and congregants of the aforesaid community, of whatever quality they may be, to recognize, obey, and respect the persons commissioned by us and duly elected as the true and legitimate regents, without the least resistance or opposition; to observe their orders and dispositions and to put aside any hastiness, discord, and legal proceedings, trusting that each and every one will be ready to contribute to the welfare, quiet, and peace of the Jewish community in order to make the rule of the aforesaid parnassims pleasant, peaceful, and useful, and in order to bring about our wholesome intention, aimed solely at the welfare of the community; under penalty that all who may act contrary to these our dispositions will be punished as disturbers of the common peace.

And that our resolution, before the election of the regents takes place, shall be announced in both synagogues, in order that everyone may be acquainted with it, and will act accordingly.

Herewith,
Very Honorable Gentlemen!
May you honorable ones abide under God's holy protection.
      Your very honorable and affectionate friend,
      the governor general of the Colony of Surinam,
      (Signed)
        WICHERS.

No. XXIII [b]

Following the content of our dispositions given above, concerning the memorandum of the deputies of the mahamad and general junta:

We have decided to choose, from among the regents and adjuncts, five persons, and from among the leading members, two persons, making a total of seven regents, as is indicated in our resolution.

To wit, according to their rank as adjuncts and the age of the members, the following:

Adjuncts.
- No. 1. *Isaac de la Parra.*
- 2. *David de Is. C. Nassy.*
- 3. *David Nunes Monsanto.*
- 4. *Jacob Henriques de Barrios Jr.*
- 5. *Samuel Hobeb Brandon.*

Members.
- 6. *Moses Para de Leon.*
- 7. *Samuel H. de la Parra.*

In case these refuse to accept this our election and commission, those who are unwilling shall be subject to a fine of 500 gulden in accordance with the direction established by the resolution of the junta under date of July 9, 1782, for the benefit of the poor fund. Those who are commissioned as regents shall remain free and unhindered so that after the end of this their service and the fulfillment of our commission they may be discharged from it or may continue as adjuncts at their own desire.

In regard to the presidency and further arrangements, we grant to your worthy selves the power to decide and to make resolutions.

We declare herewith, in regard to the person of *Isaack de la Parra,* that notwithstanding this our new election, he shall not be able to function in the same office as regent until after the time of service of his brother, the present functioning regent *David de la Parra,* shall expire, and that during this time the aforesaid *David de la Parra,* in his office as regent, shall continue to the end of his years of regentship.

Since, as a result of this election, the adjunct treasurer, *D. J. Cohen Nassy,* is named as regent, and since someone else should now act as adjunct treasurer, we therefore permit the same *D. J. C. Nassy* to select someone from the collegium of the mahamad to serve in his place as authorized treasurer, remaining during the time he shall function as regent, and he shall be free, at the end of the years of his commission, to resume his office of adjunct treasurer.

Furthermore, we authorize the aforesaid regents to appoint without delay, in place of a treasurer or *Gabay,* a collector of all the funds of the community, under a proper bond, in order to keep all the salaries in their proper condition.

Herewith, very worthy gentlemen!

And committing your worthy selves to the holy protection of God, I remain,

    Your worthy selves' affectionate friend,
    the governor general of the Colony of Surinam,
    (Signed)
        WICHERS

[No. XXIV.]

YOUR HIGH POWERS

We have found ourselves honored by the respected order and resolution of May 18 of last year [1785] of Your High Powers, in that Your Highnesses have made use of our consideration and advice in regard to the accompanying request of Messieurs *W. J. P. Muntz, M. H. van Lobbrecht, P. S. Hansen, N. C. Lemmers, G. G. Vogt, P. Bogel* and *P. Sichtermans,* all advocates, and *J. J. Leysner, G. Conynenberg, M. H. Wolff, T. Lolkes,* and *J. H. Helper,* all solicitors, admitted and pleading before the court of civil justice in the Colony of Surinam, containing, for reasons mentioned therein, the request that Your High Powers may find it good and decree that no Jews, heathens, Mohammedans or other unbelievers may be admitted or appointed as advocates or solicitors in any courts or collegia of justice in the Colony of Surinam, either individually or generally in the colony of this state [Holland], or as such may be able to plead before any courts of justice here or may be able to undertake or present any requests, memorials, or briefs.

Inasmuch as the suppliants have not covered their request to Your High Powers with any reasons or proofs, we would have found ourselves embarrassed in noteworthy manner to fulfill the worthy requests and orders of Your High Powers, since the request presented by a Jewish solicitor, Monsieur *Pereira de Leon,* to the court of civil justice in the Colony of Surinam has given no occasion for this address of the advocates and solicitors of Surinam to Your High Powers. Consequently there arose in the colony an antidotal request to the court of civil justice from the greater part of the aforesaid advocates and solicitors. The court has sent this to us.

Herein are set in order the reasons given by the suppliants, with further information to be judged. So with full confidence we shall bring to the knowledge of Your High Powers our thoughts and views on the former work and on this subject. For this we shall begin, with due respect, with an adjoined copy of the missive written to us about this circumstance by the court of civil justice, together with the documents that appertain to it.

If Your High Powers will examine this missive for a moment, it will undoubtedly become clear to Your Highnesses that the court of civil justice, although it agreed in chilly manner (*propria auctoritate*) to the request of the Jewish advocate *de Leon* to be permitted to plead, as solicitor, it nonetheless made clear its inclination towards the suppliant, which is possible not to be seen at once, and there should be substantial and weighty consideration for the following because of the notable number of the inhabitants of the Jewish faith who live in the Colony of Surinam and who make up nearly two-thirds of the total [white] inhabitants here.

And if we should add anything to this, we can do nothing else than to confirm this inclination of the court of civil justice, and declare before Your High Powers that the Jews who have settled here for many years have fulfilled all the duties of true and obedient inhabitants, have paid their taxes and fulfilled other obligations willingly, and have always shown a peaceable submission and reverence for their authority.

We find, from these considerations, reasons enough to advise against the request of the Surinam advocates and solicitors, insofar as it would apply to the Jewish community. We are all the more convinced of this in that we feel sure that in the aforesaid antidotal request of the same advocates and solicitors to the court of civil justice in the Colony of Surinam, nothing is to be found against the admission of a Jewish solicitor there nor is it against the rules.

Although these advocates and solicitors have, with much diligence, assembled many reasons, all these, in our opinion, do not constitute an exclusive right of theirs. So in no way can they prove or could there by any proofs, namely, that through any right any court of civil justice could forbid the admission of Jewish solicitors, whatever they themselves may judge about the circumstances.

It avails nothing to adduce the laws of emperors of the Roman [Catholic] faith of olden times, which also has, on the whole, nothing to do with the case, since all creeds, including the Roman Catholic, would be excluded. Even if there should be a local exemption, as in Frisia, or whether mention is made only of advocates and not of solicitors, this makes no difference. The only certain truth is, on the one hand, that these two professions, in occupation, name, and remuneration, are different, and on the other hand, that all penal prohibitory laws are excluded through interpretation for other objects, and, besides, are often limited.

Furthermore, Your High Powers, always united in regard to the welfare of the colony, there has been among the Jews, without contradiction, what deserves an especial attention and protection, with freedom and tolerance on the part of our community, that they may always remain in proper condition and honor, under whatever disposition they may lodge, and this should not be denied without weighty reasons. Thus we do not find any difficulty in advising Your High Powers to clarify the request of the aforesaid Surinam advocates and solicitors as far as the Jewish community is concerned, so that the latter should not be affected by it, and at the same time to authorize it by ordering the governor and the council of civil justice in the colony that in regard to the request of the solicitor Monsieur *Pireira de Leon,* as well as all others that may be presented in the future by other Jews for admission as solicitors, these requests should be laid before them and should be disposed of by them in whatever way, according to the circumstances of the matters, they shall think ought to be done.

Herewith, etc.

Amsterdam, July 28, 1786.

NOTES TO THE INTRODUCTION

¹ See his [Voltaire's] *Treatise on Tolerance* [*Traité sur la Tolérance* (Geneva, 1763)], which ought only to be regarded as a complete treatise on philosophical fanaticism.

² One should recall what [Voltaire] himself said: "I did more in my time than Luther and Calvin" [*J'ai fait plus en mon temps que Luther et Calvin*]. ("Epistle to the Author of the [Book *The*] *Three Impostors*" [which is Epistle No. 97 in Vol. 9 of *Oeuvres Complètes de Voltaire* (Paris: Armand-Aubrée, 1831]).

³ Pope Gregory IX testified in their behalf "that they are in no way guilty of the crimes which the Christians impute to them in order to get possession of their goods while abusing their religion, in order to give some color to their avarice." And in the year 1236, he wrote another letter from Rieti, dated September 9, in which he said "that the Christians exercise against them unheard of cruelties, and take no heed of the fact that they owe to the Jews the foundations of their religion." *(Letter of a Mylord to His Correspondent in Paris,* London, 1767, pp. 25 and 62.)

⁴ To know the hatred of the latter [Bartolocci], let one read just in his *Bibliothèque Rabinique* [*Bibliotheca Magna Rabbinica*] his malignant accusations against Rabbi Manasseh [ben Israel] in Holland. See on this *Histoire Universelle,* translated from English, Volume 23, pp. 582 and 583.

⁵ See *Nomologie* [*Nomologia o Discursos Legales*] of [Immanuel] Aboab, Part 2, pp. 304 *et seq.* (Amsterdam, 1629).

⁶ Alexandro and Alvaro Nunes da Costa served in Holland as agents of the court of Lisbon. On them and on the following one may consult Gregorio Lety [*sic*—Leti] in his *Compendium of the Heroiç Virtues* [*Raguagli Historici e Politici o Vero Compendio delle Virtù Heroiche* (Amsterdam, 1700)] Part II, p. 123.
Francisco Xavier d'Olivera, secretary of the embassy of the king of Portugal, in his voyage to Holland. [See Antoine Guené']s *Lettres de Quelques Juifs à Monsieur de Voltaire,* Volume 1, pp. 20 *et seq.* (Paris, 1775).

⁷ Machados was one of the favorites of King William, and this monarch recognized that he had rendered great services to his armies in Flanders.

⁸ Count de Belmonte was employed by the court of Madrid as its agent in Holland, and was honored by the emperor with the title of baron, and later with that of count.

⁹ The Texeiras were agents of the king of Sweden in Holland and at Hamburg.

[10] Soasso was created baron of Avernas by the king of Spain.

[11] Francisco Molo was employed by the king of Poland in Holland.

[12] Dard. Bo. de Mesquita was the resident of Charles Ernst, marquis of Brandenburg, duke of Prussia, and [was] general agent in Holland of the duke of Brunswick and Lunebourg. His son-in-law was Francisco Fernando Mora, who held eminent posts in Brazil and in Etruria. See further on them *L'établissement des Juifs en Hollande,* by Miguel de Barrios, at the end.

[13] D'Aguilar was made a baron by the emperor and was employed by the queen of Hungary as her treasurer; he then, with the permission of the empress-queen, retired to London, where he died in the year 1764 or 1765. *Letter of a Mylord,* p. 56.

[14] Gradis is too well-known in France to require mention, and we shall cite in regard to him only what [François de Baculard] d'Arnaud reports of him in Volume 2 of *Délassement[s] de l'Homme Sensible* [Paris, 1783], p. 49. The sum which he was able to sacrifice in favor of his debtors amounts to much more than 200,000 livres.

[15] In what respects is Mendelssohn not celebrated? His works, translated into nearly all the languages of Europe, are justly regarded as masterpieces of acuteness in metaphysics and in good morals.

We could, without much trouble, augment this list with many other persons of the Jewish community who were able to distinguish themselves in the past century, principally those who produced great works, such as Don Anthonio Henriques Gomes, Isabel de Correa, [Miguel de] Silveira, and several others.

[16] "In the 12th century the Jews established universities or academies in the vicinity of Nîmes; this community then produced men commendable for their learning. Rabbi Abraham, professor at Vauvert, saw that some of his disciples came from very far distant countries. He often added to the gift of his knowledge that of a part of his means in order to supply the needs of his indigent pupils." See the abridgment of the *Histoire de la Ville de Nîmes* (Amsterdam 1767), pp. 24 and 25; and what is still more remarkable, as the author continues: *"If we did not have certain monuments for this part of the history of the human spirit (literature), one would find it very difficult today to persuade oneself that a Jew ever had this generosity; and that it is to this community that one owes, in Europe, the renaissance of literature and of the fine arts."* *Ibid.* See *Lettre sur les Juifs,* of Baron [Jean Baptiste] de Cloots du Val de Grace, pp. 69 to 73 (Berlin, 1783). *Ibid.* for the branch of sciences. [Juan Alvarez] de Colmenar, *Annales d'Espagne et de Portugal,* Part 4, p. 8, Amsterdam, [1741,] in 4°. Joseph Scaliger, author of the 16th century, *Sur les Années Judaïques,* book 8. Perhaps the first epic poem which appeared on astronomy was that of Rabbi [Solomon Ibn] Gabirol, an author of the 12th century, although his system is founded only on that of Ptolemy, which was then in vogue.

We shall, furthermore, call our readers' attention to the parallel between certain pieces of the poetry of our rabbis and those of the greatest poets of France, J[ean]. B[aptiste]. Rousseau [1671-1741] and Voltaire, the latter the one who attributed to the Jews the crassest ignorance, although the pieces of the rabbis will lose much because of the literal rendering of the Hebrew, and because they are in prose, which often causes the loss of the charms of the most beautiful poetic composition. We have chosen pieces which have a certain affinity, yet differ in time by some six centuries; but genius is of all times. Let us look at these pieces. We shall make use of the translation of Monsieur [Mardochée] Ventura, *Prière[s Journalières à l'Usage] des Juifs* [*Portugais ou Espagnols*], Volume 3, pp. 198, 442, and 443, at Nice [1772].

Voltaire, *Henriade*.
Take care lest you surrender yourself to feeble reason;
God has made you to love Him, and not to understand Him.
Invisible to your eyes, let Him reign in your heart:
He confounds injustice, pardons error; but He also punishes every deliberate error.
Mortal, open your eyes, when His sun enlighten you.

Seventh Chant.

[French translation from] Hebrew.
Mortal, take counsel with yourself, dispose your heart, understand in your inmost being, and consider what you are and whence you take your origin, who has strengthened you, who has given you intelligence and what force makes you move? Consider the power of God, and awaken your soul from its sleepiness, prudently examine His works, but take care not to approach His existence too closely when you wish to inquire into what was at the beginning, what will be at the end, and what is hidden and beyond human intelligence.

Page 198.

J. B. Rousseau, Stanzas.
 Man during his life is
 A perfect mirror of sorrows.
 As soon as he breathes, he weeps, he cries
 And seems to foresee his misfortunes.
 In his infancy there are always tears,
 A schoolmaster who bears sadness
 Books of all colors,
 Punishments of every kind.
 Ardent and impetuous youth
 Places him in a still worse state.
 Creditors, a mistress,
 Torment him like a galley-slave.
 In mature age, other struggles.
 Ambition urges him on.
 Riches, honors, glory,
 Family needs, all this agitates him.
 When old, he is despised, he is avoided.
 Bad humor, infirmities,
 Coughing gravel, gout, phlegm
 Beset his decline.
 As climax of calamity
 A Director masters him.
 He finally dies, little regretted.
 It was worth the pain of being born.
  Oeuvres de J. B. Rousseau,
  Volume II, page 335.

Rabbi Gabirol.
Man from his existence is oppressed, beaten, mortified, and afflicted. From his beginning he is a straw which the wind carries away. As soon as he comes forth from his mother's womb, he passes the night in groanings, and the day in sadness. Today he is lifted up, tomorrow he is gnawed by worms. A straw makes him recoil, a thorn wounds him. If he has abundance, he becomes wicked; if he lacks bread, he becomes a criminal. He comes to the world and he does not know why; he rejoices, and he does not know over what; he lives, and does not know how long. During his infancy he follows his own depravity; when reason begins to give strength to his spirit, he seeks vigilantly to accumulate property. At all times he is subject to inquietudes and to accidents which unexpectedly befall him in life, until he becomes a burden to himself and his honey is transformed into vipers' gall. When the inconveniences of his old age increase, his spirit grows weak, children make a fool of him, they become his masters. He is a burden to the people of his family, and he is disregarded by his own relatives.
 Pages 443 and 444.

For the field of metaphysics, let the writings of the rabbis Jehudah Halevi and Bahya ibn Pakuda of the 12th century, especially their treatises on the existence and unity of God, and on the immortality of the soul be consulted. Let them be compared without prejudice with those of modern metaphysicians and judgment given. But, unfortunately, those are not writings which one reads and examines in order to judge. The Talmud, its fancies, its Oriental apologues [allegories] (according to the definition thereof given by our antagonists) is what occupies the critics. Has [Jean de Boyer] the Marquis d'Argens in his scholarly memoirs on human intelligence made as many researches on the former as he has made on the latter? If the Talmud exists and if the famous Maimonides had the strength to comment on it, do not several others exist? Did not Newton, the great Newton, make commentaries in the same manner? Whatever the fantasies of all the rabbis may amount to altogether, do they contain more stupidities than the theological sermons and musings of various other nations? See

Mém[oires]. du Marq[uis]. de Pombal, Volume III, pp. 176 and 230, and several others. [For Pope Paul IV's remark,] see Louis Guyon, *Diverses Leçons,* Volumes 2 and 9, p. 485.

[17] See *Abrégé du Procès Fait aux Juifs de Metz* (Paris, [published] by Leonard, 1670). A reading of the documents which confirm the alleged crime of having sacrificed a Christian child during the days of Passover will revolt [against the charge even] the most anti-Jewish political leader and jurist.

[18] The *Code Noir,* printed in 1680 or 1682. Never has a work received a title more analogous to its contents than this one. It appears rather to designate the blackness of fanaticism and of religious intolerance than the color of the Negroes which gave it its title.

[19] See the *Letter of a Mylord to His Correspondent in Paris* (1767).

[20] See the *Political Reform of the Jews,* by Monsieur Dohm, p. 106.

[21] See *Brieven over Demerary en Essequibo, tusschen Aristodemus en Sincerus* ["Letters about Demerary and Essequibo between Aristodemus and Sincerus"], Volume I, supporting document L. G., p. 70 (Amsterdam, 1785). [The seventeenth-century polemicist Johann Andreas] Eisenmenger and all the enemies of the Jews together were certainly not more rabid against them than these Areopagists [judges] of Demerary and of Essequibo (belonging to a republic [Holland] which knew how to protect the Jews splendidly) before the eyes and to the astonishment of the entire world, and that, too, in these times, and solely for fear of having them as competitors in their unfortunate colonies. We shall say a little about this work, but in the meanwhile we shall merely remark that these gentlemen ought rather to think about their own disordered affairs than to write to the disadvantage of another community. See the advertisement in the *Courier du Bas Rhin* of August 25, 1787, No. 65.

NOTES TO PART I

[1] [Mariana, *Historia*], Vol. 9, pp. 189-90.

[2] *Historie der Jooden, of vervolg van Flavius Josephus* ["History of the Jews, or Continuation of Flavius Josephus"], chapters 6, 7, and 8, pp. 516 *et seq.* (Amsterdam, [published by] van Gulik, 1784).

[3] See *Ibidem*, pp. 596-608.

[4] *Historie der Jooden*, p. 509.

[5] *Ibidem*, p. 193.

[6] In his [Montesquieu's] *Esprit des Loix*, Book XXI, p. 310.

[7] Raynal, vol. 5, p. 8 (Geneva edition, 1781). See also Bielfeld, *Institutions Politiques*, vol. 3, § 13, p. 17 (Leyden edition, 1772); and *L'Histoire Universelle*, translated from English, vol. 23, pp. 527 *et seq.*

[8] See [Philip van] Limborch, *Collat. amici* [*sic*—*P. a L. de Veritate Religionis Christianae, Amica Collatio cum Erudito Judaeo* (Gouda, 1687)?], p. 102.

[9] *Ibidem*, same page.

[10] See also in Cardoso, *L'histoire des Juifs Établis à Paraïba au Brésil; en ensuite Retirés en Hollande*, and what happened to the Jew [Isaac] de Castro Tartas, who left America and was burned by the Inquisition in Portugal, in 1650 [*sic*—actually, December, 1647].

[10a] *Calomnies des Hébreux* (Amsterdam, 1679), p. 824.

[11] [Basnage,] *Histoire des Juifs*, vol. 9, p. 292; Don Miguel de Barrios, *Maison de Jacob*, pp. 12-13; [A.] Du Lignon, *Bibliothèque Judaïque*, p. 38 (Leyden, 1769); [Jan] Wagenaar, *Amsterdam in zyn Opkomst* (Amsterdam, [published by] Tirion, 1765), p. 219, part 3, and several others.

[12] de Barrios, pp. 2-3.

[13] [de Barrios,] *op. cit.*, p. 67.

[14] [Franciseus Lievens] Kersteman, [*Hollandsch*] *Rechtsgeleerd Woordenboek*, article "Jooden"; *Richesse de la Hollande*, vol. I, p. 501.

[15] [Wagenaar,] *op. cit.*, part 3, p. 324.

[16] See *Richesse de la Hollande*, vol. II, pp. 425 *et seq.*

[17] *Ibidem*, p. 483.

[18] *Richesse de la Hollande,* vol. I, p. 501.

[19] See Martinière, *Dict. Géographique,* article "Brésil," p. 458, column ii., and *Tegenwoordige Staat van America* ["Present-Day State of America"] (Amsterdam, [published by] Tirion, 1767), volume II, p. 291.

[20] See Mig[uel]. de Barrios, *Govierno Popular Judaico,* p. 28; *Vida de Ishak Uziel,* p. 46; and his *Histoire dele poetas y escritores de la Nation Juive Portugaise* [sic—*Relacion de los Poetas y Escriptores Españoles de la Nacion Judayca*: "History of Spanish Jewish Poets and Writers"], where are found [remarks about] those who came from Brazil to Amsterdam, pp. 53-60; Du Lignon, p. 196; *Histoire Universelle,* vol. 53, p. 584, in the notes.

[21] See, on this history, *Voyage du Chevalier du Marchais,* by Fr. [Jean Baptiste] Labat, vol. 3, pp. 79-84; Raynal, *Hist. Phil.,* vol. 7, p. 19, according to what is reported in *Beschryving van Guyane* ["Description of Guiana"], by [Jan Jacob] Hartsink (Amsterdam, 1770), volume I, pp. 161 *et seq.,* in quarto.

[22] See [Geerlof] Suiker[s], [*Algemene Kerkelyke en Wereldyke*] *Geschiedenisse[n des Bekenden Aard-klodts* . . .], vol. 2, chapter 35, article 12.

[23] *Voyage du Chevalier du Marchais,* vol. 3, p. 93; Hartsink, op. cit., vol. I, p. 163.

[24] See *Tegenwoordige Staat van America,* vol. II, p. 540.

[25] See also [Raynal,] *Histoire Philos[ophique]. et Polit[ique]. des Isles Françaises dans les Indes Occidentales* (Lausanne, 1784), pp. 62 *et seq.*

[26] See [La Condamine,] *Voyage à la Rivière des Amazones* (Maastricht, 1778), p. 209.

[27] [Jacques Nicolas] Bellin, *Déscription [Géographique] de la Guyane,* p. 14; *Tegenwoordige Staat van America,* vol. II, p. 512.

[28] [Hartsink, *Beschryving,*] vol. II, in English and in Dutch, pp. 522-58.

[29] [La Porte, *Voyageur,*] pp. 326-92, vol. XI.

[30] It was not until several years later, when the clearing of the lowlands was begun, that water mills were constructed in Surinam.

[31] See, on this, *Richesse de la Hollande,* vol. I, p. 304.

[32] As contained in *Tegenwoordige Staat van America,* vol. II, p. 450.

[33] [Fermin, *Tableau,*] p. 3.

[34] See Document No. II, dated August 16, 1665.

[35] See Document No. III. See also *Histoire Générale des Voyages,* vol. 21, p. 75 (Amsterdam, 1774); and Hartsink, vol. 2, p. 559; [Fermin,] *Tableau de Surinam,* p. 231.

[36] See Document No. IV.

HISTORY OF SURINAM 233

[37] Raynal, vol. 7, p. 272.

[38] See Hartsink, vol. 2, p. 599.

[39] See Hartsink, vol. 2, p. 600.

[40] See on Aboab, *Entretiens sur Divers Sujets d'Histoire, de Réligion et de Critique* ["Discourses on Various Historical, Religious, and Critical Subjects"] (London, 1770), pp. 13 *et seq.*, during his sojourn in Surinam.

[41] See the remonstrance and the response, in Hartsink, pp. 608-12.

[42] According to [Eduard] van Zur[c]k, *Codex Batavus*, p. 217.

[43] [Hartsink,] pp. 612-14.

[44] See on this *Richesse de la Hollande,* vol. I, p. 245.

[45] *Richesse de la Hollande,* vol. I, p. 284.

[46] *Richesse de la Hollande,* vol. I, p. 263, in the notes.

[47] In his [Hartsink's] *Histoire de la Guyane,* p. 676.

[48] Hartsink, p. 674.

[49] We cannot conceive on what basis Bellin gives the assurance that, in the year 1683, at the arrival of Governor Sommelsdyk, there were already to be counted in Surinam up to six hundred families who were settled there; this would make a population of 3,000 whites, with the exception of the number of almost 1,500 who left for Jamaica, etc. Besides, the Jewish population was calculated at one-third of that of the Christians, and from the number of families whom we find to have been in Surinam about the year 1690, we can calculate the population at only 300 to 350 families in general, which (at five persons per family) would make almost 1,800 inhabitants. See Bellin, *Disc. Géographique*, part 2, p. 113.

[50] Manuscript, *Ibidem;* Hartsink, pp. 676-80; [Raynal,] *Hist. Philos. et Polit. des Isles Françaises,* p. 30.

[51] See the register of the Jewish community.

[52] Hartsink, p. 681.

[53] *Ibidem,* p. 680.

[54] [Hartsink,] pp. 691-94.

[55] [Fermin, *Tableau,*] p. 111.

[56] See the Act signed by Cassart, October 27, 1712, in Hartsink, pp. 714, 720, and 722.

[57] [Hartsink,] pp. 693-94.

[58] Hartsink, p. 756.

[59] [*Rich. de la Holl.,*] vol. I, p. 294.

[60] See Hartsink, p. 695.

[61] Hartsink, p. 726.

[62] *Ibidem,* p. 727.

[63] This letter and the reply thereto, dated June, 1707, are to be found in the archives.

[64] Hartsink, p. 741.

[65] [Fermin, *Tableau,*] p. 253.

[66] According to Hartsink, p. 741. As for what concerns the commodities and the period of their introduction into the colony, in contradiction to all that the historians of Surinam say, we have made our researches about this, and with great care and exactitude, and we have succeeded in drawing up a general table of all the commodities of the colony exported to Europe from the beginning of this century up to our own day. This will be found at the end of the first part of this work.

In this table it will be seen that despite the general supposition which has been commonly adopted, to the effect that the lands of the colony were suitable only for sugar, coffee, cacao, and, at the present time, cotton, there were many attempts made with regard to other commodities which would have had very favorable results, if the inconstancy of the colonists had permitted it [ie., had not made it impossible]. Tobacco, for example, was begun from 1706, and year after year a sufficiently large quantity thereof was exported even in this time of experiments, and even in 1749 30,000 pounds were exported to Holland.

Annatto [roucou] had a more brilliant good fortune, for, started in pits on several small holdings, where it had been planted more as a curiosity than for the purpose of making it an article of trade, from 100 to 7,000 pounds a year were sent to Holland.

On indigo, the introduction of which all the authors attribute tô the efforts of Monsieur van Jever and Officer l'Estrade, see [Fermin,] *Tableau de Surinam,* p. . . .; Hartsink, p. 742. In the year 1764, or thereabout, it had already been cultivated in Surinam since 1708, and two years later until the year 1722, from 150 to 1,328 pounds had been sent to Holland. It was entirely abandoned in order to introduce coffee, the first beans of which were brought in 1720, as we have noted above.

Cacao, which, according to Hartsink, p. 741, and *Tableau de Surinam,* p. 256, was introduced in 1733, and cotton in 1735, were cultivated in Surinam from 1706 on.

Besides these products, the old inhabitants of the colony made their speculations on all sorts of commercial products, even to the extraction of raw wax from the honeycombs formed by the bees in the trees of the immense forests of the colony, situated at the source of the Surinam river. They even made attempts with regard to the minerals of the colony, and in the year 1736 five ounces of fine gold were sent to Holland. This encouraged the formation of a private company expressly for mining in 1742, but it had no results. (See on this Hartsink, pp. 744-54.)

HISTORY OF SURINAM 235

The above-mentioned *Tableau* will indicate several other exportable commodities of the colony. If one applied oneself thereto, it would extend the work to all classes of the citizens. Why is it that people abandoned everything in order to devote themselves only to sugar, coffee, and cotton, which require for their cultivation means of which the greatest part of the colonists are destitute? In order to reply to this argument, one has only to cite the inconstancy of the colonists, since experience has shown us a thousand times that each new commodity easily caused them to change the cultivations which they practiced. We have seen that after the introduction of coffee, a large part of sugar cultivation was abandoned; cacao is losing out on its cultivation little by little; cotton is at present in vogue, and the first commodities which chance will bring here will lead to the abandonment of these in their turn. If only the colonists who have so few means at the present time occupied themselves with working on other branches of agriculture than on coffee and on cotton! Why do they forget dyewood? Why do they forget copaïba balm, wax, tobacco, and even annatto [roucou], which do not require so many Negroes for this work? See on this subject the learned reflections of Monsieur Firmin [Fermin] in his *Tableau de Surinam*, pp. 257 *et seq.*

[67] [Hartsink,] pp. 755-57.

[68] [Bielfeld,] *Institutions Politiques* [2 vols., The Hague, 1760], vol. 3, p. 18, Leyden, 1772; Du Lignon, *Bibliothèque Judaïque*, p. 39; [Isaac] de Pinto, *Apologie des Juifs*, p. 17; the dictionaries of Martinière and Savary [des Bruslons] on the word "Amsterdam"; and several others.

[69] According to Hartsink, pp. 728-39.

[70] Hartsink, pp. 758-67; *Richesse de la Hollande*, vol. I, pp. 305-16; *Tableau de Surinam*, pp. 138, 141, and 154.

[71] Hartsink, p. 756.

[72] In order to confirm all this, in contradiction to what Hartsink says, p. 766, one can ask the Negroes of Juca, our new allies, the truth of this fact, and then one will know that they had two names for this village of Creoles destroyed by Nassy: *Gri-gri* and *Nassy Broko*. "Gri-gri," in the jargon of the country, or Negro-English, metaphorically signifies the sound which naked feet make on the ground, when one runs swiftly. "Dem ron gri-gri" means, "they ran away very quickly." "Nassy Broko" means, "Nassy demolished it," because "Broko" means, alike, "to demolish," "to rupture," "to break," "to ruin," etc.

[73] See all this more in detail in *La Richesse de la Hollande*, vol. I, pp. 305-25.

[74] See two resolutions of the Council of March 10 and 12, 1750, Document No. X, 1 and 2 L°.

[75] [Hartsink,] pp. 779 *et seq.*

[76] See Document No. II.

[77] [Hartsink,] p. 876.

[78] Document No. XV.

[79] See these proceedings in the collection of Mauritius, folio vol. 3.

[80] Nos. XIII, XIV, and XV.

[81] See Justificatory Document, No. XIII.

[82] See the Letter of Her Royal Highness to the regents, dated August 22, 1754, Justificatory Document, No. XIV.

[83] See Justificatory Document, No. XV.

[84] And which one can see in greater detail in Hartsink, pp. 777 and 779; [Fermin,] *Tableau de Surinam,* pp. 145-50.

[85] Despite the assurance of these authors, exact researches persuade us—and what we have heard from these allies confirms it to us—that the number of those of Juca in general in a condition to bear arms did not amount at that time to more than 350 or 400, and those of Saramaca to from 550 to 600. This makes a number of at most 1,000 men, and if we further allow each one five or six persons for their families, the result will amount to no more than nearly 6,000. Let us still add another third, if that is desirable, and there will be found only about 8,000 to 9,000 souls! This number is at present diminished to the point at which, according to the most exact researches, there are probably in Juca from 1,800 to 2,000, and in Saramaca 3,000 to 4,000 souls, which makes a total of 5,000 to 6,000.

[86] Hartsink, p. 793.

[87] Hartsink, p. 799.

[88] See, in addition, for the details of this peace, [Fermin,] *Tableau de Surinam,* pp. 154-72; *Richesse de la Hollande,* vol. I, pp. 325-32.

[89] [Hartsink,] pp. 779-813.

[90] See on this subject the letter which a doctor of the Sorbonne wrote to Monsieur J. [*sic*—Isaac] de Pinto, very well known in the republic of letters for his works and who died at The Hague on September 20, 1787, on the subject of his apology for the Jews against the writings of Monsieur de Voltaire. The extract from this letter is printed in an anonymous work of a Venetian, under the title of *Reflexions Critiques sur l'Apologie pour la Nation Juive,* by Monsieur J. [*sic*] de Pinto (London, 1768).

[91] It was forbidden to the citizens of whatever conditions they were in and for any case which there might be, to go to the villages of Juca and Saramaca, belonging to our new allies. We do not know whether this prohibition has not contributed for a long time to keeping these Negroes in their bad habits, and to maintaining their hatred against the whites for a longer time.

[92] [*Brieven over Demerary en Essequibo,*] p. 73.

[93] When one disputes those who adhere to the opinion of attributing everything to the ignorance of the Jews on agriculture, they divert their specious judgments to the multitude of their [the Jews'] festivals, which give birth, they say, to idle-

ness and to malignity among their Negroes. The Jews, however, have only fourteen days of festivals, not counting Saturdays (which are exchanged for Sundays), namely: in April, Passover, four days; in June, their Pentecost [*Shavuot*], two days; in July, their fast [*Tisha B'Av*], one day; and in October, the New Year, the Day of Atonement, and Booths [*Sukkot*], seven days, which makes altogether fourteen days a year; and on these days and their Saturdays, the Negroes still work for them on their lands, as is done in Santo Domingo [Hispaniola], in Cayenne [French Guiana], and elsewhere. These fourteen days of loss for the Jewish planters in each year are not at all an object sufficiently considerable on which to build up a system to the prejudice of a portion of the human race. The said work on Essequebo, [*Brieven over Demerary en Essequibo,*] pp. 72-73, where it is said again that "the Jews, not being able to work as much as the Christians, force their slaves to work harder in order to make up for the loss of their days of rest, etc.," is erroneous. Here in Surinam, they are accused of bad examples which they set for their slaves, because they work too little and because of their festivals and Sabbath days; and there at Demmerary (where it is said that information has been received from Surinam) they are accused of giving their slaves too much work. Are not these two accusations contradictory? But this matters very little to these gentlemen, for this is not the first time that they contradict themselves and reason falsely when it is a question of bearing down on the Jews.

[94] Sam. Nassy and Jeos. Sarphaty were notaries public, as are the Jews at London. Jacob Polak was assistant receiver of the office of taxes. Abm. Nunez was sworn land-surveyor, who served Christians and Jews alike. Doctor Ladesma was the physician of the hospital, Abm. de Barrios and Eliazer, etc., were sworn clerks of various countinghouses, J. H. Brandon was collector of the fees of the secretariat. All that they have at present is leave to serve as solicitors before the commissioners of petty cases and, moreover, the number of only two Jews can be admitted thereto.

[95] Document XVIII.

[96] That [the theatre] of the Christians is still on the same footing as when Sansini saw it.

[97] With the exception of the general fund for the poor, the Portuguese Jewish community, despite its present decline and the contribution to the taxes of the colony and the expenses for the maintenance of its two synagogues, one at the Savane and the other at Paramaribo, has three confraternities: one for the interment of the dead and the maintenance of the cemeteries; the second for the furnishing of shrouds, coffins, and tombstones, etc., and for the support of poor families during the seven days of mourning; and the third for aiding the sick and supplying them with their needs. The three together are a matter of almost four thousand florins a year given for the subsistence of the poor, with the further exception of six to eight thousand florins which [the community] spends annually together with the general fund for the support of the families of widows, of orphans, and of those who are not in a position to earn their livelihood, without counting the payments made for physicians and for medicine, etc. Well, great God, with what resources? Their industry [alone]. Honest Christians, friendly

philosophers, profound politicians, and finally, sovereigns, open your eyes for once on this unfortunate community, and you authors of the libel that has gone forth from Essequebo and Demmerary, blush for your sentiments, stop calumniating the Portuguese Jews in regard to the charity that they exercise towards their brethren. J. C. [Jesus Christ] himself preached it, and the heart of a sensitive man prescribes it.

[98] We agree that there are among the Jews many dissensions, as among other peoples; but nevertheless those who say that they are friends are so truly in the full force of the term; firm, constant, and always with candor, they know how to appreciate this heavenly gift of friendship and in consequence to sacrifice whatever is necessary in order to maintain it. Many circumstances, many small complaints must cooperate before this link, once strengthened, can be broken. But once it has been broken, they become terrible to one another, and it is because of their impetuosity in this respect that their enmities break out in Surinam more than those of the Christians.

[99] Nevertheless, we admit with pleasure (and we would even be ingrates if we failed to acknowledge it) the acts of friendship for which some Jews are indebted to some Christians of the colony; but in generalizing this fact, we observe that the number of these Christians is so small that their goodness and their benevolence become almost useless for the general body of the Jewish community [which must face] the rest of the inhabitants, who are not at all informed by the same sentiment. Besides, everyone wishes to be impressed by visible objects; what does it matter to the Jewish community that it has individuals beloved, so to speak, in secret or clandestinely, by several persons of distinction, when these same Jews are not honored in their own homes by these Christians? Frequent visits made to the Jews; inviting them at some time to their festivals; making them little by little familiar with the other persons of their company; encouraging thereby their wives and children—[this] implies some merit in the Jewish community and will open the eyes of those who are the most prejudiced against it; but [for Christians] to protect some of them, even to love them without rendering the object, so to speak, visible, implies only an individual affection and redounds very little to the benefit of the Jewish community in general. We are, by constant deeds, imbued with feelings of the goodness of Governor Wichers, of Colonel Frederici, of the Councillors Lemmers, de Graaf and several others, of Doctor Schilling, and of several individuals. We glory in meriting their affections; yet (may this outburst of our heart in favor of the body of the Jewish community be permitted us) do not these gentlemen act rather as virtuous and reasonable men than as citizens of the first rank who can set the tone, and edify the rest of the inhabitants of the colony, towards the Jews?

[100] *Letter of the Jews to Monsieur de Voltaire* [sic—Guené, *Lettres de Quelques Juifs,*] vol. I, p. 23.

[101] See a scintilla of this truth in Document No. XX of October 15, 1784, after the death of Governor Texier, and during the absence of the prosecutor, Monsieur Wichers.

[102] See Justificatory Document, No. XIX.

[103] See hereon the prospectus, Document No. XXI, and the letter of the governor, Document No. XXII.

[104] Governor Wichers was able to add to his benefactions the employment of under-clerks of the warehouse of foodstuffs for the cordon established at the Savane, with which he favored J. H. de Barrios (who died, regretted by his friends, in December, 1786), an employment which, despite its small importance, gave some hope to the Jewish community, in view of the fact that up to that time there had been no example of any Jew's having been employed in the military establishment of the colony.

[105] See the details of this festival in the description which was made thereof in Dutch, and which was presented as a feeble homage to the Lords Proprietors. These details were printed at Amsterdam by Dronsberg in 1786, and before this work had been made public in the colony, the regents took care to pay their homage, in the name of the Jewish community, to the governor and to the administrative councillors, furnishing them a sufficient number of copies thereof. This elicited thanks to them on the part of the council, with assurances of good will towards the Jewish community.

[106] See Justificatory Document, No. XXIV.

[107] We do not deny that there are some very rich people among the Jews: among the Portuguese [the Sephardim,] there are some persons and families who still possess from 50,000 even up to 400,000 florins of capital, accumulated in great part through their capacity in business and in trade and commerce with the English, etc. Others probably still have from 20,000 to 50,000 florins of capital, employed in work in the woods, which yields a very high annual income. Among the German [Ashkenazic] Jews there are some capitalists who possess up to 150,000 and 200,000 florins, and a large proportion who have sufficient funds for their maintenance, for that of the poor which we have noted, and for contributions for the synagogues and other relief which is given to the needy. But since the rest of the Jewish community (in number more than two-thirds) are poor, it is only they, their sufferings, their few resources, and the hindrances which they experience in their trading, that we have in mind in everything to be found in the text of this note.

[108] Here is the summary of the questions of Monsieur Dohm, contained in his letter, the copy of which is in the preface to this Essay:

1st. On the advantages which the government of Surinam accords to the Jewish community.

2nd. If any distinction is made there between our Jewish community and the other inhabitants of the colony.

3rd. If all occupations, professions, and kinds of commerce are permitted to them.

4th. If the Jewish community there enjoys the right to possess plantations in full ownership.

5th. If the Jewish community there pays special taxes to the colony, as in several countries.

6th. If, as in several countries, the number of their families there must be restricted.

7th. If the Jewish community is able to defend the fatherland as soldiers, or as civil or military officers.

8th. On historical notices; on the fate which the colony has suffered from its beginning with the date of its founding, and the changes which the privileges of the Jewish community met with.

9th. On the political and moral condition of the colony in general, and on the feelings which the wise and enlightened justice of the government should have inspired in the Christians toward the Jews.

NOTES TO PART II

[1] The cultivation of cotton has much increased but since the first ten years of the last reckoning produced very little cotton, the average per year has amounted to only 750,000 pounds.

[2] In [Fermin's] *Tableau de Surinam,* p. 371, a barrel of sugar is figured at 60 florins; here at 112.10 florins.
Coffee at 8½ sous; here at 10½ sous.
Cacao at 6½ sous; here at 5 sous.
Cotton at 8 sous; here at 21 sous.

[3] In the period of twenty-six years from 1750 to 1776, the colony produced year after year the following averages: (See *Tableau de Surinam,* p. 372, for the year 1771, and p. 373 for the year 1775):
Every year, 20,572,122 pounds of coffee, and from 1777 to the end of 1787
Every year, 12,064,878 pounds, a decline of
  8,507,244 pounds of coffee.
  22,127½ barrels of sugar up to 1776.
  15,872 up to 1787.
  6,255 fewer barrels of sugar.
  1,366,669 pounds of cacao up to 1776.
  701,362 up to 1787.
  665,307 fewer pounds of cacao.
  572,214 pounds of cotton up to 1776.
  851,483½ up to 1787.
  279,269½ more pounds of cotton.

[4] To appreciate the lot of the unfortunate planters in Surinam, one has only to deduct, from the total of their annual revenue of 9,289,109 florins, the sum of 1,214,693 florins for the freight of the vessels, and the expenses for the revenue of the products which we have mentioned above, and this sum, added to the 829,188 florins for merchandise, locks, etc., sent from Holland for the plantations, according to the calculation which we have given in this work, and also the annual wages of the directors and commanders to the number of 1,090 persons on 545 estates, at an average of 500 florins each, which amounts to the sum of 45,000 florins. The taxes on the products of the estates, which can be reckoned altogether at nearly 600,000 florins, and also the interest of 6 percent on a debt of 60,000,000 which the colony owes, make the sum of 3,600,000. These sums altogether make a total of 7,478,881 florins, so that there remains as profit for the planters to meet the mortality and the flight of the slaves, the repair of the buildings, unforeseen and extraordinary expenses, etc., only the sum of 2,210,228

florins, again without counting the 10 percent which the proprietors in Holland pay for the administration of their properties, which can be reckoned at least as two-thirds of the total revenue of nearly 6,200,000 florins, of which the 10 percent amounts to an annual expense of 620,000 florins.

[5] The English trade which has just been mentioned is an absolute necessity for the colony; it is absolutely impossible to do without it. However, one remarkable thing is the importation of an immense quantity of English boards which are made in America, and which do considerable harm to the wood plantations of the colony. It is never permitted in any place whatsoever to import there manufactures, etc., which are made there, especially when the local people are in general in a position to supply the needs of each individual.

[6] Firmin [Fermin] says, in his claimed general description of Surinam in two large volumes [*Tableau de Surinam*], vol. 1, p. 24, that the houses were all without windows, because of the great heat, a mistake which was copied by the *Histoire Générale des Voyages* and by the *Voyageur François*.

[7] According to appearances, it seems that the place where the city is situated and all that portion of ground, filled with marshes, which drains to the north, was formed by some early revolution of nature; the quantity of shells, a marine product which is found there, gives reason to believe this. The rest of the colony, on the contrary, is filled with large mountains and a prodigious number of hills intersected by great plains thirty leagues inland; but the places near the seashore are swampy and filled with woods and bushes.

[8] See their civil separation from the Portuguese [Sephardim] in this work.

[9] This matter is true. A decent Jew, well-read and of good judgment, had a Negress as his concubine, who gave him several children who were reared in the [Dutch] Reformed religion. He later legitimately married off his eldest daughter to a Roman Catholic widower, a man of much merit but who, unfortunately, had, by his first marriage, a son who, born in Russia, was raised in the Greek [Orthodox] religion. Thus the father was Jewish, the mother pagan, the husband Catholic, the wife Calvinist, and his son a Greek schismatic. After the husband died, his wife became a strict Anglican.

[10] See, on this article, Firmin's mistake [in *Tableau de Surinam*,] p. 241.

[11] [Raynal,] vol. 4, p. 337.

[12] Printed at Geneva, by Pellet, 1781.

[13] See [Raynal,] *Hist. Phil.* (Geneva, 1781), vol. 2, p. 75.

[14]
On the plantations	1,090
In the city	955
Portuguese Jews	834
Germans	477
	3,356
Mulattoes and freed Negroes	650
	4,006

HISTORY OF SURINAM 243

[15] Of these fifty vessels, there are some which carry from 16,000 to 30,000 florins worth of freight, so that one can calculate, without exaggeration, for each vessel, 16,000 florins of exported freight.

[16] These bills of two, four, and ten shillings and of ten florins, and the notes of 50 to 500 florins, were devised in 1764. They are signed by two administrative councillors, and by the collector of the countinghouse of moderate charges, who is the one who signs the stamped papers. And in the middle there is affixed the seal of the colony. See Hartsink, pp. 857 and 858.

[17] See on this subject the lie uttered against the Jews in the libel of Essequebo [*Brieven over Demerary*] regarding the introduction of this debased currency: Justificatory Document of the first volume.

[18] We give notice that in this description we are considering only the Creoles; one must not confuse the other inhabitants of the colony with them. Extremely sensitive and compassionate, equally stubborn and capricious, they have vices and peculiarities which are characteristic only of them, and which have nothing in common with those which are to be met with in Europe. Sacrificing always to love, they are not especially enthusiastic about sex, nor so passionate and intrepid as to dare everything in order to make conquests therein. *Of those treasons, of those base deeds which soil the annals of all peoples,* says Monsieur Raynal, *one would never be able to cite a shameful crime which has been committed by a Creole.* See vol. 6, p. 167.

[19] The art which the Africans have of taming snakes of a certain species is not unknown. Monsieur de la Flotte's essay on the Indies [*Essais Historiques sur l'Inde* (Paris, 1769)] demonstrates this, and what we see being done by the Negroes of Huida convinces us thereof sufficiently so as not to suppose it so astonishing as to believe it a miracle, like those who attach themselves to this Negress.

[20] So many researches on the cure of this disease, and always fruitlessly, have been made in America that we are tempted to believe that it was only by venereal diseases of the most fatal kind that this Negro was attacked. Perhaps if this idea is accepted in Surinam, more progress will be made in the case of those who are attacked by so-called elephantiasis. May the symptoms and the horrible signs which accompany this illness not befall us! For if one reads the brochure of the physician [Francisco?] Sanchez, translated into French by Professor [Hieronymus David?] Gaubius, on the appearance of venereal disease in Europe, it will be seen that it has at least a complete analogy to this frightful disease, both in regard to the marks and to the other symptoms. To strengthen this idea, we have the experience of the little effect produced here by the new discoveries made by the Spaniards in Peru and extolled by all the journals and literary gazettes. According to a memoir read at the college for researches into nature by Jos. d'Anaria, a Jewish surgeon and accoucheur.

[21] The college is composed of a president, who is the governor [of the colony], of a treasurer, a secretary, and a sufficient number of active members who take care of all that is needed for the maintenance of the college, as well as of a large number of honorary members. Meetings are held there once a month, and

memoranda provided by the members in general are read there. The contents thereof are never other than the agriculture of the country, its natural history, and all that has reference to physics and to medicine. There are observed there, with the greatest exactness, the state of the atmosphere, the pressure of the air, the winds that prevail more constantly in each month, together with the degrees of cold and of heat, according to the thermometer and the barometer. These observations are due to the assiduity and the patience of Doctor Schilling. This society, whose useful goal does honor to those who have established it, cannot make any noticeable progress because the honorary members and those who reside on the plantations (and who have some leisure to make observations) do not contribute to furnish the least thing. Nevertheless, the memoranda which have already been read publicly, but have not yet been printed, would amount to several printed volumes, in quarto.

[22] See *Lives of the Dutch Governors in the East Indies,* in quarto, p. 219.

INDEX

A

ABENATAN, S. H. MORON, JUNIOR, 218
ABOAB, 35; IMMANUEL, 226; ISAAC, 24, 233; RAPHAEL, 194
Academies, 227
Accoucheurs, 156, 243
Administrative council, 38, 46-49, 54, 57, 62-63, 65-71, 74, 76-77, 80-81, 84-85, 90, 93, 106, 108, 110-11, 115-16, 127, 133-38, 141, 146, 176-79, 182, 188, 195-99, 206, 211, 235, 239, 243; *see also* High Council
Admirals, 31, 34, 49
Advisors, 138; *see also* Preadvisors
Advocates, 113, 118, 138-39, 223-25; *see also* Attorneys
Africans, 67, 143, 146, 243
Aged, the, 137
Agents, 17, 84, 93-94, 98, 101, 131, 147-48, 201, 226-27
Agriculture, 24, 26, 36, 49, 63-64, 80, 84, 95-99, 101-2, 116, 125, 185-86, 216, 218, 235-36, 244
Almonries, 137
Amazon Country, South America, 27, 125
America, xi, 8, 18, 22, 24, 27-30, 32, 36, 39, 49, 52, 84-85, 92-93, 99, 126, 129, 131-33, 141-43, 145-46, 153, 164-66, 190, 231, 242-43; *see also* North America, South America, United States
American Philosophic Society, XI
Amsterdam, xi, 4, 17, 21-23, 36-37, 43, 46, 48, 51, 53, 55, 82, 90, 111, 156, 163-64, 185, 188, 190, 203-4, 225, 232, 235, 239

Amusements, 167
Anglicans, 242
Animals, 101-2, 128, 147; *see also* Cattle
Annatto; *see* ROUCOU
ANNE OF ORANGE AND NASSAU, 22, 79-82, 200-206
Antigua, 32
Anti-Jewish prejudice, 8, 10-11, 15, 77, 85, 98, 104, 230
Antwerp, 20
Apologists, xii, 15, 236
Apothecaries, 141, 156, 162
Archives, 7-8, 26, 30, 33, 35, 43, 45-47, 50, 55, 58, 61, 68, 72, 103, 120, 134, 148-49
Ark, 149
Army; *see* Military
ARRIAS, ISAAC, 193-94; Js., 67-68
Arts, 22; *see also* Fine arts
Ascamoth, 81, 117, 203-5, 219-20; *see also* Ecclesiasticism, Institutions
Ashkenazim, xi, 3, 63-64, 134, 207, 211, 213, 239; *see also* German Jews
Assassinations, 176
Assayers, 141
Astronomy, 227
Atheism, 105
Atonement Day; *see* Kippur
Attorneys, 113, 118; powers of, 93, 139
AUCA (Jew), 71
Auctions, 119, 148
Auditors, 138, 180-81
Authority, 220, 224
Autonomy, ix, 60
AZEVEDO, ISAAC, 96

245

B

Bakers, 106
Balsam, 186
Banishment, 205
Bankruptcy, 199
Barbados, 28, 32-33
Bark, 174
BARRIOS, ABM. DE, 237; JACOB HENRIQUES (ENRIQUES) DE, JR., 12, 80-81, 218, 221, 239; MIGUEL DE, 21, 23, 25, 227, 231-32
Beechwood, 49, 172-74
Beer, 145, 147
Belles-lettres, 155
Berbice, 52, 89
Bergendaal (plantation), 58
Berlin, 6-7, 13
Bigotry, 18, 64, 104-5, 111, 136, 140, 230
Blacks; see Negroes
Boa Vizinhanca (plantation), 98
Boards, 242
BOLS, ABRAHAM, 182, 194
Boni, 108, 127
Bookkeepers, 119
Books, 6, 8, 12-13, 21, 45, 53, 56, 105, 112, 117, 163-64, 166, 215, 217-19; see also Publications
Booths; see Feast of Tabernacles
Bordeaux, 20
Botanists, 148
Bramspunt, 28
BRANDON, D. H., 218; J., 26; J. H., 237; SAMUEL HOHEB, 4, 12, 218, 221
Brandy, 145, 147
Brazil, 10, 20, 23-24, 26, 96, 227, 232
Breda, 31; see also Treaties
Bricks, 132, 134, 144
BRITTO (BRITTON), AB. (ABM.) DE, 68, 71; IS. DE, 202
Brokerage, 22
BUENO BIBAL, A., 218
Buildings, 84, 91, 110, 129, 132, 134, 136, 241
Burghers, ix

Burial, 30, 102, 108, 116, 133, 189, 210, 212, 237
Bush Negroes, x

C

Caap de Goede Hoop (plantation), 98
Cabarets, 166-67
Cabo Verde (plantation), 98
Cacao, 56, 98, 128-30, 147, 169-72, 234-35, 241
Calvinism, 21, 39, 127, 136, 185, 242
Cananama River, 31, 191
Canavinika, 196
Cantors, 134
Cape of Willoughby of Parham, 28
Capital, capitalists, 49, 147, 239
Capitation-tax, 146
Captains, 30, 32, 42, 44-45, 49, 54, 60, 65-70, 72, 75, 108, 127, 144, 191, 196, 211
Cards, 167
Caribbean islands, 143
Carpenters, 55, 141
Carriages, 147, 167
CARRILHOS (CARRELHO; CARILHO; CARRILHO), IS., 65, 69, 75, 77, 79-80, 106, 197
CASERES, HENRIQUE DE, 194
CASSARD (CASSART), JACQUES, 31, 49-54, 58-59, 64-65, 233
Casseneka, 196
Cassewine, 56, 58-59, 70
Catholicism, 15, 19, 21, 38, 135-36, 224, 242
Cattle, 151
CAUCANARS, IS., 117, 218
Cayenne, 10, 24-26, 28-30, 32, 44-45, 49, 105, 152, 183, 190, 237
Cemeteries, 30, 149, 237
Ceremonies, 43, 50, 63, 75, 88, 105, 136, 156, 189; see also Customs
Chaises, 147
Chambers of commerce, 186
Charpente, 101

INDEX 247

Chartered Society of Surinam, 37, 176, 190, 194-95, 197, 207-8
Chartered West India Company; *see* Dutch West India Company
Charters, X, 25, 27, 29, 52, 184; *see also* Grants
Children, 62, 71, 85, 102, 104, 137, 153, 155, 163, 214, 230, 238, 242
Chinese, 114
Christianity, ix-x, 9, 13-14, 17-18, 23, 25, 33, 35-36, 46, 50, 55, 57-58, 61, 66-67, 69-70, 72-73, 75, 80, 83, 85, 92, 94, 96-102, 104, 108, 110, 112-14, 121, 127, 133-36, 140, 144, 149, 152, 154, 156, 164, 167, 187, 198, 214, 226, 230, 233, 237-38, 240; *see also* Anglicans; Calvinism; Catholicism; Dutch Reformed Religion; Greek Orthodoxy; Jesuits, Lutherans; Moravian Brethren; Non-Jews; Papists; Protestants; Reformed Protestants
Chronicle of Xarises, 17
Cid, Isaac Gabay, 194
Citizens, citizenship, x-xi, 5, 13, 18, 21, 42, 45, 49-50, 54, 60, 63-65, 67-68, 70-72, 75, 77, 84, 86-88, 94, 107-8, 125, 127, 139, 185, 188, 196-97, 207, 210-12, 235-36, 238
Citizens' Company, 106
Civic life, 6
Civilians, 65-66, 68, 88
Classes, social and economic, 166-67; *see also* Lower-middle class, Middle class, White Collar class
Clerks, 113, 119, 142, 182, 199, 237, 239
Climate, 132, 152-53
Cloth, clothing, 145
Code Noir, 18, 230
Coffee, 56, 83, 93, 98, 128-30, 146-47, 166, 169-72, 234-35, 241
Collectors, 237, 243
College of Literature; *see* Docendo Docemur
Colleges, 163-64, 243
Colonels, 117, 126-27, 164, 179, 238

Colonies, colonists, x, 9, 26-32, 34-39, 41-56, 58-61, 64-67, 72-76, 78, 81-85, 89-93, 95-96, 98-99, 101, 103, 113, 118-19, 125-26, 128-29, 142-46, 154, 162-63, 166-67, 175-76, 179-81, 183-88, 193-94, 198, 201-2, 206, 214, 219, 223-25, 230, 234-35, 238-40, 241-42
Comedy, 167
Commandants, commanders, 38, 41-42, 55, 109, 127, 142, 175-78, 180, 190-91, 241
Commandos, 196-97
Commissioners, 76-77, 79-80, 82, 85, 118, 141, 177, 180, 198, 207, 237; Commission (commissioners) of small cases, 137-38, 147
Commowine, 56, 58, 84, 100, 134; River, 28, 42, 56, 65, 70, 91, 99-100, 126, 128-29, 131, 151, 197
Communion, 135
Community, Jewish, x-xi, 4, 8-9, 11, 13, 15-16, 18, 22, 26, 30, 33, 36, 39-40, 43, 45-46, 48, 50-51, 55-56, 58-64, 67, 72-73, 75, 77-81, 95, 97, 99-101, 103-21, 129, 139-40, 142, 151-52, 188-89, 192-96, 199, 202-4, 206, 210-12, 214, 224-25, 227, 233, 238-40; *see also* German Jews, Jews
Company of Equinoctial France, 25; of Rohan, 28; of the North Cape, 24-25
Competition, 119, 151, 230
Confiscation, 193
Confraternities, 237
Constables, 180
Contracts, 184
Controllers, 137-38, 180-82
Conversion, 17
Copaiba balm, 235
Copename River, 29, 57
Copyists, 199-200
Corcipines, 27
Cordon, 90-91, 109, 127, 146, 149-50, 152, 239

Coromantin, 57, 67
Correspondence; see Letters
Cottica, 84, 100; River, 65, 91, 99, 128
Cotton, 56, 128-30, 146-47, 166, 169-72, 234-35, 241
Council, councillors, 138, 147, 187, 189-90, 192, 225, 238; Council of civil justice, 38, 137, 139, 181; Council of civil procedure, 139; Council of the Nineteen, 183, 187; High Council, 76; see also Administrative council
Countinghouses, 113, 119, 237, 243
Courts, 20, 60, 64, 81, 106, 118, 135-39, 141, 148, 166, 180, 182, 187, 189, 193, 198, 200, 208, 210-13, 223-24
Crafts, 13
Credit, 18, 83-84, 93, 97-98, 100, 130-31, 143
Creditors, 121
Creoles, 68-69, 155-56, 164, 235, 243
Crime, 36, 60, 120, 138, 151, 187, 196
Crockery, 145
Culture, ix, xi, 20, 26, 109, 121
Curaçao, x
Customs, 100, 105, 111-12, 134-35, 189, 219; see also Ceremonies

D

DA COSTA, ALEXANDER (ALEXANDRO), 17, 226; ALVARO NUNEZ (NUNES), 17, 226; BENTO, 194; ISAAK, 194
DACOSTA, 30; ABRAHAM, 79-80
D'ANARIA, IMANUEL, 218; JOS., 243
Dancing, 152, 155, 159, 167
D'AVILAR, JACOB, 66
Day of Atonement; see Kippur
DE LA PARRA; see Parra
DE LEON, MOSES PARA, 4, 12, 118, 218, 222; PEREIRA, 223, 225
Deaths, 97, 107-10, 130, 136, 138, 156-57, 175-76, 178-82, 236, 238-39

Debts, debtors, 9, 37, 57, 61, 82-84, 92-93, 95, 97, 100, 136, 143, 193, 227, 241
Decrees, 105-106, 212-13
Deists, xi
DEL MONTE, BIENVENIDA, 67
DEMEDINA, ABM. DE SAMUEL ROBLES, 218
Demerary (Demmerary), 18, 34, 51, 91, 99, 125, 230, 237-38
DEMESQUITA, ABRAHAM BUENO, 218; ISACK DE ABRAHAM BUENO, 218
Deputies, 60, 189, 193, 197, 201, 206, 208, 220-21; see also Regents
Descanco (plantation), 98
Dessau, 6
Diet, 153-54
Directors and Regents, 38, 176, 178-81, 190, 194-97, 199-200, 204-5, 211, 220, 241
Disabilities, ix
Disasters, 100, 105, 209
Discrimination, 18, 22
Diseases, xi, 153-54, 243; see also Elephantiasis, Leprosy, Sicknesses, Venereal
Disputes, 187, 198, 201-2, 204-5, 238
Docendo Docemur (College of Literature), 6, 117, 213-19
Documents, 9, 30-31, 75-77, 80, 140, 183-225, 230
Dogmas, 100
DOHM, CHRISTIAN WILHELM VON, ix, 5-8, 11-14, 17-18, 27, 121, 239
"Dou" (Surinam order), 142
DRAGO, ISAAC, 194
Drie Gebroeders (plantation), 98
Drunkenness, 166-67
Drygoods, 144-45
Dutch Guiana; see Surinam
Dutch Jews, 22
Dutch language, xi, 48, 106, 109-10, 134, 163-65, 167-68, 183, 217, 239
Dutch Reformed Religion, 185, 187, 242

INDEX

Dutch Republic, 9, 23-26, 30, 34, 52-53, 62, 83, 89-90, 130-31, 143, 186, 209-10; *see also* Holland, States General
Dutch, the, IX-XI, 8, 20, 23-25, 29, 31-34, 37, 49, 57, 120, 125-26, 140, 146, 175, 187, 192
Dutch West India Company, 24-25, 34, 37, 53, 96, 145, 176, 183
Dutch West Indies, 119, 186, 209
Dyestuffs, 56, 186
Dyewood, 172-74, 235

E

East Indies, 20, 177, 244
Ecclesiasticism, 20, 105, 114, 139, 147-48, 193, 203-4; *see also* Ascamoth
Economic life, x, 13, 18, 21-24, 26, 33, 37, 52-53, 63, 110, 115-17, 119-20, 125, 131, 137, 139, 145, 147, 151, 166, 184, 188, 214, 216, 218, 234, 237, 239, 242; *see also* Retail trade
Edict of Nantes, 36
Edicts, 47-48, 138
Education, XI, 5, 16, 44, 105, 112, 154, 163, 165, 214
Egalitarianism, xi
Egypt, 125
Elections, 220, 222
Elephantiasis, 243
Emancipation, ix-x
Empiricists, 156-57, 162
Employees, 102, 141, 148, 175
Employment, 60, 95, 239
England, 20, 28, 30, 32, 34, 36, 52, 175, 178, 181, 189
English language, xi, 183; *see also* Negro-English
English, the, ix-x, 25, 28-36, 40, 49, 51-52, 57, 60, 82, 96, 119, 131, 146, 175, 179, 188, 190-92, 194, 209, 239, 242
Enlightenment, x
Ensigns, 127, 197
Epidemics, xi

Equity, 9
Eracubo River, 31, 191
Essequibo (Essequebo), 18, 34, 51, 96, 99, 125, 187, 230, 237-38, 243
Established church, 136
Estates, 100-101, 241
Ethnicism, 111
Eucharist, 135
Eulogies, 109
Europe, ix-x, 6, 13, 15-17, 19, 23, 27-28, 36, 40, 43, 46, 52, 56, 62-64, 97, 110, 114, 117, 131, 133, 136, 141, 143, 153-54, 156, 163-66, 175, 178, 214, 227, 234, 243
Exchange; *see* Letters of exchange
Exemptions, ix, 183, 185
Exile, 20, 120
Exploicteurs, 148
Exports, 146, 169, 181-82, 234-35
Expulsions, 10, 19

F

Factories; *see* Manufactories, Mills
Factors, 119
Family, families, 13, 16, 23-24, 28, 44, 72, 85-87, 103, 113, 119-20, 137, 151, 191, 233, 236-37, 239
Fanaticism, 26, 75, 105, 210, 226, 230
Fasts, 108, 208-9, 237
Feast of Tabernacles, 152
Fees, 146-48, 186, 237
FERNANDES, SAMUEL, 218
Festivals, 43, 95, 97, 100, 102, 104, 152, 189, 236-38; *see also* Feast of Tabernacles, Holidays, Kippur, New Year, Passover, Shavuot
Fez, 17
Fiefs, 184
Finance, 138-39, 219
Fine arts, 116, 227
Fines, 222
Fiscals; *see* Prosecutors
Fish, 131, 185-86
Flanders, 226
Flour, 131, 145

FONSECA, ALANS D', 194; JOS. GABAY, 218
Foodstuffs, 128-29, 143-45, 149, 151, 239
Foreclosures, 94-95, 97-98
Foreigners, 108
Forests, 89, 101, 234, 239
Forgers, 121
Fort New Amsterdam, 64, 126
Fort Zeelandia, 28, 131, 133, 191
Fortresses, forts, 28, 30-31, 40-46, 50, 54, 64-65, 126, 190
France, 17, 26, 32, 43, 49, 52, 61, 227
Franchises, 105, 121
Freedom, 9, 18, 21, 23, 50, 78, 144, 152, 167, 185, 210, 225; of religion, 22, 135, 139, 184
Freemasons, 167
Freight, 130, 143-44, 241, 243
French Guiana; see Cayenne
French language, ix, xi-xii, 5-6, 10, 134, 163, 165, 183, 208, 217, 228, 243
French Revolution, xi
French, the, 21, 24-25, 27-28, 30, 32, 42, 44, 48-50, 52, 119, 136, 140, 148, 163, 190
Furniture, 144, 167

G

Gabay; see Treasurers
Gelderland Plantation, 57, 96, 98
Geography, 214, 218-19
German Jews, 3, 6-7, 44, 63-64, 104, 106, 110, 120-21, 129, 132, 134, 141-42, 154, 156, 207, 239, 242; see also Ashkenazim
German language, 6
Germany, 6, 61
Gin, 147, 166
God, 15, 21, 88, 113, 136, 209-10, 218, 229
Gold, 19-20, 156, 172-73, 185, 234
GOMES, ANTHONIO HENRIQUES, 227

Gospels (New Testament), 15
Government, 137-39, 141, 182, 198, 239-40, 242
Governors, 24, 28, 30, 32-35, 38-39, 41, 43-44, 46-49, 53, 55, 59, 64-65, 68-70, 73-81, 84, 89, 94, 106-10, 115-18, 121, 127, 132, 135, 137-38, 148, 152, 163-64, 175-81, 188-89, 192-97, 199-200, 206-7, 210-13, 215, 218, 221, 233, 239, 243
GRADIS (family), 17, 227
Grants, IX, 29-30, 37, 54, 60; see also Charters
Grease-merchants, 106, 145
Greek Orthodoxy, 242
Greeks, 136, 242
Guardians, 141
Guiana, 18, 25-30, 57, 96, 126, 153, 164; see also Cayenne, Surinam
Guilds, 22
Guilgal (plantation), 98
Gums, 172-73, 186
Goosen (plantation), 98
Gorcum, 76

H

Haarlem Society of Sciences, 22
Hague, The, 106, 111, 156, 236
Half-breeds, 105
Hamburg, 20, 226
Hamlets, 40, 131
Hardware, 143, 145
Hats, 145
Hebraists, 16
Hebrew language, 228
Hensel Militia, 197
High Council, 76
"High Germans"; see Ashkenazim, German Jews
Hispaniola, 143, 237
History, 216, 219
Holidays, 30, 57, 100, 108-9; see also Festivals

INDEX

Holland, xi-xii, 4, 6-12, 14, 18-23, 25-26, 30-32, 36, 38-39, 43-44, 47-48, 51-52, 54-55, 57, 62, 74-76, 78-80, 82, 84, 89-90, 92-101, 103, 105-7, 110-11, 117-18, 128, 130-31, 135, 140, 143-44, 148, 162, 164, 172-74, 177-78, 182, 190, 210, 216, 219, 223, 226-27, 230-31, 234, 241-42; *see also* Dutch Republic, States General, United Provinces, West Friesland
Horses, 131, 147, 151, 167
Hospitals, 44, 47, 133, 149-51, 162, 237
Houses, 132-33, 135-37, 147, 149, 151, 185, 215, 242
Hudson River, ix
Humanism, xi
Humanity, 209

I

Iberia, 19; *see also* Portugal, Spain
Immigration, ix, 19-20, 22
Immortality, 229
Immunities, ix, 6, 62-63, 75, 113, 121, 125
Imports, 144, 146-47, 181-82, 242
Imposts, 185; *see also* Taxes
Indians, 27, 35, 38, 40-41, 45, 53, 66-68, 131, 160
Indies, 177, 243; *see also* East Indies, West Indies
Indigo, 172-73, 234
Industry, 20
Inheritance, 141
Inquisition, 19-21, 23, 36, 105, 193, 231
Institutions, 105, 114-15, 117; *see also* Ascamoth
Insurance, 144
Interest, 53-54, 82-83, 92, 95, 97, 101, 143, 241
Intermarriage, 63
Iron, 145
Italy, 16-17, 19, 25, 61, 92

J

Jamaica, 25, 32, 38, 70, 96, 233
Jesuits, 17, 92, 163
JESUS (of Nazareth), 15, 62, 116, 238
Jewish community; *see* Community
Jewish quarter, 106
Jews, ix-xii, 5-11, 13, 15-23, 25-26, 28-33, 35-36, 39, 42-43, 45-51, 54-55, 57-63, 64-75, 77-78, 80-83, 85-88, 93-106, 110-16, 120-21, 128, 135-37, 139-40, 142, 144, 150, 152, 154, 156, 164, 167, 184, 188, 191, 193, 198, 200-201, 212, 223-28, 230, 233, 236-39; 242-43; *see also* Ashkenazim; Community; German Jews; Portuguese Jews
Joden Savane; *see* Savane
Journals, 88
Juca, 59, 71, 85-86, 88, 127, 235-36; creek, 59, 71
Judaism, 16, 20-21, 24, 100
Judges, 187-89, 198, 230
Junta, 219-22
Jurators, 61, 106-7
Jurisprudence, 61, 116
Justice, 5, 9, 14, 184, 186, 196-97, 240; *see also* Courts

K

Kings, 224, 226-27
Kippur (Atonement Day), 21, 68

L

La Rochelle, 25
LADESMA, DOCTOR, 237
Land, 30, 39, 96-100, 130-32, 139, 141, 147-48, 153, 183, 188-89, 191, 200, 232, 234, 237
Languages, 154, 163, 165, 214, 227
LASATTE, GABRIEL DE, 197
Laws, 60, 62, 81, 112, 114, 117, 146, 210, 224

Lawsuits, 17, 67, 69, 76, 78-79, 97, 106, 148, 166, 187
Lectures, xi, 164, 217; see also Sermons
Legislature, 115, 175
Leisure, 215, 244
LEON; see de Leon
Leprosy, 117
Letters, 6-8, 11-15, 23, 35, 45-48, 54-55, 59, 75, 81, 97, 106, 111, 117, 121, 144, 162, 168, 194-95, 197, 200, 218, 220, 226, 234, 236, 238-39
Letters of Aristodemus and Sincerus, 96, 125
Letters of exchange, 94-95
Letters on Essequibo and Demerary, 78
Letters patent, 18
Lettre Politico-Théologico-Morale sur les Juifs (Nassy), xii
Lettres de quelques Juifs à Monsieur de Voltaire, 74
Levies, 49-50
LEVY, AARON, 21; RAPHAEL, 18
Liberal arts, 214
Liberalism, xi
Libraries, xi, 164, 215
Lieutenant colonels, 90, 126-27, 164, 218; generals, 190
Lieutenants, 65, 67, 70, 88, 127
Life, 166-67
Liquor, 154, 166
Lisbon, 20, 226
Literary societies, xi, 163-64
Literature, 116-17, 121, 163-64, 214-16, 227
Liturgy, x
Livorno, 25
Loans, 92
LOBO, DANIEL JN., JR., 218
Locksmiths, 141
London, 19, 227, 237
Lords of the Colony, 46, 48, 63-64
Lotteries, 23
Lower-middle class, x
Lutherans, 134, 137, 140

Luxury, 22-23, 53, 57, 74, 82, 84, 94, 100, 129, 131, 142, 145, 151
Lyceums, xi
Lyon, 136

M

MACHADO (family), 17; IMMANUEL, 58-59, 226
Madrid, 226
Magistrates, 18, 43, 51, 62, 65, 78, 90, 110, 139, 141, 189
Mahamad, 60, 208, 210, 219-22
Major generals, 127, 178
Majors, 85, 126
Male-midwives, 141
Managers, 101, 113, 119, 136, 142, 167-68
MANASSEH BEN ISRAEL, 226
Manufactories, manufactures, 22, 242
Marony River, 28-29, 89
Maroons, Marrons, X, 50
Marriage, 26, 39, 41, 44, 61-63, 102, 189, 242
Marshals, 193
Martinique, 32
Masons, 141
Mass, 135
Massacres, 58
Matapica River, 128
Mathematics, 218
Mauritzburg, 150-51
Mayors, 55
Meat, 145
Medicine, 22, 121, 137, 141, 156, 159-60, 162, 164, 216, 237, 243
MENDELSSOHN, MOSES, 17, 227
Mendicants, 137
Mercantilism, x
Merchandise, 23, 29, 34, 119, 141, 143-44, 186, 191, 206, 241
Merchants, x, 9, 18, 57, 82, 84, 92-93, 95, 98, 101, 119, 143-44, 147, 190
Merchant-shippers, x
MESQUITA (family), 17, 46; DARD. BO. DE, 227

INDEX   253

Messengers, 200
MESSIACH, DANIEL, 194
Metals, 20
Metaphysics, 227, 229
Metz, 17
MEZA (family), 24, 35; ISAAK, 194
Middle class, x
Military, x, 13, 23, 41, 121, 127, 133, 137-38, 141, 179, 197, 211, 239-40; *see also* Soldiers
Mills, 29, 32-33, 44, 56, 128, 232
Minerals, 185-86, 234
Mining, 234
Ministers, 134-35, 148; *see also* Priests, Rabbis
Minorities, ix
Minors, 141
Mohammedans, 223
Molasses, 131, 141, 146
MOLO (family), 17
Money, 36, 53-54, 72-73, 82-84, 93-95, 97, 100-101, 108, 113, 143-45, 156, 191, 243
MONSANTO, DAVID NUNES, 4, 12, 218, 221
Montserrat, 32
Moors, 20
Morality, 15-16, 82, 105, 112, 116, 121, 219, 227, 240
Moravian Brethren, 134
MORERY (writer), 17
Mortality, 29, 143, 241
Mortgages, 83, 92
Mot Creek, 126
Mourning, 237
Mulattoes, xi, 71, 105-6, 132, 141-42, 146, 242
Mules, 131, 151
Music, 155
Mythology, 218

N

NAAR, ISAK, 218; MOSES, 70-71, 196-97
NAHAR, M. H., 218
Naples, 110
Nassau-Siegen, 20, 24

NASSY (family), 24, 35, 87; DAVID AND ASSOCIATES, 183-88
NASSY, DAVID DE ISAAC COHEN, XI-XII, 4, 12, 24-25, 65-70, 193, 218-22, 235; ESTHER, 17; GRACIA, 17; Is. C., 71-72, 106-7; ISAAC (ISAK), 68, 79, 81, 106-7, 201-2; J., 81; JOSEPH, 31, 61, 190; SAMUEL C., 30, 39-40, 42-43, 45-48, 61, 103, 148, 190-91, 194, 196, 237
Natives, 28, 35, 40
Natural history, 109, 163, 244
Nature, 116, 152, 163-64, 216, 243
Navigation, 23, 37, 130, 184, 216; *see also* Ships
Navy, 23, 49
Negro-English, 135, 154
Negroes, x, 50-51, 55, 57, 59, 66-71, 73, 76, 78, 82, 85-86, 88-90, 93, 101, 106, 120, 126-27, 132, 134-35, 141-46, 151, 153-63, 167, 193, 196-97, 230, 235-36, 242-43; *see also* Bush Negroes, Maroons, Runaway slaves
Neighbors, 215
New Amsterdam, ix, 28
New Christians, 19-20
New World, IX, 24-25, 125-26, 131; *see also* America, North America, United States
New Year, 237
New York, 31
Nieuw Middelburg, 40
Nieuwe Star (plantation), 98
Nîmes, 227
North America, ix-x, 31, 108; *see also* United States
Notaries, XI, 61, 106, 190, 237
NUNES, AB., 61; JACOB, 194
NUNEZ, ABM., 237

O

Oaths, 81, 147, 189
Occupations, 13
Officers, 13, 61, 66-67, 71-72, 90, 109, 113, 127, 197, 240; of justice, 113

Onobo (plantation), 59, 84
Optics, 164
Ordonnateurs, 152
Organ, 134-35
Orientalism, 229
Orinoco River, 125
Orphans, 137, 141, 237
Ostracism, 120-21
Ottomans, 19

P

Paganism, 135-36, 223, 242
Palmaribo, Palmeneribo (plantation), 59, 84
Para creek, 57-58, 93, 127-28; River, 29, 40, 56-57
Paraïba, Brazil, 231
Paramaribo, ix-xi, 28, 40, 42, 47-48, 57, 63-64, 73, 93, 96, 106-9, 121, 126-29, 131, 134, 139, 141-42, 149, 151-52, 164, 194, 197, 199, 201, 204, 206, 211-12, 220, 237
Paramburg, 40
PARDO, 99
Parents, 155, 163, 214
PAREYRA, ISAACK, 193
Parham, 40, 175
Parhams-Punt, 28
Paris, 13, 18
Parnassim; see Regents
PARRA, MESSIEURS DE LA, 87-88; DAVID DE LA, 222; ISHAK (IS., ISAAC, ISAACK) DE LA, 4, 12, 218, 221-22; JEOS. DE LA, 218; M. DE LA, 218; SAL. DE LA, 86; SAMUEL H. DE LA, 4, 12, 218, 222
Passover, 220, 230, 237
Patrons, 183, 185-86
Paulus (creek), 128
Peace, 201-6, 220-21
Peddlers, x
Peninica, 58
Pensionaries, 76
Pensions, 110

Pentateuch, 44
Pentecost; *see* Shavuot
PEREIRA (family), 24
PEREYRA, 59; MANUEL, 58, 67
Perica, 128, 134
Periodicals, 168, 209, 216, 243
Persecutions, 17-18, 26, 36, 54, 61, 105
Peru, 243
Pharmacies, 133, 156
Philadelphia, xi
Philanthropy, 238-39
Philosophers, philosophy, 6, 15-16, 103, 216, 219
Physicians, xi, 109, 117, 133, 141, 150, 154, 156-57, 160, 164, 218, 236-37, 243; *see also* Surgeons
Physics, 164, 244
PINTO, ISAAC (ISHAK) DE, 49, 74, 106, 111, 235-36
Plantations, planters, X-XI, 9, 13, 32, 40, 44, 50-51, 54-57, 64, 66-67, 76, 80-84, 86, 88, 90-91, 93-102, 113, 119-20, 127-31, 134-36, 142-45, 147, 151-53, 160, 162, 166-67, 196, 198, 201-2, 237, 239, 241-42, 244
Poetry, 23-24, 67, 155, 163-64, 227
POLAK, ARON, 99; JACOB, 237
Poland, 6, 227
Police, 119, 186
Political life, x-xi, 5, 12, 18, 51-52, 60, 62, 89, 92, 103, 112, 121, 137-39, 141, 166, 206, 216, 240; reform, 18
Pomo Negroes, 85
Poor, the, 62, 101-2, 104, 112-13, 119-20, 132, 134, 137, 151, 167, 206, 222, 237
Popes, 17, 19, 226
Population, 121, 131, 141-43; *see also* Statistics
Porcelain, 145
Ports, 126, 145, 147
Portugal, 10, 19-21, 24, 26, 52, 105, 226, 231

INDEX

Portuguese Jews, ix-x, 3-4, 6, 12, 21, 23, 44, 60, 63-64, 86, 104, 110, 117-21, 127, 129, 132, 134, 139, 141-42, 148-49, 155-56, 163-65, 176, 196-98, 200-201, 203-8, 211, 213, 219-21, 237-39, 242
Portuguese language, xi, 5, 42, 108, 165, 217
Post office, 147
PRADO, ISAAC R. DE, 194
Prairies, 148-49
Prayer, 87-88, 208-10
Preadvisors, 137-38, 180-81; *see also* Advisors
Prejudice, 12, 22, 25, 43, 54, 62, 72, 78, 83, 103, 109, 111-12, 114, 118, 120, 136, 140, 194, 238; *see also* Anti-Jewish, Bigotry
Prices, 56, 97, 147, 151
Priests, 15, 134-35
Privileges, ix-x, xii, 14, 21, 27, 30-31, 34, 39, 43, 46-48, 55, 60-64, 75, 80-81, 102-5, 107, 109-10, 112-13, 115-16, 120-21, 139-40, 148, 176, 183, 185, 188-89, 192-94, 196-98, 202, 205-6, 213, 219, 240
Professions, x, 22, 224
Profits, 9, 100-102, 119, 130-31, 143-45, 147, 241
Prohibitions, 109-10
Property, 26-27, 61, 63, 100, 132, 141, 148, 188, 191-93, 206, 242
Proprietors, 50, 52-55, 60-61, 64-65, 72-77, 80-84, 90, 98-101, 103-4, 106-7, 111, 115-18, 126, 128, 131, 135, 138, 140, 143-44, 146, 148, 176, 239, 242
Prosecutors, 62, 67, 79, 109-10, 120, 137-38, 148, 163, 175, 177-82, 196
Protestants, x, 21, 60, 134-35
Providence (plantation), 59, 84
Prussia, 6, 14
Public office, 20, 30, 60, 188, 200, 202

Publications, XI, 6, 8

R

Rabbis, xi, 16, 43, 61, 227-29
Rain, 153
Real estate, 19
Rebels, 41-42, 59, 65-66, 68, 70-71, 91
Receivers, 147, 187, 237
Reformed Protestants, 133-34, 137, 148, 185
Reforms, 219-20; political, 6, 18
Regents, ix-xi, 4, 6-7, 9, 12, 43, 46-48, 51, 55, 58, 60-61, 63, 75-77, 79-81, 105, 111, 115, 117-18, 120-21, 139, 149, 195, 197, 199-201, 203-8, 211-13, 220-22, 236, 239
Religion, ix, xi, 15, 22, 26, 39, 48, 72, 88, 95, 104-5, 120, 134
Rent, 147
Retail trade, 119
Retour (plantation), 86
Revenues, 9, 53, 121, 129, 143-44, 241-42
Revolts, revolutions, x, 28, 33, 35, 41, 50-52, 58, 67-68, 83, 86, 89, 102, 108, 114
Rights, ix, xii, 5-6, 14, 55, 107, 125, 194
Rio Negro, 126
Ritual, x, 61, 136
Rivers, ix, 27-32, 40, 52, 56, 65, 70, 89, 91, 96, 98-99, 125-26, 128, 131, 148, 151-53, 183-84, 190-91, 193
Roads, 147, 151
Rome, x
Roucou, 56, 169-70, 234-35
Rum, 131, 166
Runaway slaves, x, 50-51, 57-59, 65-67, 69-71, 73-74, 82, 84, 86, 88, 90-91, 93, 108, 127, 146, 180, 197; *see also* Slavery
Russia, 242

S

Sabbath, 108, 189, 212, 220, 237
Sailors, 166
St. Domingue, 143
St. Eustatius, 119, 209
Salaries, 222
Sales, 146, 148, 209
Salt, 145
Santo Domingo, 237
Saramaca (Saramacke), 57, 59, 66, 70, 74, 85-86, 88, 127, 197, 236; River, 28, 57, 66, 89, 131
Sarcasm, 15
SARPHATY, JEOS., 237
SARRUCO, MEZA DAVID, 218
Sarua, 56, 67
SARVATY, JEOS., 61
Satire, 74
Saturday, 21, 87, 108, 237
Savane, x, 29-30, 39, 44, 50, 57-59, 63, 71, 77, 91, 99-100, 106, 108-9, 118, 121, 139, 142, 148-52, 208, 220, 237, 239
Schiedam, 76
Schismatics, 136, 242
Scholars, 15, 17
Schools, 137, 185, 189, 214
Science, xi, 22, 155, 165, 214
Scrolls of the Law, 50, 149
Secretaries, secretariat, 107, 137-39, 177, 181-82, 191-92, 194, 199-200, 226, 237
Sephardim, ix-x, 3, 63-64, 119, 134, 239, 242; *see also* Portuguese Jews, Spanish Jews
Sermons, 134-35; *see also* Lectures
Servants, 141, 185
Settlements, settlers, 28-30, 39, 42, 49, 53, 56-58, 63-68, 71, 75, 82-86, 89-91, 93-94, 96-99, 103-5, 108, 121, 125-26, 128-29, 131, 137, 142-44, 146-48, 153, 162, 164, 166-67, 188, 192-93, 196, 198, 201, 206, 219, 224, 234, 239, 243
Sex, 243
Shavuot (Pentecost), 237
Sheriffs, 186-87

Ships, 28, 30-32, 34, 40, 42, 44, 46, 49, 52, 126, 130-31, 143-44, 146, 172-74, 186, 241, 243; *see also* Navigation
Shopkeepers, shops, x, 119, 143-45
Sick, care of, 133, 150, 156-60, 237
Sicknesses, 28, 102, 150, 153-54; *see also* Diseases
SILVA, ARON DE, 194
SILVEIRA, MIGUEL DE, 227
Silver, 19-20, 185
Sinnamary River, 190-91
Slavery, slaves, x, 32-34, 44, 49-51, 57-59, 65-66, 70-71, 82-84, 86-87, 89, 92, 94-98, 100, 104, 106, 119, 127, 130-31, 134, 141-43, 146, 151, 161, 167, 187, 196-97, 237, 241; *see also* Runaway slaves
SOARES, S. G., 218
SOASO (SOASSO), MONSIEUR, 79, 81, 227
SOASSO (family), 17
Social life, x-xi, 154, 214
Social welfare, xi
Societies, xi, 24, 109, 112; *see also* Literary societies
Society of Rohan, 24
Soldiers, 13, 24, 30, 32, 38, 41, 43-44, 50, 53, 65, 68, 76, 79-80, 89-90, 126-27, 133, 137, 151, 209, 240; *see also* Military
Solicitors, 118, 139, 223-25, 237
SOLIS (landowner), 30
Sorbonne, 236
Soul, 229
South America, x, 12, 27, 52, 126
Spain, 10, 19-21, 52, 163, 227, 243
Spanish Jews, 21, 23, 156
Spanish language, x-xi, 5, 23, 25, 45, 67, 163, 165, 217
Spanish Main, x
Speculation, 234
States General, 22, 34, 36-38, 54, 60, 62-63, 74-76, 79, 89-90, 117, 127, 135, 137, 175, 203; *see also* Dutch Republic, Holland
Statesmen, 6, 13

Statistics, ix-x, 19, 21-22, 32-35, 37, 44, 49, 56-58, 60, 63-64, 68, 73, 80, 84, 89, 98, 128-32, 138-39, 141-44, 146-47, 151, 169-74, 181, 187, 222, 227, 233-34, 236-37, 239, 241-43
Stocks, 22
Strangers, 112
Subalterns, 66, 68
Sugar industry, x, 26, 29, 32-33, 44, 49, 55-57, 83, 98, 128-30, 141, 145-47, 169-72, 234-35, 241
Sukkot; see Feast of Tabernacles
Sunday, 39, 46, 48, 134, 193, 195-96, 237
Superstitions, 64, 105, 135
Surgeons, 133, 141, 156, 162, 243; see also Physicians
Surina (province), 27; River, 27, 59, 65, 68, 70
Surinaamse Lettervrienden, 164
Surinam, ix-xi, 3-8, 10-12, 20, 25-34, 36-38, 41-46, 49-52, 54, 56, 59-62, 64, 70, 72, 75-76, 79-81, 83, 92-94, 96-103, 105, 108, 115-16, 121, 126-27, 129-31, 134-35, 139-40, 143, 145, 148, 150, 152-53, 155-56, 160, 163-67, 169, 172-75, 177, 190-92, 194-98, 200-208, 210-11, 213, 222-25, 232-34, 237-38, 241-43; River, 40, 42, 57, 65, 91, 96-100, 126, 128-29, 131, 148, 234
Surinamsburg, 40
Surines, 27
Surveyors, 61, 141, 237
Sweden, 226
Synagogues, xi, 21, 29-30, 39, 47, 51, 63, 75, 99, 102, 118, 134, 148, 152, 184-85, 195, 197, 201, 204, 206-8, 210, 219, 221, 237, 239
Syndics, 46
Syrup, 141

T

Talmud, 229
TARTAS, ISAAC DE CASTRO, 231

Taverns, 147
Taxes, 9, 13, 52, 54, 64, 73-74, 91, 102, 107, 112, 141, 146-47, 185-87, 224, 237, 239, 241
Tempaty, 58-59, 71, 84, 108
TEXEIRA (family), 17, 226
TEXIER, BERNARD, 108-10, 116, 163-64, 178-81, 210-12, 238
Theatres, 109-10, 167, 237
Theft, 142
Thirty Years' War, x
Thorarica, 189
Timber, 29, 128
Tisha B'Av, 237
Tithes, 185
Tobacco, 29, 56, 131, 169-71, 234-35
Tolerance, x, 12, 15, 21, 136, 140, 210, 225
Tombstones, 237
Torrica, 30
Towns, x, 40; see also Urban, Villages
Trade; see Economic life, Retail
Translations, translators, 6-7, 12, 48, 106, 108, 135, 183, 227-28, 243
Travel, 184, 186
Treason, 243
Treasurers, 201-2, 204, 219-20, 222, 227
Treaties of peace, 31, 73-74, 84-86, 108, 236; Breda, 32-34; Westminster, 34
Trees, 129, 132-33, 147
Tribunals, 60, 64, 81, 106, 137-39, 189
Turks, 101
Tuscany, 16, 61

U

Über die bürgerliche Verbesserung der Juden (Dohm), 6
Unbelievers, 223
United Provinces (Netherlands), 4, 24, 32, 34, 37, 52, 118, 203; see also Holland

United States, xi, *see also* America
Universities, xi, 227
Urban areas, x, 28, 40, 101, 120, 128, 139, 141-43, 242; *see also* Towns, Villages
Utensils, 145
Utrecht, 150

V

Venereal diseases, 243
Venetians, 236
VENTURA, MORDOCHÉE, 228
Vice-admirals, 43, 61, 175
VIEIRA, J. E., 182, 208
Villages, 40, 59, 68-69, 71-72, 85, 88-89, 127, 151-52, 235
Votes, 199, 202, 206

W

Wages, 127, 147-48, 181, 241
War, wars, 30, 34, 36-37, 42-44, 49-52, 65, 93, 108, 126, 189, 209; *see also* Thirty Years
Warehouses, 239
Water, 150
Wax, 172-73, 234-35
Wealth, 19-20, 22-24, 26, 36, 46, 56, 60, 62, 64, 66-67, 75, 94, 99-100, 105, 108, 125, 167, 239
West Friesland, 62
West Indies, 20, 183
Westminster; *see* Treaties
Whale oil, 131
White-collar class x

Whites, x, 35, 40-41, 50, 58, 68, 70-72, 75, 85, 87-88, 106, 132, 141-43, 146, 151, 153, 156, 159, 161, 219, 225, 233, 236
Widows, widowers, 237, 242
Wild Coast (West Indies), 183, 187
WILLIAM IV (Prince of Orange), 76, 79, 226
Wills, 61, 184, 189
Wine, 145, 147, 154
Witchcraft, 160
Women, 16-17, 61, 110, 112, 120, 142, 149, 154, 156, 160-62, 238
Women's gallery, 149
Wood, 91, 128-29, 132, 134, 147, 242; *see also* Forests
Work, workers, workmen, 49, 64, 83, 99-100, 102, 193, 237
Worship, x, 113, 134, 136, 184, 189
Writers, 5-6, 9, 16, 18, 21, 27, 29, 51, 66, 72, 84, 86, 92, 103, 121-22, 125, 152, 218
Writ-servers, 113

Y

Yellow fever, xi
Young, 110, 214-15, 217-18

Z

Zeeland, 28, 30-35, 37-38, 40, 52-53, 126, 131, 175-79, 181, 187, 190-92
Zeelandia (fort), 31, 40, 42